High-Performance GM LS-SERIES Cylinder Head Guide

David Grasso

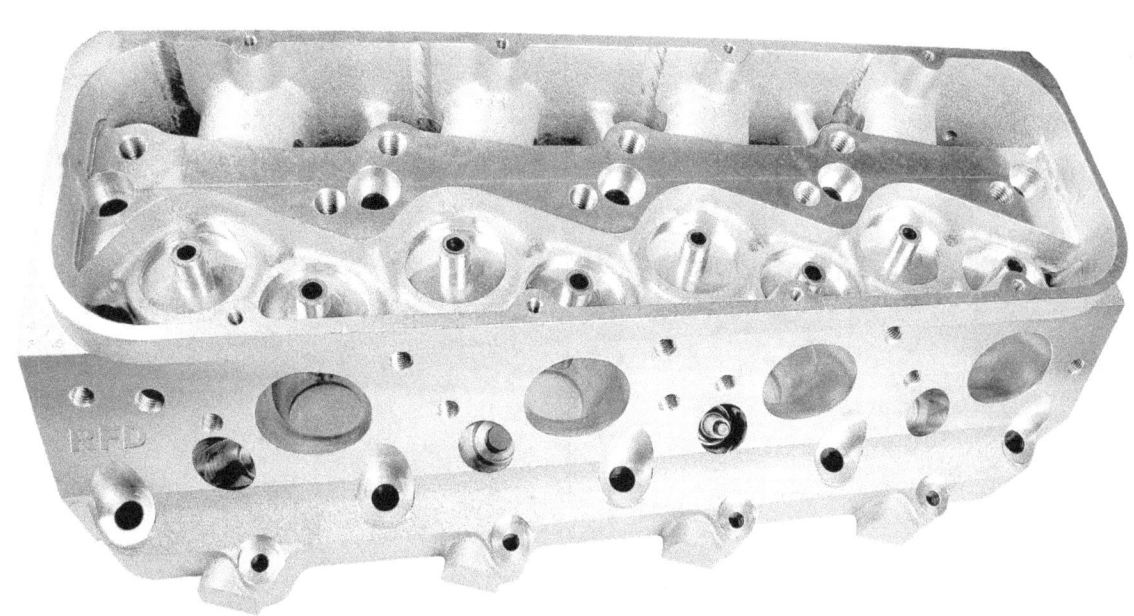

CarTech®

CarTech®

CarTech®, Inc.
Phone: 651-277-1200 or 800-551-4754
Fax: 651-277-1203
www.cartechbooks.com

© 2012 by David Grasso

All rights reserved. No part of this publication may be reproduced or utilized in any form or by any means, electronic or mechanical, including photocopying, recording, or by any information storage and retrieval system, without prior permission from the Author. All text, photographs, and artwork are the property of the Author unless otherwise noted or credited.

The information in this work is true and complete to the best of our knowledge. However, all information is presented without any guarantee on the part of the Author or Publisher, who also disclaim any liability incurred in connection with the use of the information.

All trademarks, trade names, model names and numbers, and other product designations referred to herein are the property of their respective owners and are used solely for identification purposes. This work is a publication of CarTech, Inc., and has not been licensed, approved, sponsored, or endorsed by any other person or entity.

Edit by Scott Parkhurst
Layout by Monica Seiberlich

ISBN 978-1-61325-431-8
Item No. SA231P

Library of Congress Cataloging-in-Publication Data

Grasso, David
  High-performance GM LS-series cylinder head guide / by David Grasso.
    p. cm.
  ISBN 978-1-934709-90-0
  1. General Motors automobiles–Motors–Cylinder heads. 2. General Motors automobiles–Motors–Modification. 3. General Motors automobiles–Performance. I. Title.

TL214.C93G73 2012
629.25'2--dc23

2012008528

Title Page: This is Eldelbrock's Victor LSR head.

Back Cover Photos

Top Left: Cylinder head porting is somewhat of a black art; gurus can spend hundreds of hours on a single set of heads with a grinder, various grits of sandpaper, welder, and epoxy. CNC machines, however, allow you to replicate a particular set of well-ported heads over and over again, and in half the time. The LS market has embraced this technology in providing programs for virtually every factory or aftermarket casting. West Coast Cylinder Heads is among several companies that even port LS7 and LS9 heads, which come CNC-ported from GM.

Top Right: LS1 210 cc and LS1 215 cc

Middle Left: LS1 230 cc and LS1 245 cc

Middle Right: 5.3-Liter Stage 2.5

Bottom Left: 280-cc LS7

CONTENTS

Acknowledgments 5
Introduction 6

Chapter 1: The Basics 10
   Converting from Cathedral to Rectangular Port 10
   Cathedral Versus Rectangular Port 12
   Cylinder Head Theory 15

Chapter 2: Cathedral Port Cylinder Heads 17
   Factory Heads
      LS1 18
      LR4/LM4/LM7 19
      LQ4 20
      LQ9 21
      LS6/LS2 22
   Aftermarket Heads
      Advanced Induction 23
         GM 706/862 5.3-Liter LS1, 218 cc 24
         GM 243 (LS6) and 799 (LS2), 218 cc 25
         GM 243 (LS6) and 799 (LS2), 226 cc 26
      AirFlow Research 27
         LS1, 210 cc 28
         LS1, 215 cc 29
         LS1, 230 cc 30
         LS1, 245 cc 31
      Edelbrock/Lingenfelter 32
         LS1 Performer RPM, CNC 33
      Edelbrock
         LS1/LS2, E-CNC 215 34
      Livernois Motorsports 35
         LS2 Stage 2, CNC 36
         LS2 Stage 3, CNC 37
      Mast Motorsports 38
         LS1/LS6, 11-Degree Small-Bore 39
         11-Degree 6-Bolt Small-Bore 40
         12 Degree 6-Bolt Large-Bore 41
      Patriot Performance 42
         LS6/LS2 and LQ9, Stage II 43
         LS6/LS2 and LQ9, Stage III 44
         LS1, Stage II, 5.3-Liter 45
      Precision Race Components 46
         Stage 2.5, 5.3-Liter 48
         LS6 Stage 1, 6.0-Liter 49
         LS6 Stage 2.5, 6.0-Liter 50
         LS6 Stage 3, 6.0-Liter 51
         215 cc 52
         227 cc 53
         237 cc 54
      Total Engine AirFlow 55
         LS2/LS6 Stage 1 56
         LS2/LS6 Stage 2 57
      Trick Flow Specialties 58
         GenX 205 61
         GenX 215 62
         GenX 220 for LS1 63
         GenX 220 for LS2 64
         GenX 225 65
         GenX 235 66
         GenX 245 67
      Trick Flow/Total Engine AirFlow
         265 cc 68
      West Coast Cylinder Heads 69
         Edelbrock 4.8/5.3-Liter 70
         Edelbrock LS1, 215 cc 71
         Edelbrock LS2, 245 cc 72
      World Products
         Warhawk, 15-Degree, CNC 73

Chapter 3: Rectangular Port Cylinder Heads 74
   Factory Heads
      LS7 75
      L92/LS3/LSA 76
      LS9 77
   Aftermarket Heads
      Advanced Induction 78
         L92, 267 cc 79
         LS3, 275 cc 80
         LS7, 280 cc 81
      All Pro/West Coast Cylinder Heads
         LS7 82
      Arao Engineering
         LS7 Stage II, 32-Valve 83
      Brodix
         STS BR 7 273 84
      Lingenfelter Performance Engineering 85
         LS3, CNC 86
         LS9, CNC 87
         LS7, CNC 88
      Livernois Motorsports 89
         L92 Stage 3, CNC 90
         LS7, CNC 91
      Mast Motorsports 92
         LS3, 11-Degree Small-Bore 93
         LS3, 11-Degree Medium-Bore 94
         LS3, 11-Degree Large-Bore 95
         LS7, 12-Degree, 305 cc 96
      Procomp Electronics
         LS3 97
      Scoggin-Dickey Parts Center
         LS3, CNC 98

CONTENTS

Texas Speed/Precision Race Components 99
    LS3/L92, CNC 100
    LS3, 250 cc 101
    LS7, CNC 102
    LS7, 285 cc 103
VMAX Motorsports
    LS3, CNC 104
Wegner Motorsports
    LS3/L92, CNC 105
West Coast Cylinder Heads
    L92 Stage 2, CNC 106
World Products
    LS7 Warhawk 107

Chapter 4: Race Port Heads 108
All Pro/West Coast Cylinder Heads
    LSW-2 109
Arias
    LS Hemi Chevy 110

Chevrolet Performance 111
    C5R 112
    LSXDR/Livernois Motorsports 113
    LSXCT/Livernois Motorsports 114
Edelbrock Victor
    LSR/Race Flow Development 115
Mast Motorsports
    Mozez Canted Valve 116

Chapter 5: Supporting Components 117
Intake Manifolds 117
Rocker Arms 122

Chapter 6: LS Cylinder Blocks 128
Factory 128
Modified Factory 134
Aftermarket 138

Source Guide 144

ACKNOWLEDGMENTS

I would like to thank my future wife for her strength, support, and help keeping life on track during this hectic time.

Ron Mowen at Vengeance Racing, Greg Lovell at AntiVenom, Trevor Doelling at Texas Speed, and Bob Wise at Race Krafters all came through in a pinch when I needed it and are great resources for any aspiring LS-series owner.

Last, but not least, I would like to thank all the manufacturers that made this book happen. In 2011–2012 we have all been asked to do more and more at our jobs, wearing as many hats as we can, so it can be difficult to keep up with marketing and media relations. But all of the companies mentioned in this book managed to come through and meet our deadlines.

INTRODUCTION

The LS1 and its subsequent siblings are among the most formidable V-8s ever made for a production car. Add in some aftermarket parts and you can have performance only previously thought available with a radical race setup or big-block-type cubic inches. Oddly enough, the impetus for the revolutionary engine was a cylinder-head design closely related to the decades-old Ford Windsor. However, since then, the original cathedral-port design from General Motors has come a long way thanks to aftermarket manufacturers. The flow capable from the production LS3/L92 heads, to say nothing of an LS7 or canted valve head, has almost single-handedly raised the bar. Even cathedral port heads now exceed 350 cfm and 900 hp naturally aspirated. Needless to say, with the power and efficiency of LS1s, they have become extremely popular among hot rodders and racers. Chapter 1 discusses the basics of this evolution.

Chapter 2 examines the Gen III and IV small-block Chevy cylinder head market, starting with the original LS1 design and progressing to the other factory cathedral port heads such as the mighty LS6, as well as the LQ9 and LM7 truck heads, before moving on to various aftermarket offerings. Each casting and design has its own distinct advantages, so it is up to you to decipher which one best suits your needs.

For example, heavier vehicles (like trucks) may be better suited for a smaller runner cathedral port head that enables more torque. As a result, the AirFlow Research 210-cc LSX Mongoose and TrickFlow GenX 205 heads may be just what you need.

Chapter 3 focuses on rectangular port cylinder heads and Chapter 4 discusses race port heads. As many know, the C5R race head, created for the GM racing program including the championship-winning C5R Corvette, birthed the rectangular port LSX heads. Since then, General Motors has released the revolutionary L92 (and later LS3/L99) head, with flow numbers unheard of in a production engine, let alone one with as-cast ports. That, of course, was followed up with the LS7 head, which boasted even better flow numbers and CNC porting, a rarity in a production engine. In the interim, and since then, the aftermarket has been doing its best to improve upon GM designs with new castings of the L92/LS3, LS7, and C5R, as well as fresh designs to eliminate the conventional inline valve setup to suit hardcore racers.

Chapter 5 discusses several supporting components, and how they relate to LS-series cylinder heads, including intake manifolds and rocker arms. There are many choices when it comes to these key components, and this chapter provides some insight into choosing the right one for your combination that matches up to your cylinder heads.

Though typical LS-series owners are reluctant to leave behind their stamped-steel factory rockers, I cover modifications that can be made to factory heads, as well as steel and aluminum roller rockers, which helps reduce friction and wear, while providing high-RPM stability.

For solid-roller and full-on race builds, special attention should be paid to the section on shaft-mount setups. Some LS-series heads can make this a bit challenging, but nothing a quality machine shop can't handle.

Chapter 6 provides details on factory, modified factory, and aftermarket engine blocks.

INTRODUCTION

The LS1 was introduced in the 1997 Corvette, sporting 5.7 liters (346 ci) of displacement, 350 hp, and 350 ft-lbs of torque. The new (Gen III) design was a radical departure from both Gen I and Gen II small-block Chevy designs, using an aluminum block with a 3.89-inch bore and 3.62-inch stroke. The head design was a close relative of the Ford Windsor's, sporting a cathedral-shaped intake and oval exhaust ports. There were many variations on this original design, from the iron-block 4.8, 5.3, and 6.0 truck engines to the front-wheel-drive LS4. The runners and chambers varied with each application, as did output; however, all sport the same basic port shape. (Photo Courtesy General Motors)

The LS6 engine, introduced for the 2001 Corvette Z06 model, took the cathedral port to the next level and also used a larger camshaft, higher-flowing intake manifold (adopted to all LS1s thereafter), and higher compression to make 385 hp and 385 ft-lbs. Though they both utilize the same-size (2.00 intake, 1.55 exhaust) valves, the LS6 flows some 40 to 50 cfm better while still using an as-cast finish. For 2002, GM switched cam profiles to increase output to a whopping 405 hp and 400 ft-lbs. This version was also used in the 2004 CTS-V. (Photo Courtesy General Motors)

INTRODUCTION

The Gen IV platform started with the LS2 in the 2005 Corvette and GTO, though no radical departures were made from the previous Gen III until later. The LS2 had a larger 4.00-inch bore, and a few improvements to the block, but heads identical to the LS6. Using the original (2001 version) cam from the LS6, the larger-cube LS2 (364) made 400 hp and 400 ft-lbs. (Photo Courtesy General Motors)

The Corvette C5R and C6R racing programs are largely responsible for the evolution of the Gen IV. The rectangular port C5R heads gave birth to the LS7 casting as well as the more economical L92 design. (Photo Courtesy General Motors)

The mighty LS7 produced 505 hp and 470 ft-lbs using 427 ci (7.0 liters) of displacement (just like its C5R and LS7R cousins), debuting in the 2006 Corvette Z06. With an ultra-lightweight valvetrain and rotating assembly, chock full of high-end components such as titanium connecting rods and valves, dry sump lubrication, etc., the LS7 represents the pinnacle of factory Gen IV design, including the rectangular intake port (albeit with a raised runner and CNC porting). (Photo Courtesy General Motors)

INTRODUCTION

The L92 was the first Gen IV engine released in the United States, as the powerplant for the 2007 Escalade, to sport a much more economical rectangular port design that would later be the basis for nearly all Gen IVs. These heads were originally used on the L76 engine in the 2006 Holden in Australia, and then in 2008 when this model came to the United States as the Pontiac G8 GT. The high-flowing, large-runner design had mammoth valves, which easily made 361 hp and 385 ft-lbs in the detuned 6.0 G8. The L92, however, utilized a new block design with 6.2 liters (376 ci) of displacement and variable valve timing to make a conservative 403 hp and 415 ft-lbs. (Photo Courtesy General Motors)

The LS3 in the 2008 Corvette used a lower profile intake manifold and a larger camshaft to make 436 hp and 428 ft-lbs. The valvetrain was also slightly revised for the higher-revving cam. Similar versions were used in the 2009 G8 GXP and the 2010 Camaro SS, making roughly the same output. The exception being the VVT-equipped L99 that GM paired with an automatic transmission in the Camaro SS, which made 400 hp and 410 ft-lbs. Its camshaft was a much tamer design, made to provide longevity to the Active Fuel Management system (also known as Displacement on Demand), just like the G8 GT's L76. (Photo Courtesy General Motors)

The supercharged LS9, released in the 2009 Corvette ZR1, took the LS3 design to the next level, featuring a stronger alloy and less-porous casting method. Its heads mated to the block with larger-diameter head bolts for better clamping. A number of other improvements, including CNC porting and titanium valves, helped the supercharged 6.2 push out 638 hp and 604 ft-lbs. The LSA bridged the gap between the LS3 and the LS9, making a more conservative 556 hp and 551 ft-lbs, while debuting in the 2009 Cadillac CTS-V. The LSA uses a smaller (1.9 liters) supercharger to force air through a more durable casting than the factory LS3, though most of the valvetrain (except for the camshaft) is identical. (Photo Courtesy General Motors)

CHAPTER 1

THE BASICS

Before I get into the the meat of the book—the spec charts—there are a few things you need to know. They include information on converting from a cathedral port to a rectangular port, some thoughts on the merits of cathedral versus rectangular ports, and a bit of cylinder head theory.

Converting from Cathedral to Rectangular Port

Since the factory L92 cylinder heads were released, one of the hottest topics has been how to convert older (cathedral port) LS-series combinations. Thankfully it is a pretty simple head and intake swap, which lends itself well to fairly high horsepower combinations on a modest budget. And since all LS blocks have the identical (four-per-cylinder) head-bolt pattern, all LS or LSX heads are compatible. (Some aftermarket blocks have two additional head bolts on the outside and inside of the standard ones). The only exceptions are when certain heads have valves too large to fit in a particular bore. The L92/LS3 heads, for example, must be used on a 4.00-inch-or-larger bore, and the LS7 requires at least a 4.125-inch bore.

In order to utilize such mammoth intake valves in such scarce real estate, General Motors went with an offset intake rocker on the L92 head, which means converting it also requires sourcing at least a set of 8 intake rockers (if not a full set of 16). The LS7 uses a unique rocker system due to its offset intake valve and 12-degree valve angle, which is not compatible with either the LS1/LS2 or the L92/LS3. Beyond this point, the rest of the conversion largely depends on the previous chosen components and the application.

The intake manifold is the most important element in swapping from a cathedral to a rectangular port head. To match the runners, this factory LS3 (PN 12610434) or an L76 manifold are the most popular. It is important to note that there are some minor differences between the L76 and LS3 intakes, such as a screw-in MAP sensor instead of the Gen III–style clip-in; though none are of any real consequence to swapping over. These factory manifolds come as shown here with a 90-mm electronic throttle body, injectors, fuel rails, and gaskets. (Photo Courtesy General Motors)

THE BASICS

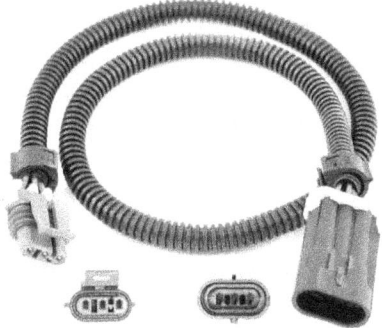

Because the LS3/L76 now places the MAP sensor at the front, just behind the throttle body, a MAP extension such as this one from Caspers is also needed. You may choose to extend the wires themselves, but for $34 you can save yourself the hassle.

To utilize the Gen IV–style injectors that come on an LS3, L76, or LS7 intake manifold with an LS1 wiring harness you need injector adapters. The Gen III injector style is known as EV1 and the Gen IV is known as EV6, so look for an EV1 to EV6 injector adapter kit from Caspers Electronics or FAST.

All rectangular port heads use offset intake rockers to accommodate the massive valves. With factory rocker setups you can get away with just changing the intake rockers; however, changing the whole set or going with an aftermarket variation are also options. In either case, extra clearance may be needed on the valve covers.

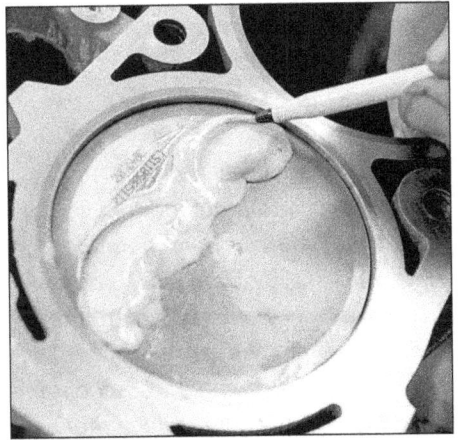

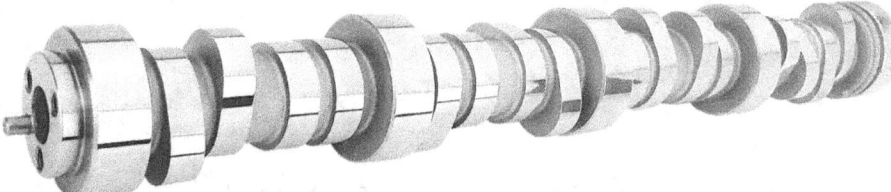

Because the valve sizes and combustion chambers are different, it may be necessary to check piston-to-valve clearance in applications with larger camshafts. Without changing pistons there is a slight mismatch in the pistons' valve reliefs, which can affect clearance.

Generally speaking, cathedral port heads have much better exhaust flow than rectangular ports, which is why cam grinds tend to have more exhaust duration with a rectangular port. For optimum performance, changing cams is recommended, though not necessarily a must. (Photo Courtesy Comp Cams)

With factory valve covers, some grinding may be required to clear the offset intake rocker. This is particularly true on older LS1 designs (on the passenger side mainly), though LS2 and LS6 or later-style valve covers should have no issues. Aftermarket valve covers are usually made to clear bulky aftermarket rockers; if they don't clear, a simple set of spacers from UMI can be used to rectify this problem.

The much different intake runner shape also necessitates a different intake manifold. It is important to note that the factory intakes come complete with injectors, fuel rails, gaskets, and a 90-mm electronic throttle body. However, neither the injectors nor throttle body is compatible with a factory LS1 wiring harness and computer. This is most commonly rectified by purchasing injector plug adapters (such as those from FAST or Caspers Electronics), a 90-mm cable throttle body, and a cable bracket.

It is also worth mentioning that the vacuum line to the rear of the manifold sometimes requires lengthening, as do the wires to the MAP sensor. Those using a carburetor simply need to transfer the old carb to the new intake, assuming its size is still appropriate for the new combination.

Experienced builders, particularly those who are accustomed to building high-compression engines with larger camshafts using tight clearances, may be wondering one or both of two things: how are these heads going to match the valve reliefs on the pistons and how well will the old cam work with the new heads?

If high-compression pistons with LS1-style valve reliefs are in the engine, there is a slight misalignment due to the offset and much larger intake valves with the new heads. In a more street-friendly engine with plenty of piston-to-valve clearance this doesn't factor in, but those running lots of duration and lift with a smaller chamber may need to swap out the pistons.

Cam specs also see quite a bit of variation between cathedral and rectangular ports, most often to compensate for a more choked exhaust port. Depending on the difference in the two heads, this is not to say that gains can't be had without switching cams, but experience shows that most often there is a considerable performance increase from doing so.

Cathedral Versus Rectangular Port

Believe it or not, there is no clear-cut winner between cathedral and rectangular ports, despite the hoopla that rectangular port heads have gotten. In large-cubic-inch and full-on race applications, it appears that rectangular ports have the advantage, but at least one aftermarket cathedral casting (TrickFlow Specialties) has proven to have enormous potential with additional CNC or hand porting—boasting more than 700 hp on a naturally aspirated 440 street engine. And with the latest designs from Air-Flow Research and Mast Motorsports, we may see even more powerful combinations using cathedral heads.

Using the old ET Performance 11-degree, 255-cc cathedral port castings, extensively hand-ported by Gregg Good and matched to a custom Beck sheet-metal intake manifold, Joe Huneycutt's 2002 Camaro is one of the fastest all-engine LSX combinations ever built. The large, solid-roller camshaft spins the little 403-ci engine more than 10,000 rpm, which makes well over 900 hp. This wild 15.8:1, dry sump race engine proves that cathedral ports can be used in high-lift, high-duration, high-RPM applications. Using a highly modified factory 6-speed manual transmission Joe has gone as fast as 8.69 at 156 mph in the quarter-mile.

THE BASICS

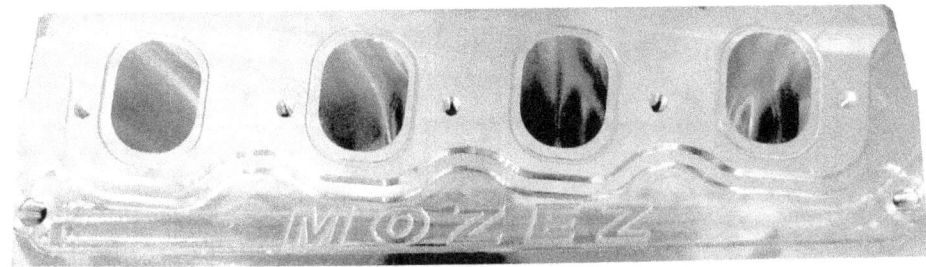

In reality, neither a cathedral nor rectangular port is optimum. An oval port, such as the Mast Motorsports Mozez canted-valve race head shown here, provides the best overall flow because there are no sharp edges to restrict it. (Photo Courtesy Mast Motorsports)

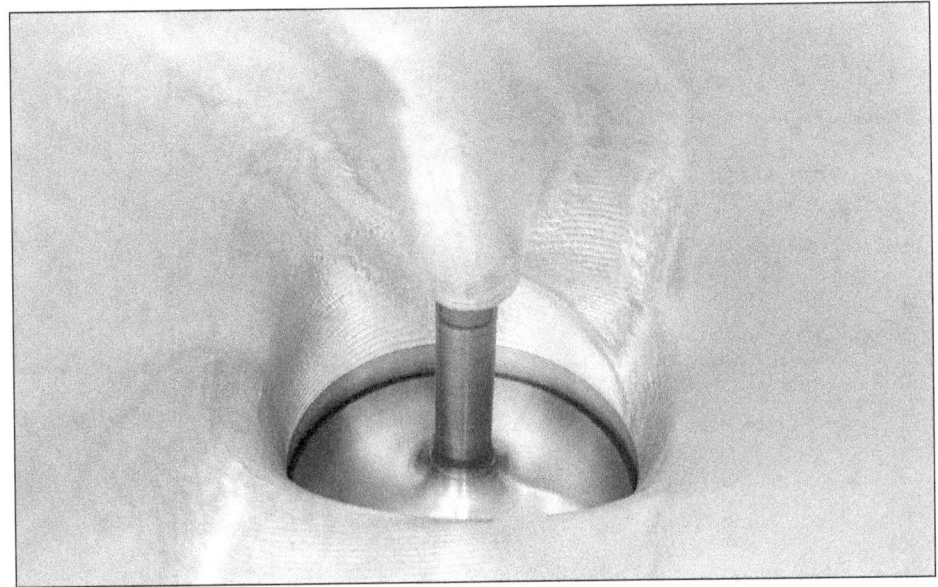

According to cylinder head design theory, neither head is actually the best design—the sharp edges associated with both create resistance in airflow. However, it is important to note that quality rectangular port designs actually use more of a rounded (oval) shape, though they are referred to as rectangular. This started with the C5R head and continues in most newly designed race heads. Quality head porters even use epoxy to further smooth out these edges.

This brings me to the point that not all rectangular heads are created equal. There are many different port shapes, the basic two being the L92/LS3 and the LS7. However, even among them, a CNC program or casting design could be vastly different in terms of runner shape, size, and taper. Some boast high flow numbers, but poor velocity and swirl. Others can be a total home run. As you navigate this book, try not to be obsessed or mesmerized by the flow numbers and instead consider how well the cylinder head matches the rest of your combination.

This is often where cathedral heads prove to be invaluable.

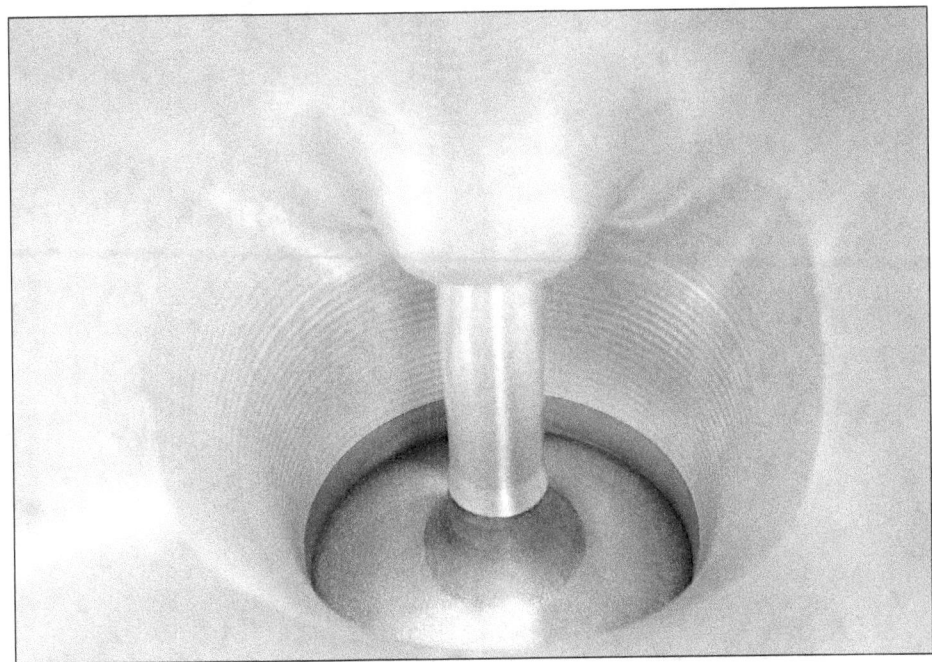

Much like the C5R before it, the LS7 has massive valves and a straight, tunnel-like runner that is effective in producing both low-RPM torque and high-RPM horsepower thanks to its large runner volume, which also manages excellent velocity. The 12-degree valve angle aids in this excellent geometry andthe large valves are accommodated by a Siamesed valve seat. Complete CNC porting on a 5-axis machine makes these some of the highest-flowing factory heads ever. (Photo Courtesy General Motors)

HIGH-PERFORMANCE GM LS-SERIES CYLINDER HEAD GUIDE

CHAPTER 1

Cylinder head porting is somewhat of a black art; gurus can spend hundreds of hours on a single set of heads with a grinder, various grits of sandpaper, welder, and epoxy. CNC machines, however, allow you to replicate a particular set of well-ported heads over and over again, and in half the time. The LS market has embraced this technology by providing programs for virtually every factory or aftermarket casting. West Coast Cylinder Heads is among several companies that even port LS7 and LS9 heads, which come CNC-ported from GM. (Photo Courtesy West Coast Cylinder Heads)

Although most can't claim 330-plus-cfm, they do provide torque, tune-ability, and drivability. On average, cathedral port heads have smaller runners (in terms of volume). Until recently, the largest intake valve you could fit was 2.08 inches. By normal standards this is considered quite large, but not compared to the 2.20-inch intake valves in an LS7 head or the 2.16-inch LS3 valves.

The enormous difference in valve size has a lot to do with the difference in flow between typical cathedral and rectangular port heads. As the result of these factors, very seldom are we comparing apples to apples. So again, I urge you to consider each cylinder head individually.

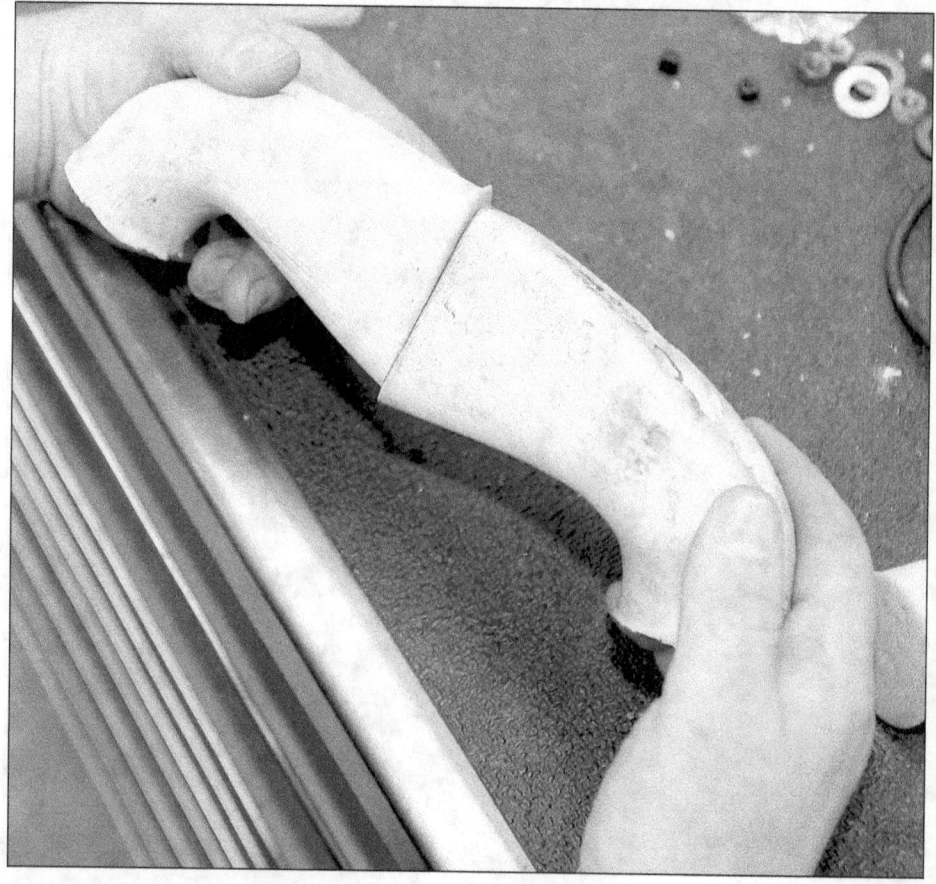

Here is a look at two molds made from Chevrolet Performance's CNC-ported L92 head (left) and an early Mast Motorsports small-bore LS3 casting (right). They are similar, though greater variation can be seen in Mast's newer castings, particularly the large-bore and splayed-valve designs.

14   HIGH-PERFORMANCE GM LS-SERIES CYLINDER HEAD GUIDE

THE BASICS

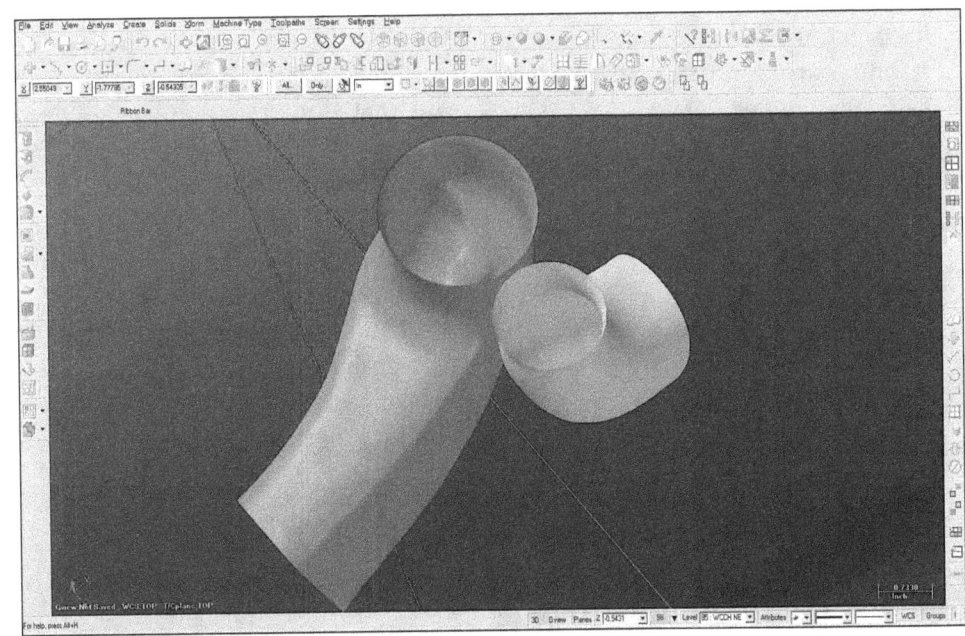

Like any CNC porter, West Coast Cylinder Heads uses CAD (computer aided design) software to create the runner design. Experienced designers know how different shapes affect flow; however, there is even software to predict how various changes alter airflow. Keep in mind that the job of the designer is also to create a "happy" port with good velocity, not just a high-flowing one.

Cylinder Head Theory

As previously mentioned, matching air speed (velocity) is almost always more important than just flow. This is why higher flow numbers on a given combination do not necessarily mean more power. At the end of the day, it is up to builders to use their experience to determine what the engine's airflow needs are.

The other parts of the induction system target horsepower and RPM range, and several other factors must be considered. For example, AirFlow Research's 230-cc LSX Mongoose head may make a perfect match for a 402- to 408-ci, naturally aspirated street combination. However, this head may also work well in a race-only setup, such as a solid-roller 346-ci LS1 that spins to 8,500 rpm or sees a lot of boost.

As much experience as it takes to select the right cylinder head, it takes even more to know how to port one. Top-notch cylinder head porters are few and far between, especially when a CNC machine does the same amount of work at a fraction of the cost. Meticulous hand porting, using epoxy to add material back in where needed, easily yields the best results, and is most often how a CNC program is designed.

Done properly, the CNC machine replicates the port shape and flow within 5 cfm. And best of all, there is no variation—each head is identical, unlike with hand porting. This is, of course, not to say all CNC heads are outstanding. A CNC head is only as good as the program and the casting it was designed on.

Head geometry, as it pertains to valve angles, valve seat angles, and port location, is particularly important and often overlooked. Changing the valve angle, when it comes to LS heads, may not provide nearly as much improvement as it has in the past (such as going from a 23-degree to a 15-degree small-block Chevy head). On the other hand, changing valve angle does allow for larger valves and a higher port, which can greatly improve performance.

LS7 heads, for example, are praised for their raised runners because air does not have a sharp angle at the short-turn radius as the result. The short-turn radius is directly related to torque, mid-range power, and top-end power. There is also something to be said for having shallower combustion chambers, which flatter valve angles allow, as they can decrease detonation and burn time, while increasing efficiency.

The combustion chamber is one of the most overlooked aspects of the cylinder head, yet its design directly affects spark timing and the distribution of fuel in the cylinder—the two other elements needed for combustion. When it comes to chambers, quench is the main focus of attention.

The quench area "squishes" the air/fuel mixture into the flame (spark plug) while also homogenizing the mixture. This flatter area of the head is crucial in meeting the piston to create necessary turbulence; however, the chamber must also complement the port design and layout. The chamber design should be heavily tailored to either lower-lift street applications or higher-lift race applications.

Street applications must stimulate torque production, while also de-shrouding the valves at lower lift. Race chambers must promote airflow stability at high lift using steeper valve seat angles.

The valve job is crucial to smoothly getting properly mixed air and fuel into the chamber, and the specs are again highly dependent on the intended lift and use. Higher valve seat angles, such as 50 to 55 degrees, are better for higher-lift flow and have less durability.

There are many factors that go into designing a good cylinder head, so please use this information wisely and look beyond just flow numbers.

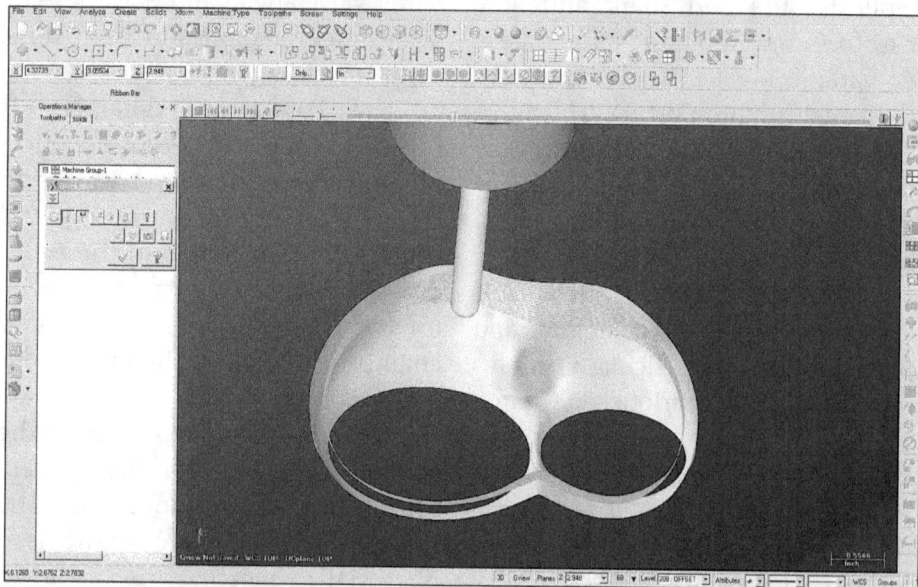

Generally speaking, GM has done its homework when it comes to combustion chamber design. However, its designs were originally meant for emissions-controlled vehicles running either regular or premium pump gas. Optimizing for a hot rod or race car sometimes requires updates such as WCCH's L92 design, which even helps stuff a 2.20-inch intake valve on its Stage 3. Just like the runners, the design is created with CAD software and the work is done on a 5-axis CNC machine.

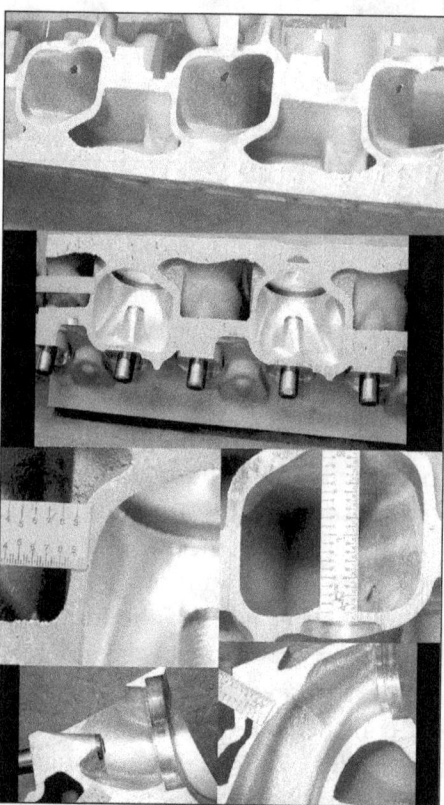

Few companies have spent as much time going back and forth between the flow bench and engine dyno as Lingenfelter Performance Engineering. Thousands of hours went into designing its LS3 CNC program, which has been completely dissected here to demonstrate wall thickness as well as runner height. Though rectangular at the opening, here you can see what the runner shape actually looks like. (Photo Courtesy Lingenfelter Performance Engineering)

CHAPTER 2

CATHEDRAL PORT CYLINDER HEADS

Cathedral port cylinder heads have been mistakenly dismissed by many in LS-series circles for being "old-tech." However, their thin cross section allows for a high-velocity and smaller-volume runner design with excellent flow. For a street car, this design means excellent throttle response, torque and average power.

Dyno tests have proven that comparable aftermarket cathedral port heads can match a rectangular port in peak power, while proving much more impressive below the curve. For road racing, a cathedral port is ideal, and has even proven to be quite capable in drag racing with an altered valve angle and larger runner sizes.

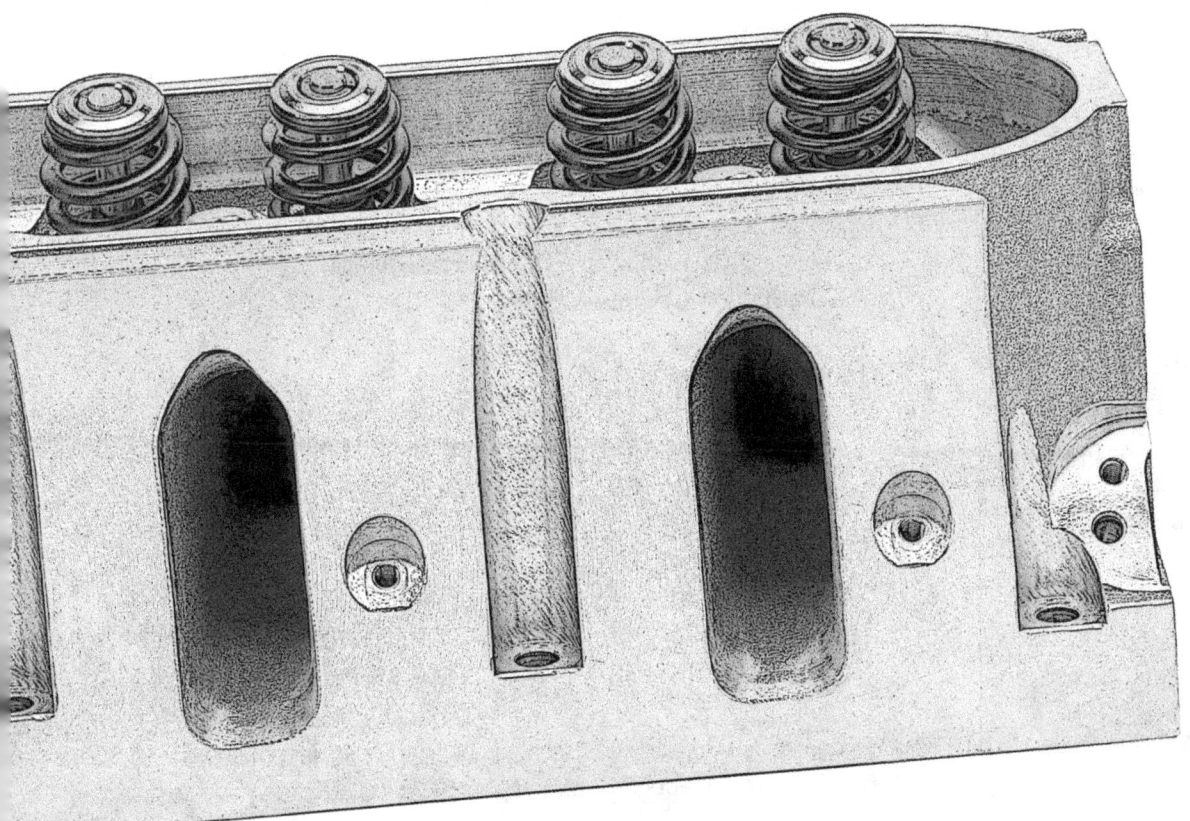

CHAPTER 2

Factory Heads

LS1

The OEM design that started it all, the original Gen III cylinder head, helped produce 350 hp using 5.7 liters of displacement. There are changes throughout the model years, which are indicated with various casting numbers (last three digits are the part number). The later "241" castings featured lighter valves, a more common center valve cover bolt configuration, and several other nuances that make them more desirable than the "853" casting. Though no longer produced by GM, all versions are fairly abundant used and work with any factory (or larger) bore. If you are new to Gen IIIs, please note that these heads are aluminum and unless otherwise noted, so is every other head in this book.

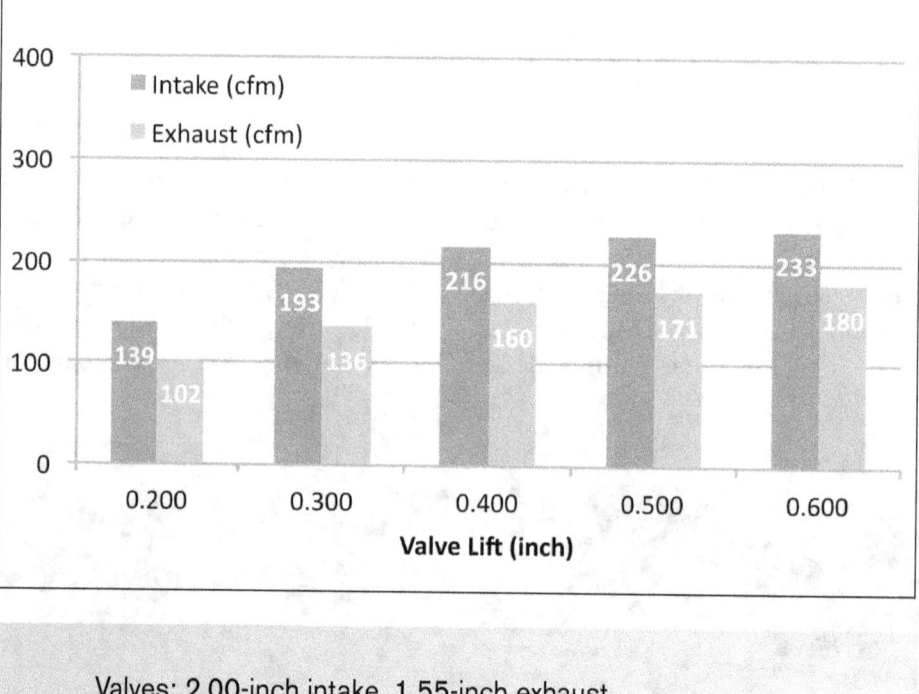

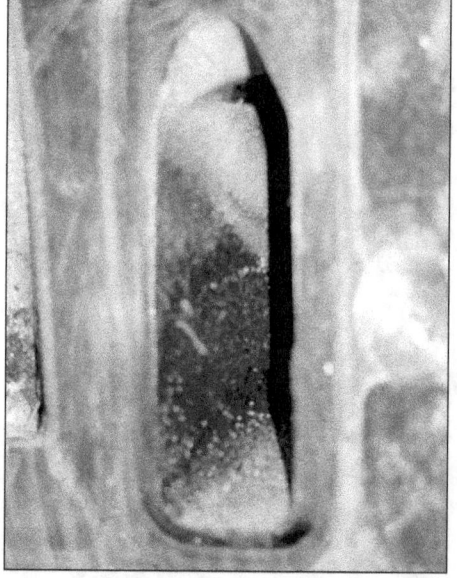

Valves: 2.00-inch intake, 1.55-inch exhaust
Combustion Chamber: 67.3 cc

Intake Runner: 200 cc
Intake (tested on a 3.90-inch bore):

Lift (inch)	.200	.300	.400	.500	.600
Flow (cfm)	139	193	216	226	233

Exhaust Runner: 70 cc
Exhaust (tested with no exhaust pipe):

Lift (inch)	.200	.300	.400	.500	.600
Flow (cfm)	102	136	160	171	180

Recommended Use: smaller cubic-inch combinations, can support more than 525 hp
Additional Features: 15-degree valve angle, 30/45/60-degree valve seat angles

CATHEDRAL PORT CYLINDER HEADS

LR4/LM4/LM7

Following directly in the engineering footprint of the LS1 casting, these cylinder heads were used on the 4.8- and 5.3-liter truck engines. The only differences between these heads and the LS1, besides the price, are the valve size and combustion chamber. Out of the box, the small valves make these heads a poor choice for performance applications, but these components are easily upgradable, which often makes for a great high-compression head that is easy on the wallet. These heads have been phased out of production in favor of higher-flowing, LS6-based castings. However, they are quite plentiful used and work with any bore size; search for casting numbers "852" and "706."

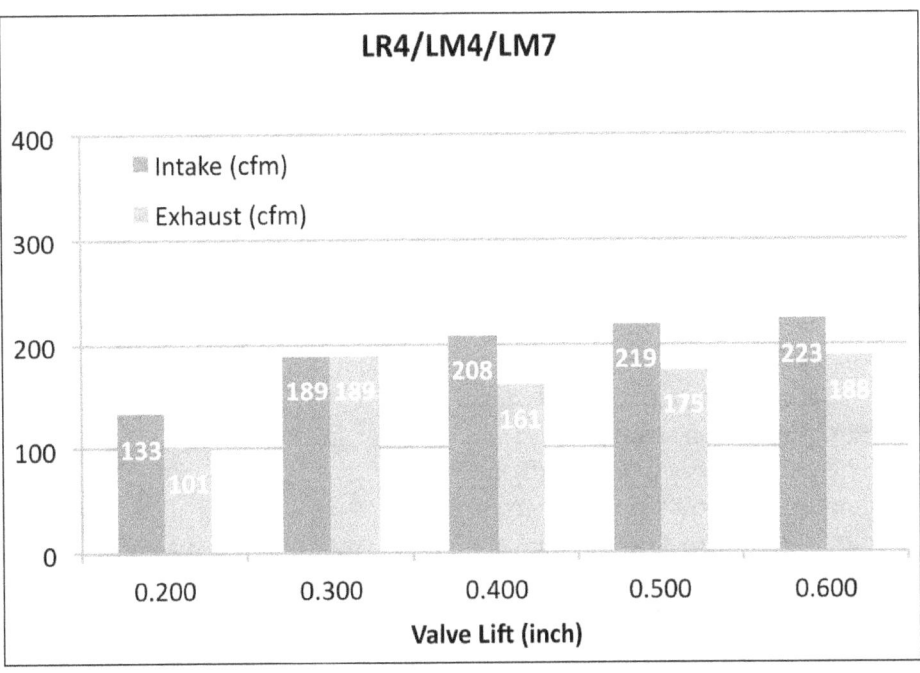

Valves: 1.89-inch intake, 1.55-inch exhaust
Combustion Chamber: 61.15 cc

Intake Runner: 200 cc
Intake:

Lift (inch)	.200	.300	.400	.500	.600
Flow (cfm)	133	189	208	219	223

Exhaust Runner: 70 cc
Exhaust:

Lift (inch)	.200	.300	.400	.500	.600
Flow (cfm)	101	189	161	175	188

Recommended Use: small cubic-inch combinations
Additional Features: 15-degree valve angle

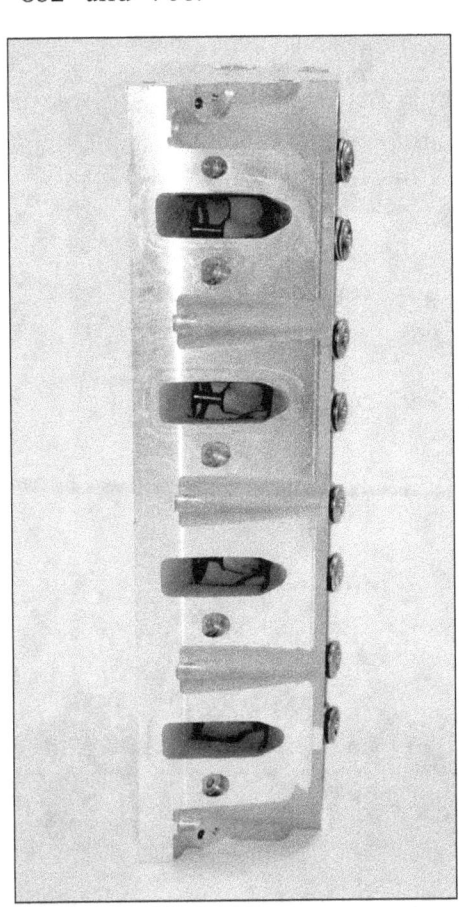

CHAPTER 2

LQ4

These heads came on low-performance 6.0-liter truck engines in two variations: "873" cast iron (1999–2000) and "317" aluminum (2001+). The early design was the only cast-iron LS head ever made, and the least desirable in a performance application. However, the later heads can be a good choice for boosted applications because they offer larger runners and combustion chambers (for lower compression) over the factory LS1 heads. Because these heads are no longer in production, they must be purchased used. Though they are not the most common, they are also not the most desirable, so the price tag is usually very reasonable and work with any bore size.

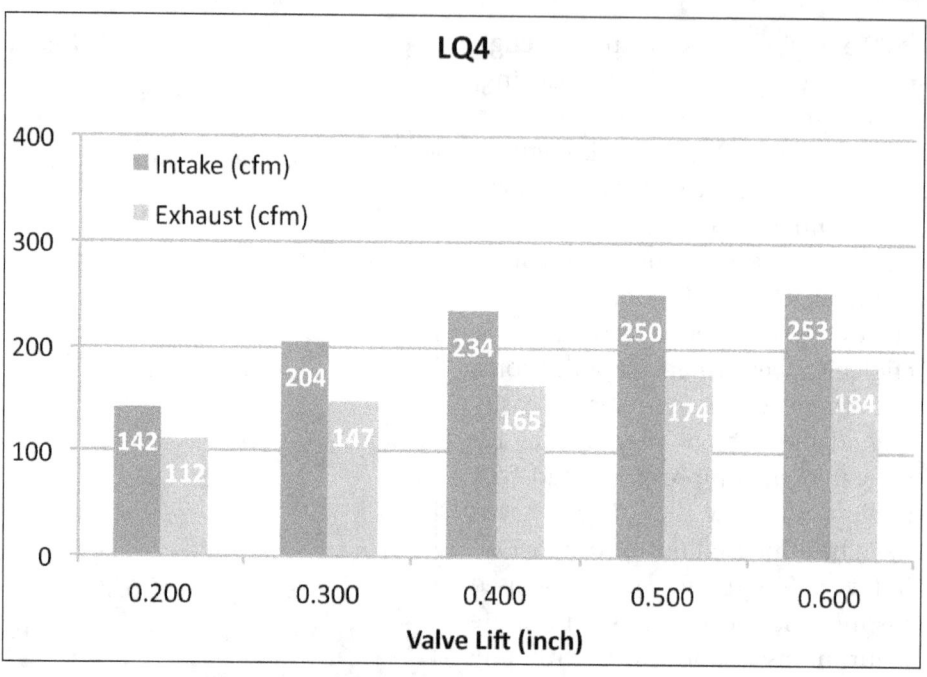

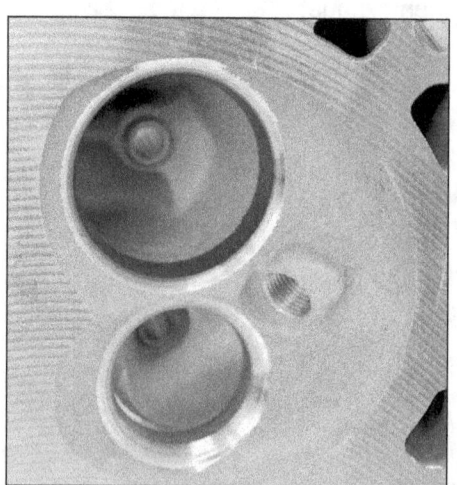

Valves: 2.00-inch intake, 1.55-inch exhaust
Combustion Chamber: 71.06 cc

Intake Runner: 210 cc
Intake (tested on a 4.030-inch bore):
   Lift (inch) .200 .300 .400 .500 .600
   Flow (cfm) 142 204 234 250 253

Exhaust Runner: 75 cc
Exhaust (tested without a pipe):
   Lift (inch) .200 .300 .400 .500 .600
   Flow (cfm) 112 147 165 174 184

Recommended Use: boosted smaller cubic-inch combinations
Additional Features: 15-degree valve angle

LQ9

The hi-po 6.0-liter truck engines, such as the Cadillac Escalade, received this variation on the LS6 head. Though the runners are identical to those on the LS6, its combustion chambers are larger, just like the LQ4. This combination of optimal runner design and larger chambers makes the "035" head (aka "317") the best of the OEMs for boost. These heads are no longer in production, replaced on 6.0- and 6.2-liter truck engines with the L92 head, but used castings are not uncommon or unreasonably expensive. Because of the small valves, these heads fit on small-bore applications (though the large chambers may be a bit much).

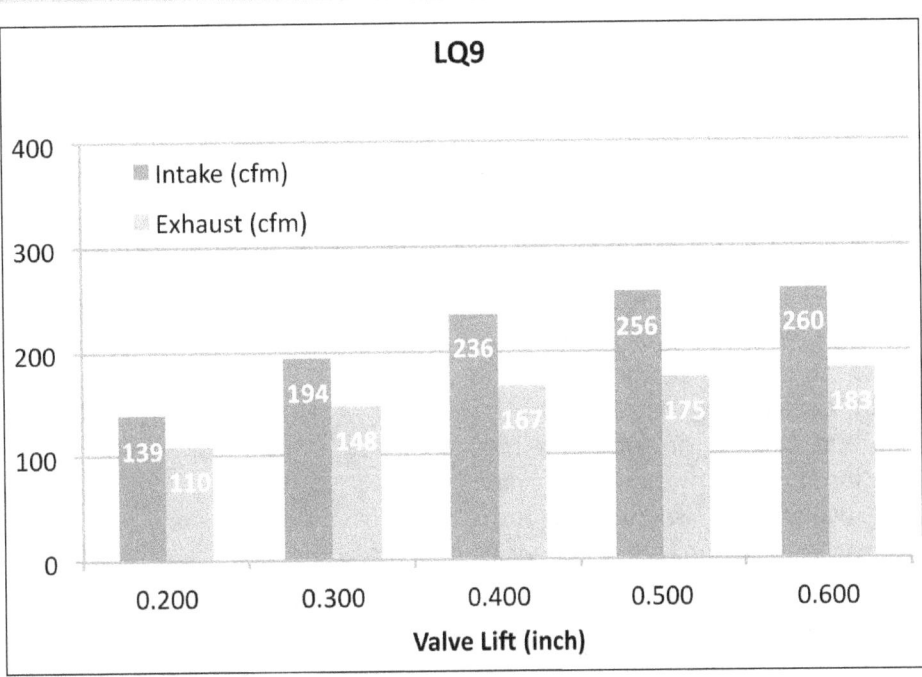

Valves: 2.00-inch intake, 1.55-inch exhaust
Combustion Chamber: 71.06 cc

Intake Runner: 210 cc
Intake:

Lift (inch)	.200	.300	.400	.500	.600
Flow (cfm)	139	194	236	256	260

Exhaust Runner: 75 cc
Exhaust:

Lift (inch)	.200	.300	.400	.500	.600
Flow (cfm)	110	148	167	175	183

Recommended Use: boosted smaller cubic-inch combinations
Additional Features: 15-degree valve angle

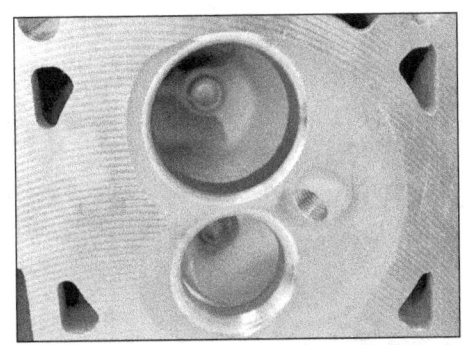
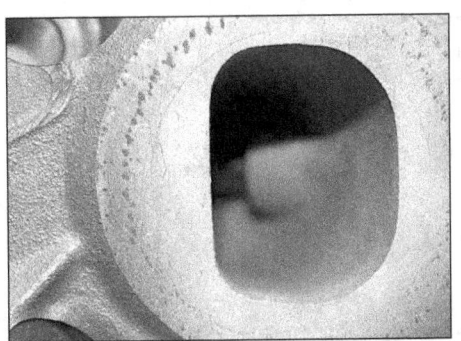
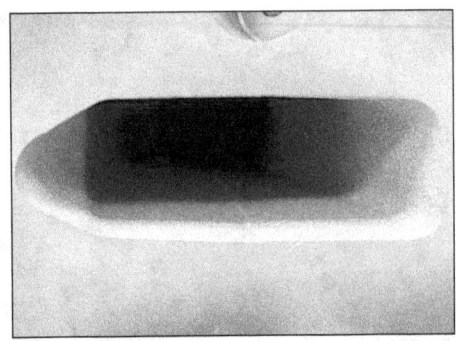

LS6/LS2

In its most potent form, these heads supported a conservatively rated 405 hp on the Z06 Corvette. The LS6 was designed specifically by GM to surpass the LS1 as the best performance head, and it did such a good job that the "243" casting was recycled on the LS2. Aside from the LQ9, which is a copy of the LS6, these are the best performing of the OEM cathedral ports. Though the LS6 and LS2 are no longer in production, brand-new bare castings are still available for around $850 from Chevrolet Performance Parts dealers. In production these heads have been repurposed on the aluminum 5.3L truck engine (L33, "799" casting), which proves that despite being originally made for a 3.90-inch bore, these heads even fit on 4.8/5.3L blocks (3.78-inch bore), and are quite abundant used.

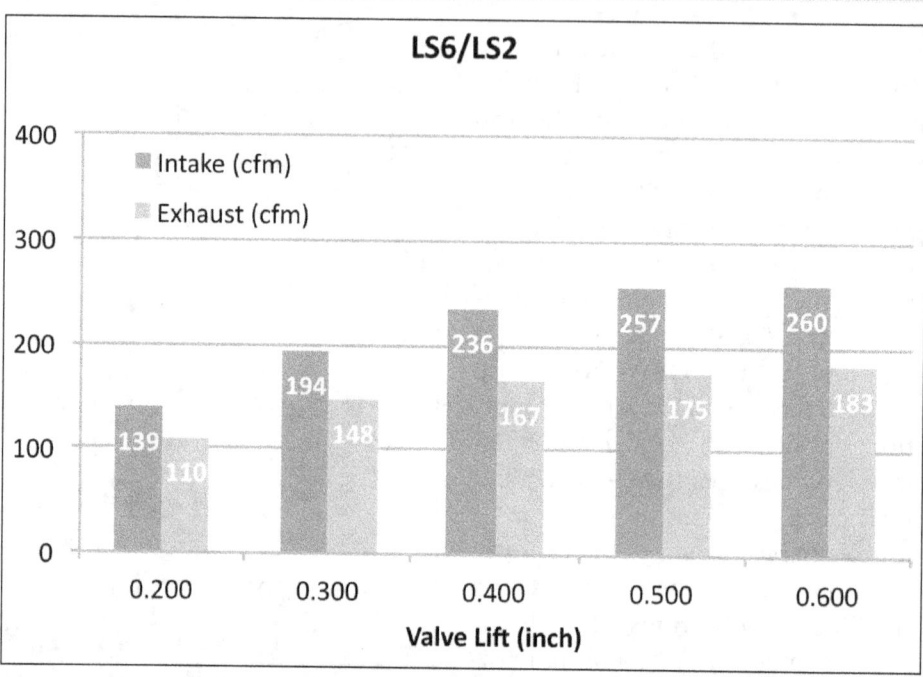

Valves: 2.00-inch intake, 1.55-inch exhaust
Combustion Chamber: 65 cc

Intake Runner: 210 cc
Intake (tested on a 4.00-inch bore):

Lift (inch)	.200	.300	.400	.500	.600
Flow (cfm)	139	194	236	257	260

Exhaust Runner: 75 cc
Exhaust (tested with no exhaust pipe):

Lift (inch)	.200	.300	.400	.500	.600
Flow (cfm)	110	148	167	175	183

Recommended Use: smaller cubic-inch combinations, can support more than 525 hp
Additional Features: 15-degree valve angle, revised "D" exhaust port and combustion chambers

CATHEDRAL PORT CYLINDER HEADS

Aftermarket Heads

Although Chevrolet has invested plenty of time and effort into engineering a fine array of cylinder heads for the LS-Series engines, it still must focus on the needs of the mass-market consumer. Aftermarket companies have no such restrictions, and can craft performance-specific castings to meet the needs of racers and hardcore enthusiasts. Some of them are custom porting jobs based on existing factory castings, while others are completely custom castings.

This means an incredibly broad range of port sizes, chamber depths, and valve options exist for the discerning LS head shopper. Whether you're designing an engine from the ground up or updating an existing powerplant, the odds are strong you'll be able to find a head that suits your needs whether you're drag racing, road racing, or off-roading. If you need to feed a big-inch stroker LS or are adding forced induction, a well-engineered head that can aid your quest for power almost certainly exists.

On the following pages you'll find the pertinent information and dimensions for just about every commercially-available aftermarket cylinder head. Please note that the flow numbers have been provided by the manufacturers, and may not be perfectly comparable because they were acquired on different equipment. Still, they should be close enough to serve your needs when looking for a particular flow range.

Includes:

GM 706/862
5.3-Liter LS1, 218 cc

GM 243 (LS6) and
799 (LS2), 218 cc

GM 243 (LS6) and
799 (LS2), 226 cc

Advanced Induction

While not the largest name in the industry, AI is well respected. This North Carolina–based shop is practically a factory for CNC head porting, with programs for the Gen II, III, and IV small-block only. Specializing in such a finite area makes AI particularly knowledgable, precise, and efficient. Each program is well thought out to appeal to a particular and common customer need. At the time of publication, AI had just completed several new heads with aftermarket and factory castings. It also offers intake manifold porting and valvetrain kits with a specially designed camshaft.

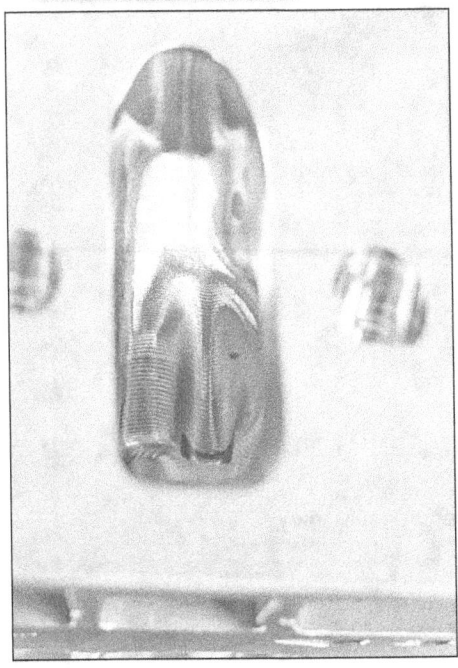

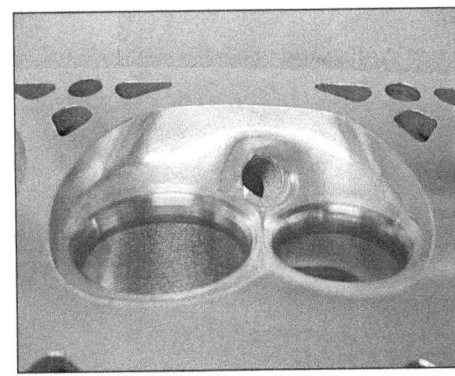

Advanced Induction
GM 706/862 5.3-Liter LS1, 218 cc

Advanced Induction (AI) takes the GM "706" casting to the next level by replacing the small factory valves with Manley Racemaster stainless-steel valves, suitable for a 3.90-inch bore. These heads boast plenty of piston-to-valve clearance for an 11:1, stock cubic-inch LS1 with a large-duration cam (without cutting piston reliefs), though cutting the chambers can easily put compression over 12:1. AI claims this reasonably priced offering is easily capable of 440 to 480 rear wheel horsepower (rwhp) with one of its cams and supporting bolt-ons in a 346-ci engine. A similar program for the "241" casting is also available. The machining and labor costs alone are $1,145 (there is a separate cost for various valves and valvesprings and other options). The buyer must supply a core. Because stock valves are used, there is no limitation on bore size.

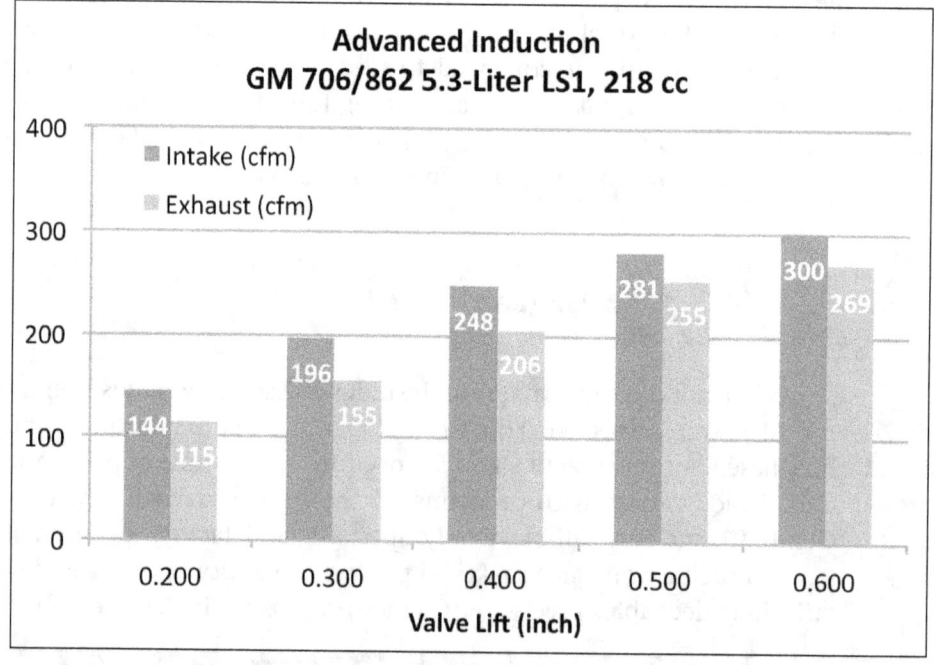

Valves: 2.00-inch intake, 1.55-inch exhaust
Combustion Chamber: 50 to 60 cc

Intake Runner: 218 cc
Intake (designed for and tested on a 3.90-inch bore):
    Lift (inch) .200 .300 .400 .500 .600
    Flow (cfm) 144   196   248   281   300

Exhaust Runner: N/A
Exhaust (tested with no exhaust pipe):
    Lift (inch) .200 .300 .400 .500 .600
    Flow (cfm) 115   155   206   255   269

Recommended Use: 327 to 383 ci, naturally aspirated or nitrous
Additional Features: new GM casting, custom-honed bronze valveguides, Manley valves, variety of valvespring options

CATHEDRAL PORT CYLINDER HEADS

Advanced Induction
GM 243 (LS6) and 799 (LS2), 218 cc

The 218-cc LS6/LS2 head is a mild upgrade from the basic performance rebuild, which boosts flow by 32.2 cfm on the intake side and 28.5 cfm on the exhaust side, at .600-inch lift, despite the more cost conscious machine work. That is not to say, of course, that the 218s don't go through the same rigorous and thorough machine work as AI's other heads: CNC-ported runners, PCD-milled deck, flanges, and valve cover rail. AI claims these heads are worth 20 to 30 rwhp over the stock, as-cast heads. The base machining and labor cost is $795, plus a $775 core charge (for brand-new heads). Additional charges apply for various components and options. The stock valves allow for any bore size.

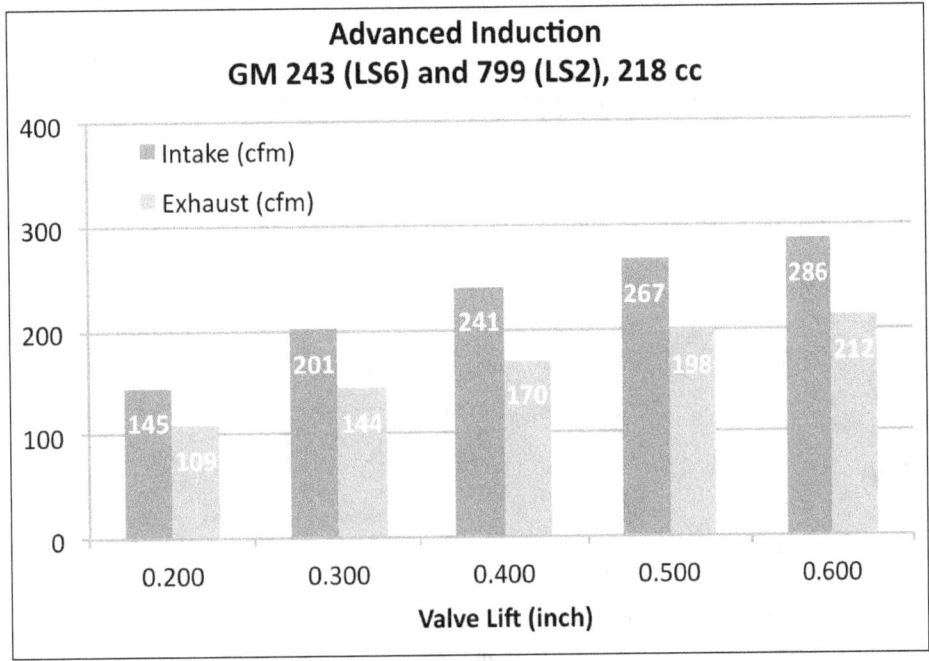

Valves: 2.00-inch intake, 1.55-inch exhaust
Combustion Chamber: 57 to 69 cc

Intake Runner: 218 cc
Intake (designed for and tested on a 3.910-inch bore):

Lift (inch)	.200	.300	.400	.500	.600
Flow (cfm)	145	201	241	267	286

Exhaust Runner: N/A
Exhaust (tested with no exhaust pipe):

Lift (inch)	.200	.300	.400	.500	.600
Flow (cfm)	109	144	170	198	212

Recommended Use: 346 to 370 ci, forced induction or naturally aspirated
Additional Features: new GM casting, custom-honed bronze liners, variety of valvespring options

CHAPTER 2

Advanced Induction
GM 243 (LS6) and 799 (LS2), 226 cc

AI's flagship cathedral port increases the port volume by 15 cc over stock, allowing up to a 41-cfm improvement over stock while still utilizing the factory GM valves (reground). Despite the larger runners, AI claims these heads produce great power under the curve, crisp throttle response, and no loss in driveability. Although the stock valves would seem to hold them back, many records are owed to these heads from stock cubic-inchers to strokers, especially on heavier vehicles such as GTOs and Trailblazer SSs. A special high-compression version is also available to allow plenty of piston-to-valve clearance for big cams with a smaller chamber and stock pistons. Machining and labor runs $995, plus a $775 core charge (for new heads); however, additional charges apply for various components and options. There is no bore size limitation.

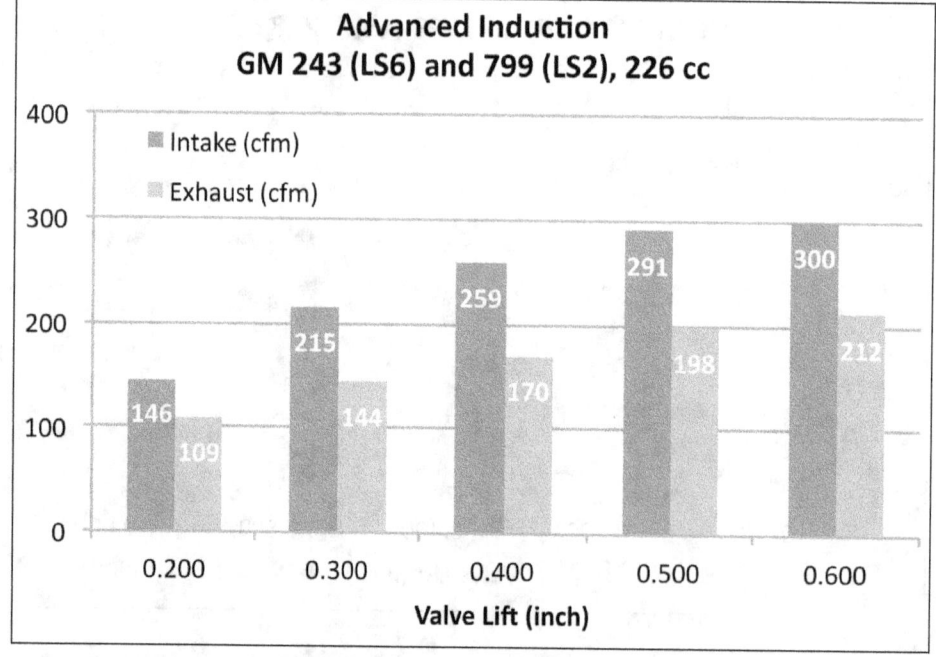

Valves: 2.00-inch intake, 1.55-inch exhaust
Combustion Chamber: 57 to 69 cc

Intake Runner: 226 cc
Intake (designed for and tested on a 4.00-inch bore):

Lift (inch)	.200	.300	.400	.500	.600
Flow (cfm)	146	215	259	291	300

Exhaust Runner: N/A
Exhaust (tested with no exhaust pipe):

Lift (inch)	.200	.300	.400	.500	.600
Flow (cfm)	109	144	170	198	212

Recommended Use: 346 to 416 ci, forced induction or naturally aspirated
Additional Features: new GM casting, custom-honed bronze valveguides, AI .625-inch beehive springs with OEM seals or Manley .660-inch-lift valvespring package with titanium retainers and Viton seals

CATHEDRAL PORT CYLINDER HEADS

Includes:

LS1, 210 cc

LS1, 215 cc

LS1, 230 cc

LS1, 245 cc

AirFlow Research

AFR is a staple in the aftermarket cylinder head market, beginning in the 1970s and pioneering CNC porting with its revolutionary tape-fed CNC machine. NHRA legends Bill "Grumpy" Jenkins and Warren Johnson both got their power from AFR aluminum heads. In the 1980s AFR loaned its services to GM and NASCAR, pioneering the use of wet flow technology. In the early 1990s the company began full production, and incorporated advanced, high-density cast-billet technology. At long last this brought full five-axis CNC-ported aluminum heads to racers at an affordable price. AFR became the first to offer aftermarket LT1/LT4 heads, the first to receive a CARB EO number, and the first to introduce an LS1/LS6 head. This family-owned and -operated organization is based in southern California, and continues to stay on the cutting edge. (Photos Courtesy AirFlow Research)

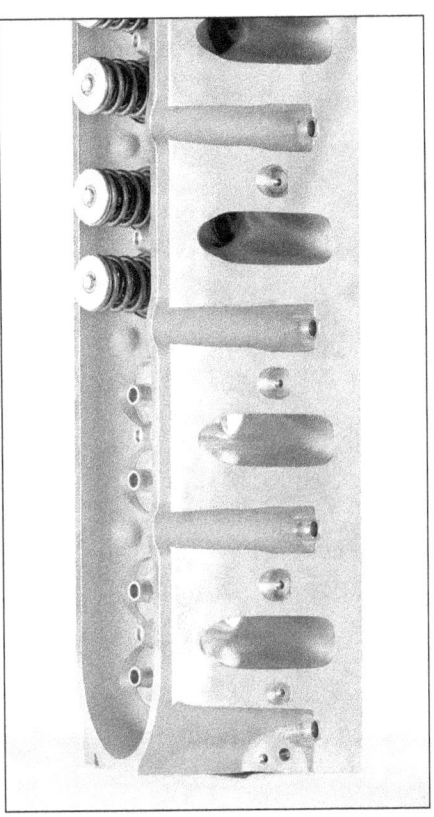
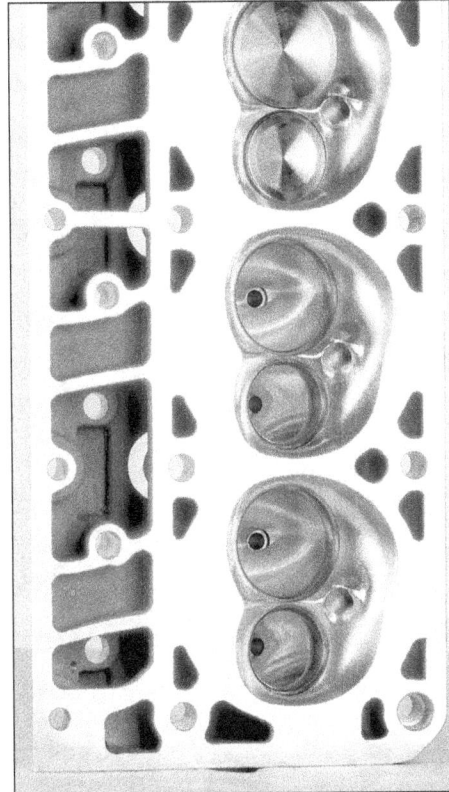

LS1 210 cc and LS1 215 cc

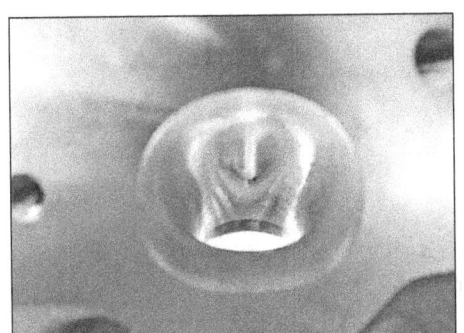

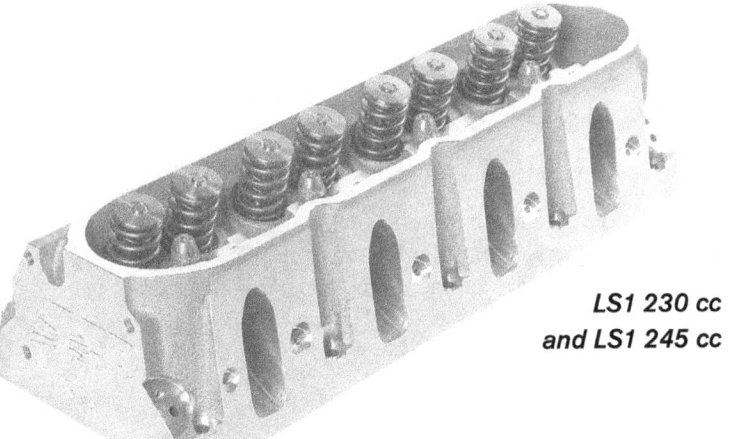

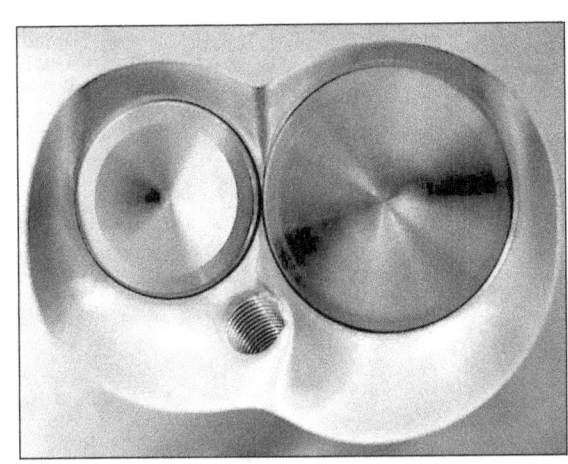

LS1 230 cc and LS1 245 cc

HIGH-PERFORMANCE GM LS-SERIES CYLINDER HEAD GUIDE

AirFlow Research
LS1, 210 cc

The small-port, high-velocity, 210-cc Mongoose is an update of the head that started it all. While others were still developing CNC programs for OEM castings, AirFlow Research (AFR) started with a clean sheet of paper and used the CNC machine to further manipulate its well-formed design. The latest iteration boasts excellent torque for smaller-cube combos, and many added features to benefit forced induction and overall durability while still compatible with factory rocker arms, intake manifold, etc. Later, center-bolt-style valve covers are required, as with all AFR castings. These heads are built for a 3.900-inch bore or larger and cost $2,400.

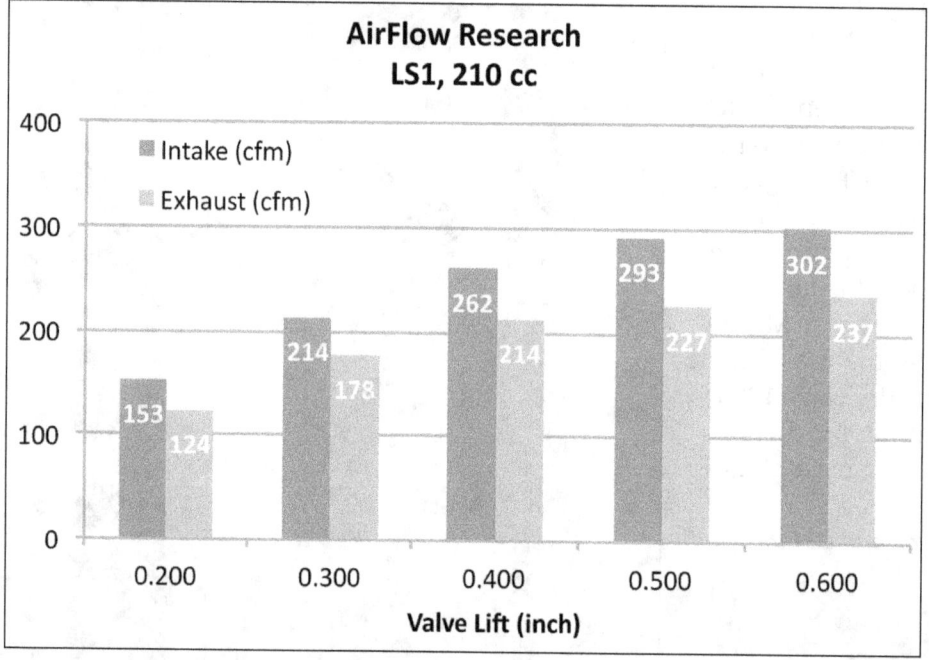

Valves: 2.020-inch intake, 1.60-inch exhaust
Combustion Chamber: 66 or 76 cc

Intake Runner: 210 cc
Intake (designed for and tested on a 3.90-inch bore):
  Lift (inch)   .200   .300   .400   .500   .600
  Flow (cfm)   153   214   262   293   302

Exhaust Runner: 84 cc
Exhaust (tested with a 1.875-inch exhaust pipe):
  Lift (inch)   .200   .300   .400   .500   .600
  Flow (cfm)   124   178   214   227   237

Recommended Use: 346 to 396 ci, forced induction or naturally aspirated
Additional Features: 1.290-inch OD valvesprings with .600-inch maximum lift, 7-degree locks and titanium retainers, bronze valveguides, 5-angle competition valve job, 3/4-inch-thick deck, reinforced rocker stud area, CARB-legal

CATHEDRAL PORT CYLINDER HEADS

AirFlow Research
LS1, 215 cc

The 215-cc Mongoose was designed specifically to maximize the 4-inch bore, and is an excellent choice for street-based applications. However, the 215-cc head can also be a good choice for aggressive or forced-induction 346-ci combinations. This fully CNC'd aftermarket casting also boasts high velocity and is still compatible with all factory equipment. Though it was designed for a 4-inch-or-larger bore, this head is also compatible with a 3.90-inch bore and simply bolts right on with factory components and fasteners. Fully assembled, the 215s go for $2,465.

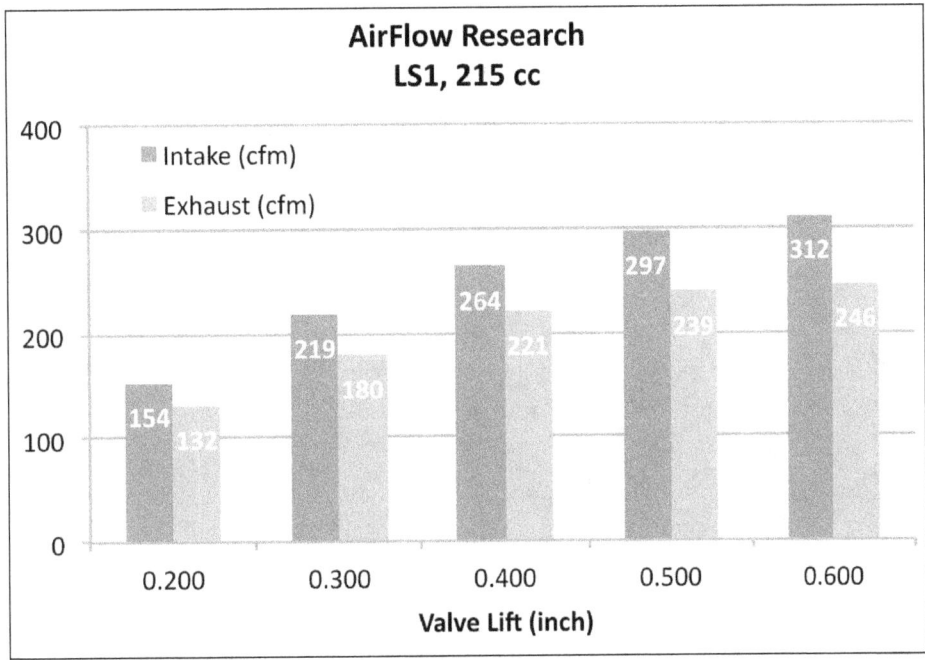

Valves: 2.020-inch intake, 1.60-inch exhaust
Combustion Chamber: 68 cc

Intake Runner: 215 cc
Intake (designed for and tested on a 4.00-inch bore):
Lift (inch)	.200	.300	.400	.500	.600
Flow (cfm)	154	219	264	297	312

Exhaust Runner: 84 cc
Exhaust (tested with a 1.875-inch exhaust pipe):
Lift (inch)	.200	.300	.400	.500	.600
Flow (cfm)	132	180	221	239	246

Recommended Use: 364 to 408 ci, forced induction or naturally aspirated
Additional Features: 1.290-inch OD valvesprings with .600-inch maximum lift, 7-degree locks and titanium retainers, bronze valveguides, 5-angle competition valve job, 3/4-inch-thick deck, reinforced rocker stud area

AirFlow Research
LS1, 230 cc

Available in small- and large-bore variations, the 230-cc Mongoose is extremely versatile and perhaps the most capable emissions-legal head on the market. For an all-out, boosted 346-ci combo this head gives up some low-end torque, but screams up top. However, it is ideal for naturally aspirated strokers (396 to 427 ci). Plenty of added features make this a competitive head for the money, especially since it is compatible with all factory equipment. The minimum bore size required is 3.90 inches, with three different chambers available; the largest of which is intended for larger bores (such as 4.060 to 4.125 inches). Total cost, fully assembled, is just under $2,600.

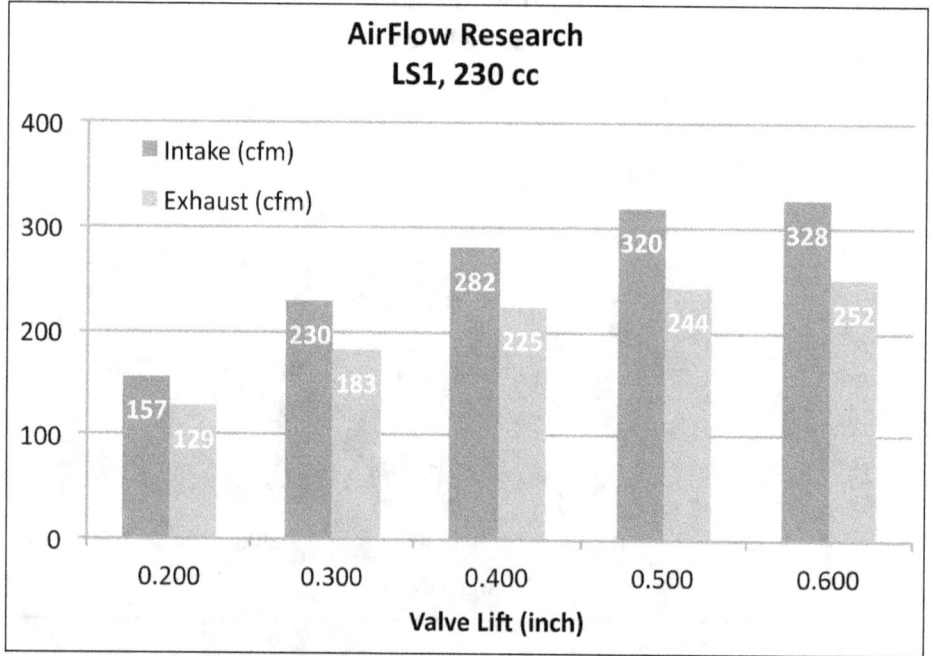

Valves: 2.080-inch intake, 1.60-inch exhaust
Combustion Chamber: 62, 65, or 72 cc

Intake Runner: 230 cc
Intake: (designed for and tested on a 4.125-inch bore):

Lift (inch)	.200	.300	.400	.500	.600
Flow (cfm)	157	230	282	320	328

Exhaust Runner: 84 cc
Exhaust (tested with a 1.875-inch exhaust pipe):

Lift (inch)	.200	.300	.400	.500	.600
Flow (cfm)	129	183	225	244	252

Recommended Use: 396 to 427 ci, forced induction or naturally aspirated
Additional Features: 1.270-inch OD valvesprings with .650-inch maximum lift, 7-degree locks and titanium retainers, bronze valveguides, 5-angle competition valve job, 3/4-inch-thick deck, reinforced rocker stud area, CARB-legal

AirFlow Research
LS1, 245 cc

The large-bore 245 cc is AFR's flagship, maximum-effort head. Machined to accept .375-inch pushrods and equipped with 1.570-inch spring pockets, this head is indeed solid roller friendly. With high-end flow reaching 360 cfm at .650-inch lift, the 245 cc is comparable to an LS7, but with greater exhaust flow. This combination enables more than 700 hp while still providing gobs of low- and mid-range torque. Like the rest of the line-up, this head still uses stock valve lengths and geometry, and is compatible with factory equipment. A 4.200-inch-bore head gasket is required; meanwhile, the heads can actually be used on a 4.00-inch-bore block (or larger). However, only the most aggressive, race-only 4.00-inch-bore combinations require such a stout head. Expect to pay $2,700 for a fully assembled set.

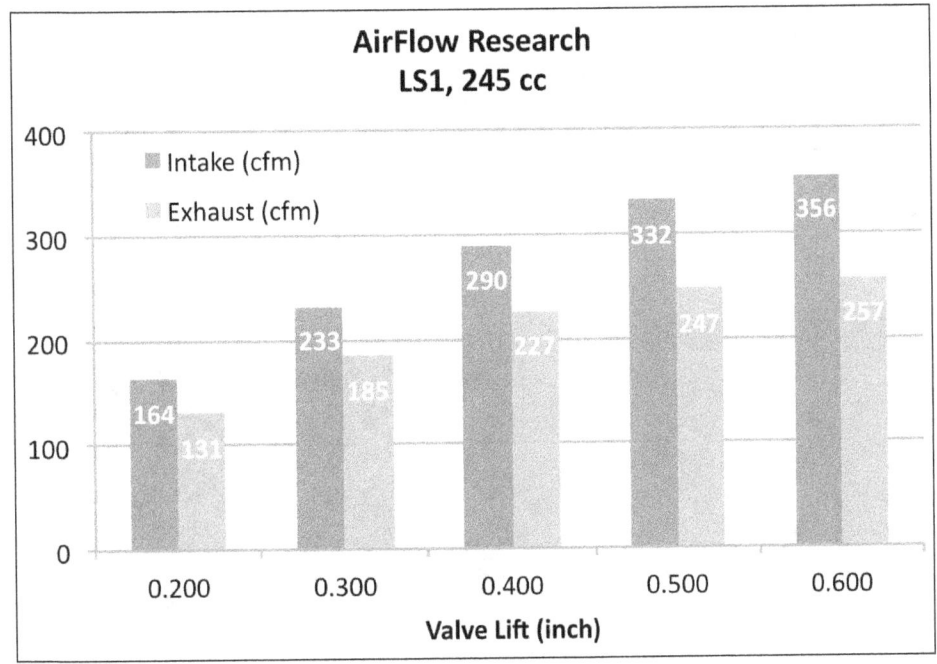

Valves: 2.160-inch intake, 1.60-inch exhaust
Combustion Chamber: 65 or 73 cc

Intake Runner: 245 cc
Intake (designed for and tested on a 4.155-inch bore):
   Lift (inch) .200 .300 .400 .500 .600
   Flow (cfm) 164 233 290 332 356

Exhaust Runner: 87 cc
Exhaust (tested with a 1.875-inch exhaust pipe):
   Lift (inch) .200 .300 .400 .500 .600
   Flow (cfm) 131 185 227 247 257

Recommended Use: 415 to 454 ci, forced induction or naturally aspirated
Additional Features: 1.270-inch OD valvesprings with .650-inch maximum lift, 7-degree locks and titanium retainers, bronze valveguides, 5-angle competition valve job, 3/4-inch-thick deck, reinforced rocker stud area

CHAPTER 2

Edelbrock/Lingenfelter

Includes:

LS1 Performer RPM, CNC

LS1/LS2, E-CNC 215

One of the oldest names in the industry is Edelbrock. Vic Edelbrock, Sr., designed and sold his first intake manifold in the late 1930s (for the Ford flathead). It wasn't until 1946, however, that the first catalogue was printed as the business was temporarily put on hold for World War II. In 1948, Vic Sr. purchased one of the industry's first engine dynamometers, which lead the way for revolutionary small-block Chevy intake manifold designs. In 1962 the company was handed to Vic Jr., following the passing of his father, who has continued the tradition of building well-tested, quality parts in Southern California. Edelbrock has its own aluminum foundries with a permanent-mold and heat-treat facility located nearby, for a 100-percent Made in the USA product. Edelbrock continues to use its resources as the basis for some incredible products from budget to high-end and street to full-on race. (Photos Courtesy Edelbrock)

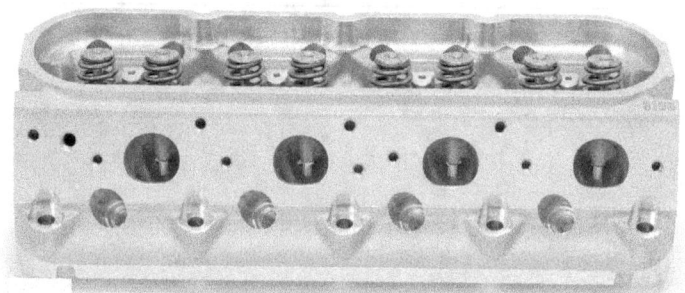

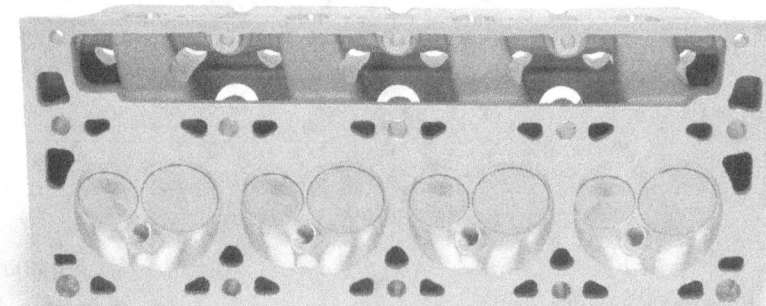

LS1 Performer RPM CNC

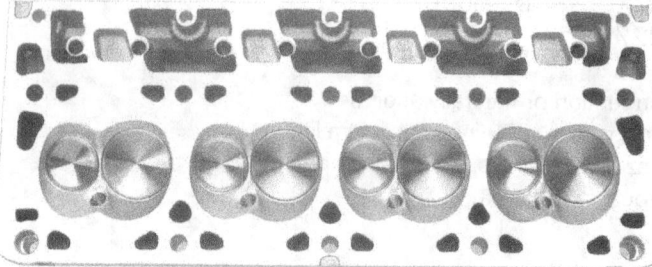

E-CNC 215 LS1/LS2

HIGH-PERFORMANCE GM LS-SERIES CYLINDER HEAD GUIDE

CATHEDRAL PORT CYLINDER HEADS

Edelbrock/Lingenfelter LS1 Performer RPM, CNC

Edelbrock worked with Lingenfelter Performance to use its aftermarket casting to create an all-out, high-flowing street/strip head. These heads come in a smaller 203-cc intake runner and a 230-cc runner for strokers. The smaller version is perfect for stock cubic-inch combos, and flows plenty of air. Plenty of other great features are afforded by the clean-sheet casting design, though these heads are compatible with factory rockers and other components. These heads bolt right on to any 3.90-inch-or-larger bore and come fully assembled for $1,350.

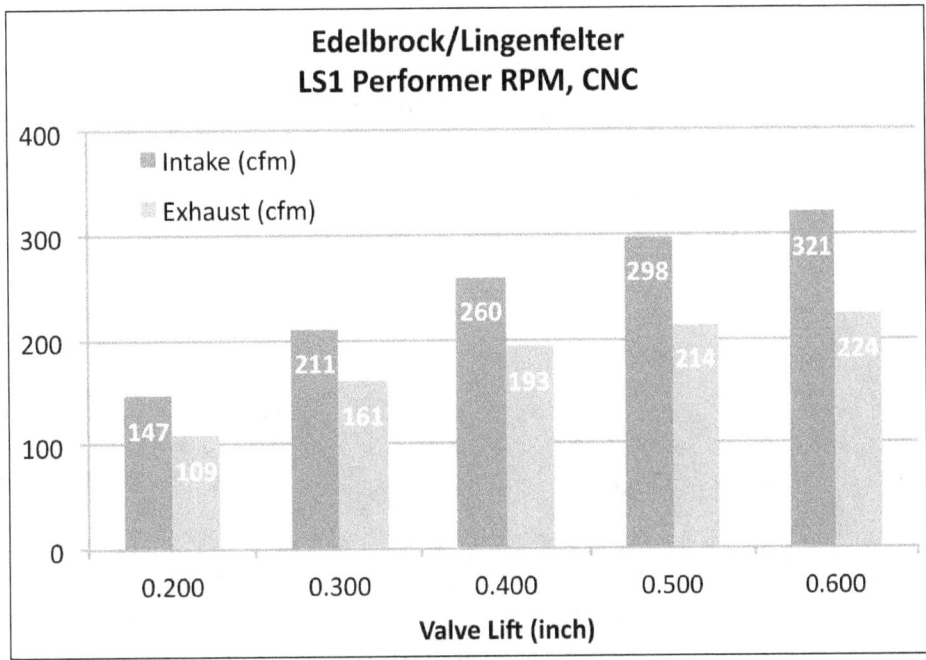

Valves: 2.02-inch intake, 1.57-inch exhaust
Combustion Chamber: 65 cc

Intake Runner: 203 cc
Intake (tested on a 4.00-inch bore):
 Lift (inch) .200 .300 .400 .500 .600
 Flow (cfm)   147   211   260   298   321

Exhaust Runner: 78 cc
Exhaust:
 Lift (inch) .200 .300 .400 .500 .600
 Flow (cfm)   109   161   193   214   224

Recommended Use: 346 to 408 ci, forced induction or naturally aspirated
Additional Features: Manganese bronze valveguides, .600-inch lift valvesprings with 1.55/1.30-inch diameter, 5/8-inch-thick deck

Edelbrock
LS1/LS2, E-CNC 215

These 50-state-legal heads are fully CNC-ported, and a nice upgrade over stock LS1, LS6, or LS2 heads. The cost is kept down, but the quality is kept up. These heads are a great choice for a stock-cube build, yet provide plenty of room to grow–giving plenty of material for further porting. The larger-than-stock sized valves are said to pose no clearance issues for even the 3.7-inch bore size. All factory equipment bolts right up including the later, center-bolt, style valve covers with factory or aftermarket fasteners. Retail price is only $1,045.

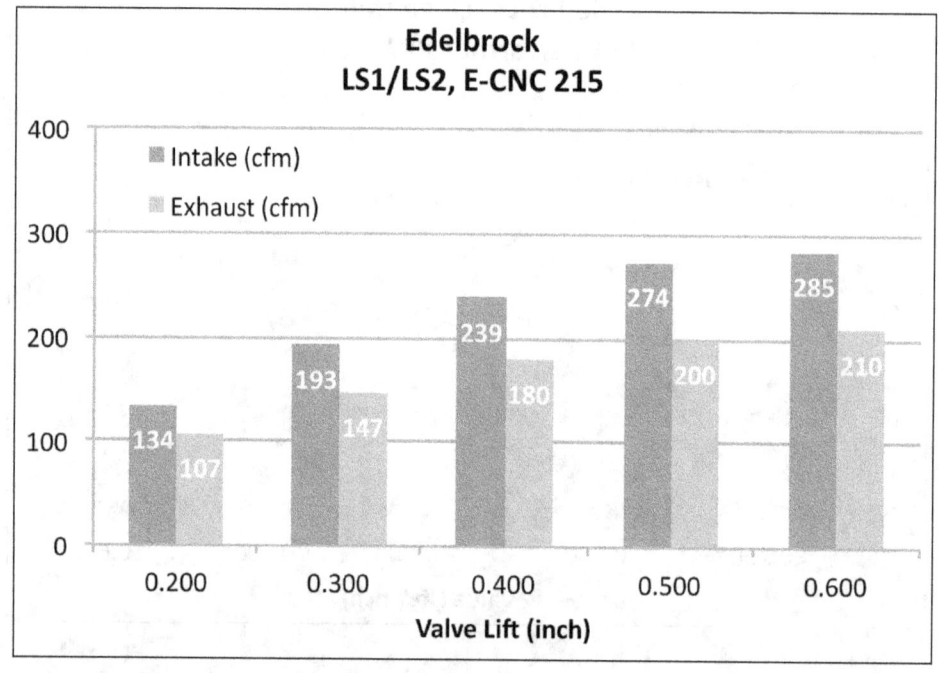

Valves: 2.02-inch intake, 1.57-inch exhaust
Combustion Chamber: 65 cc

Intake Runner: 212 cc
Intake:

Lift (inch)	.200	.300	.400	.500	.600
Flow (cfm)	134	193	239	274	285

Exhaust Runner: 76 cc
Exhaust:

Lift (inch)	.200	.300	.400	.500	.600
Flow (cfm)	107	147	180	200	210

Recommended Use: 346 to 370 ci, budget-minded
Additional Features: manganese bronze valveguides, CARB-approved, .600-inch-lift valvesprings with 1.55/1.30-inch diameter, 5/8-inch-thick deck

CATHEDRAL PORT CYLINDER HEADS

Includes:

LS2 Stage 2, CNC

LS2 Stage 3, CNC

Livernois Motorsports

Livernois has its roots in engineering, starting in 1949, becoming the first to produce aluminum radiators for automotive use as well as the tooling and machines to produce them. Over the years, the Michigan-based firm's location has enhanced its use to OEMs as well as local hot rodders. Today the same philosophy of rigorous testing and design has helped the company design many CNC programs for OEM and aftermarket castings. In the LS community, Livernois is most famous for its fifth-generation Camaro products and services, and managed to lay claim to the very first 2012 Camaro ZL1 to run a 9-second quarter-mile using a Livernois cam and CNC-ported heads. (Photos Courtesy Livernois Motorsports)

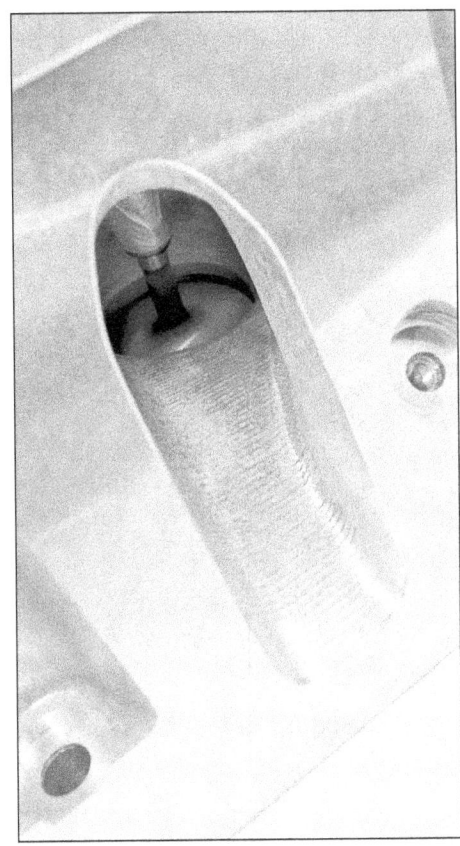
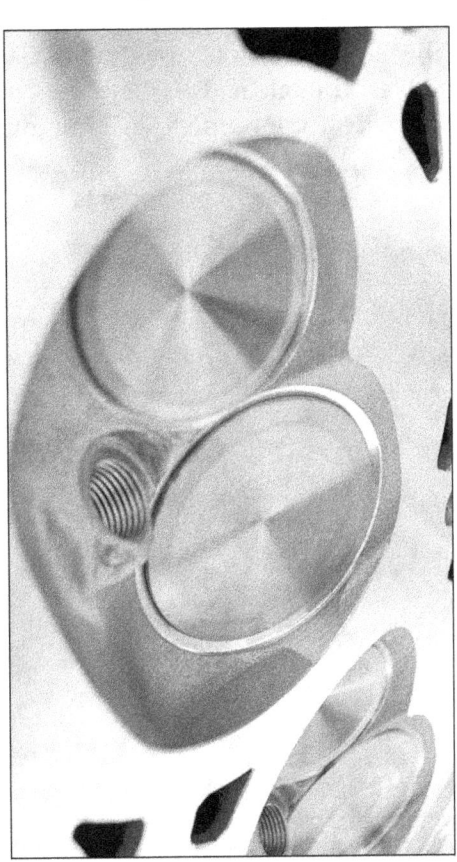
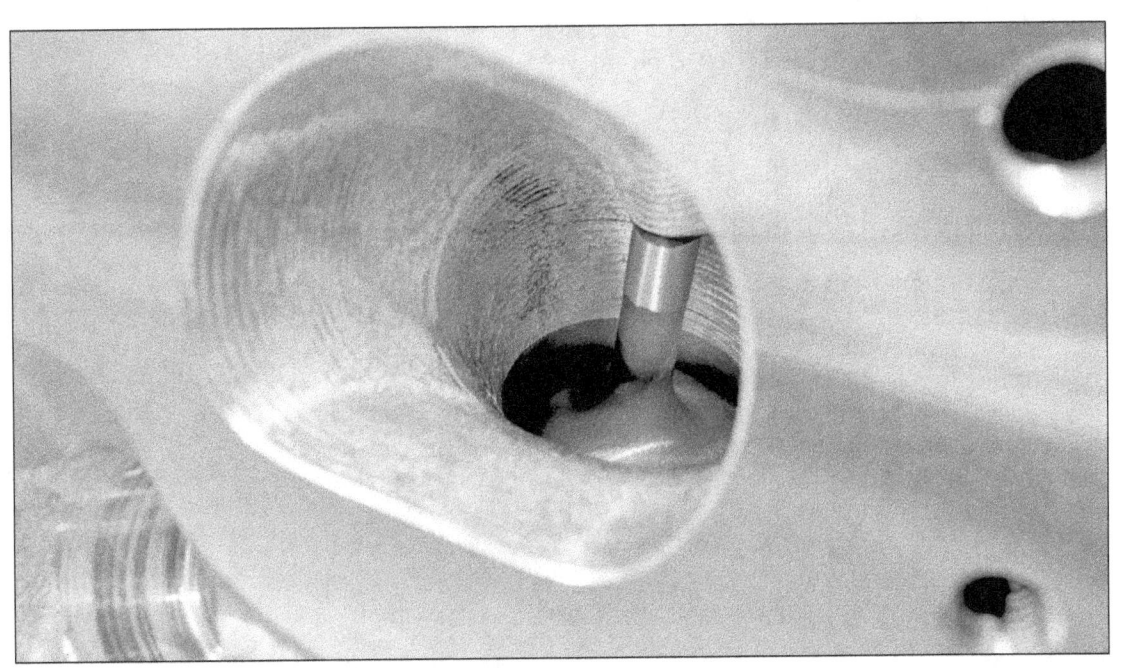

Livernois Motorsports
LS2 Stage 2, CNC

Known for its high-horsepower, boosted combinations, Livernois has several great CNC-ported stock castings starting with the LS2 Stage 2. Using a 5-axis CNC machine, the Stage 2 boasts many high-quality parts proprietary to Livernois, such as a dual-valvespring package with titanium retainers and Viton seals. The only difference between the Stage 2 and the Stage 3 is the valves, the lesser version uses new GM valves, though it does have a CNC valve job to smoothly transition into the chamber. The stock valves allow these heads to fit on the small-bore 4.8/5.7-liter blocks, and are otherwise compatible with all factory equipment. The $1,400 price tag includes the cost of the core, all components, and assembly.

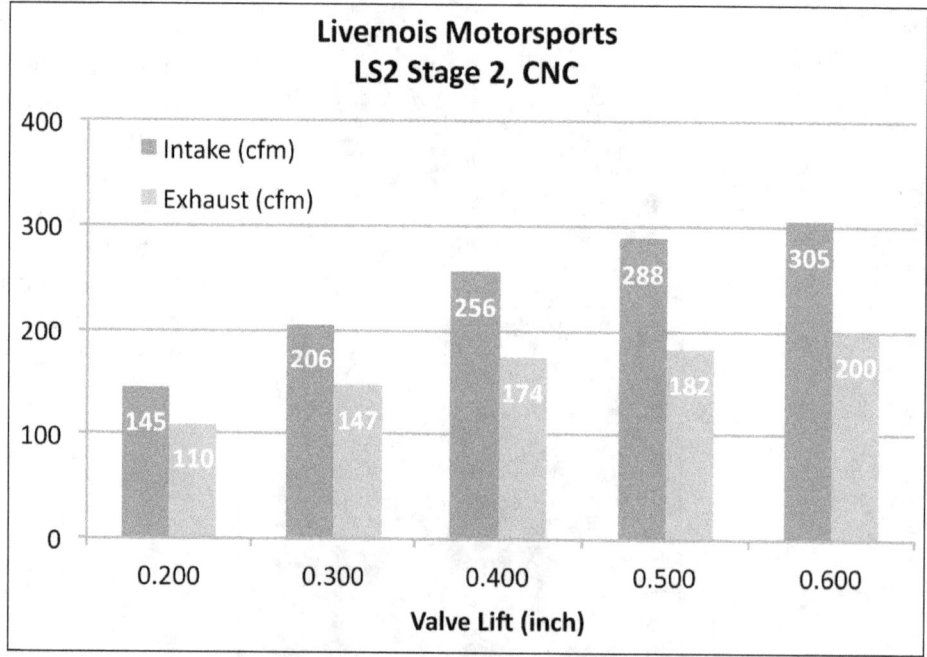

Valves: 2.00-inch intake, 1.55-inch exhaust
Combustion Chamber: 64 to 66 cc

Intake Runner: 220 cc
Intake:

Lift (inch)	.200	.300	.400	.500	.600
Flow (cfm)	145	206	256	288	305

Exhaust Runner: 85 cc
Exhaust:

Lift (inch)	.200	.300	.400	.500	.600
Flow (cfm)	110	147	174	182	200

Recommended Use: 346 to 396 ci, forced induction or naturally aspirated
Additional Features: Livernois .690-inch-lift dual valvesprings, titanium retainers, Super 7 locks, Viton valve seals

CATHEDRAL PORT CYLINDER HEADS

Livernois Motorsports
LS2 Stage 3, CNC

Livernois' 5-axis CNC machine carves up the Stage 3 heads to the tune of 310.9 cfm at .600-inch lift, which definitely takes advantage of the larger stainless valves in the higher lift range. Supercharged and nitrous applications definitely take advantage of the high-flowing exhaust port. The valve choice makes this head appropriate on a stock 3.90- or 4.00-inch bore. These added components bring the price up to $1,800, which includes the core and assembly, so they are ready to bolt up right out of the box with no other fees or charges.

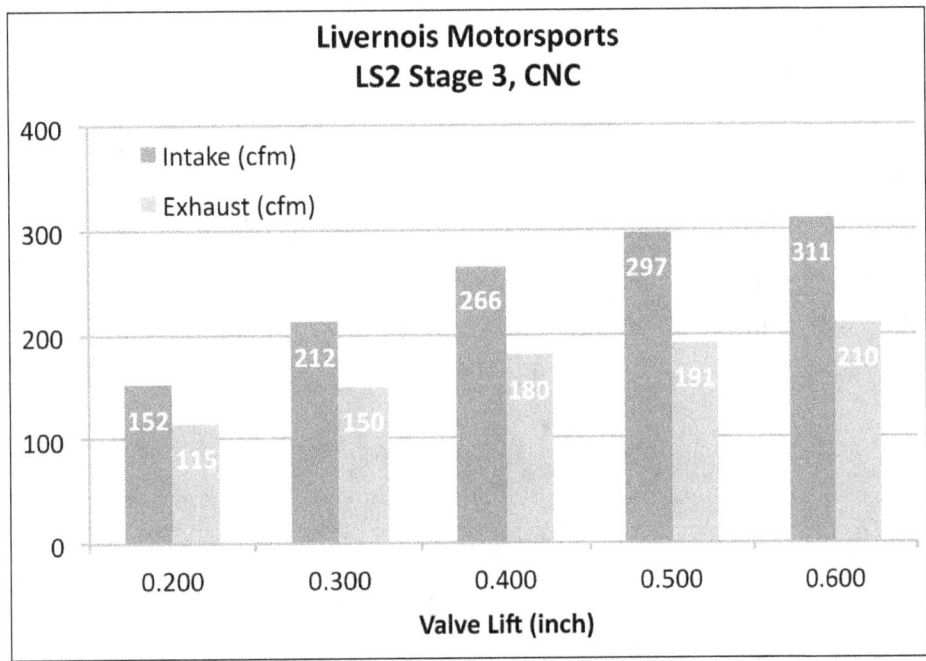

Valves: 2.020-inch intake, 1.575-inch exhaust
Combustion Chamber: 64-66 cc

Intake Runner: 220 cc
Intake:

Lift (inch)	.200	.300	.400	.500	.600
Flow (cfm)	152	212	266	297	311

Exhaust Runner: 85 cc
Exhaust:

Lift (inch)	.200	.300	.400	.500	.600
Flow (cfm)	115	150	180	191	210

Recommended Use: 346 to 402 ci, forced induction or naturally aspirated
Additional Features: Livernois .690-inch-lift dual valvesprings, titanium retainers, Super 7 locks, Viton valve seals

CHAPTER 2

Mast Motorsports

Includes:

LS1/LS6, 11-Degree Small-Bore

11-Degree 6-Bolt Small-Bore

12-Degree 6-Bolt Large-Bore

Mast is one of the newest, brightest, and fastest growing developers of LS parts. The Texas-based company was founded on the principles of engineering, developing high-quality LS components, and thorough assembly of LS crate engines—embracing new and cutting-edge technology. In addition to the engineering talents of its owner Horace Mast, it also employs Cary Chouinard, the brains behind ET Performance and Performance Inductions¬ (the first companies to develop aftermarket castings with altered valve angles). Mast is constantly developing new products for the LS market that push the design envelope for the highest performance, such as its splayed-valve designs and the canted-valve Mozez head. (Photos Courtesy Mast Motorsports)

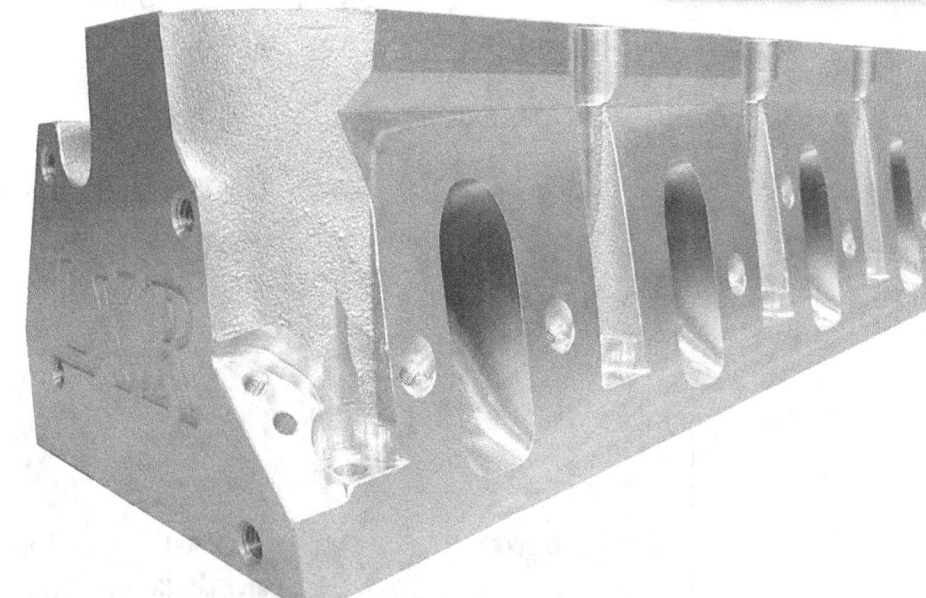

Mast Motorsports
LS1/LS6, 11-Degree Small-Bore

Similar to the ET Performance 11-degree castings of years past, which were a big game-changer, these heads are ideal in a smaller cubic-inch combination with a big-lift, high-duration cam (thanks to its flatter valve angle). The flow capabilities are unmatched at this runner size, which means torque does not suffer when bolting on Mast's fresh casting. Unlike its predecessor, the Mast 11-degree head uses any LS3-style rocker arms rather than a special set of shaft-mount rockers. Save up your pennies because these fresh castings command $1,299 each.

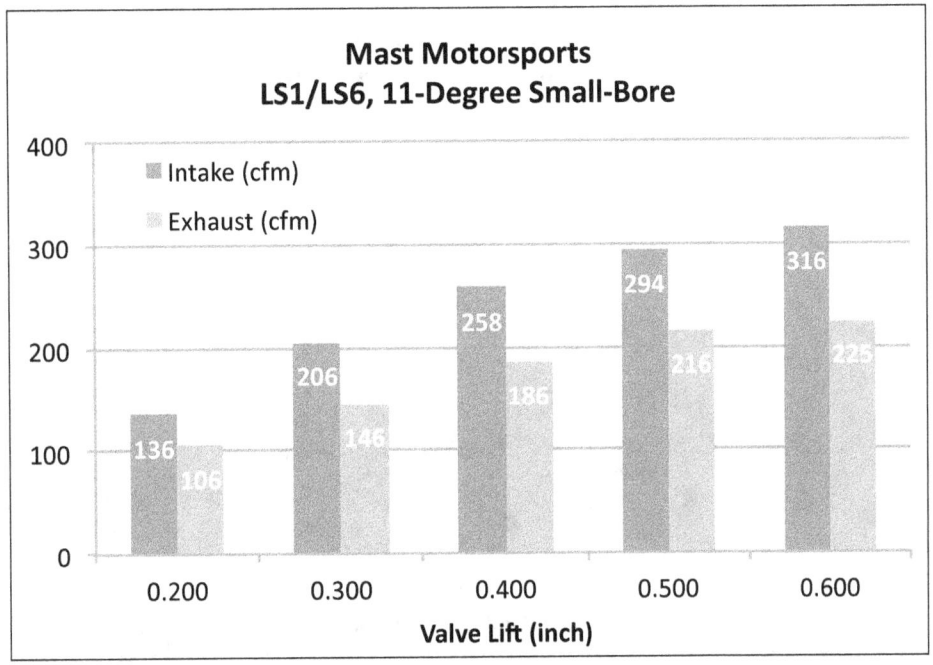

Valves: 2.040-inch intake, 1.57-inch exhaust
Combustion Chamber: 63 cc

Intake Runner: 215 cc
Intake (tested on a 3.900-inch bore):

Lift (inch)	.200	.300	.400	.500	.600
Flow (cfm)	136	206	258	294	316

Exhaust Runner: N/A cc
Exhaust:

Lift (inch)	.200	.300	.400	.500	.600
Flow (cfm)	106	146	186	216	225

Recommended Use: 346 to 383 ci, forced induction or naturally aspirated
Additional Features: 11-degree valve angle, .750-inch-thick deck, nitrided and microfinished .650-inch-lift valvesprings, lightweight stainless-steel valves, billet aluminum rocker stands, lightweight steel retainers

Mast Motorsports
11-Degree 6-Bolt Small-Bore

The 6-head-bolt provision makes this high-flowing head ideal for cubic-inch limited aftermarket block combos, or those with LS2- or LQ9-based engines who are looking to upgrade to an aftermarket block later. The runner size makes it appropriate for high-boost, smaller-cube combos, or larger-cube naturally aspirateds, with a 3.90-inch or larger bore. Medium (4.00 inch or larger) and large (4.125 inches) bore versions are also available. The added head bolts add another $200 to the price ($1,499 total), but these are also compatible with any LS3 rocker arms.

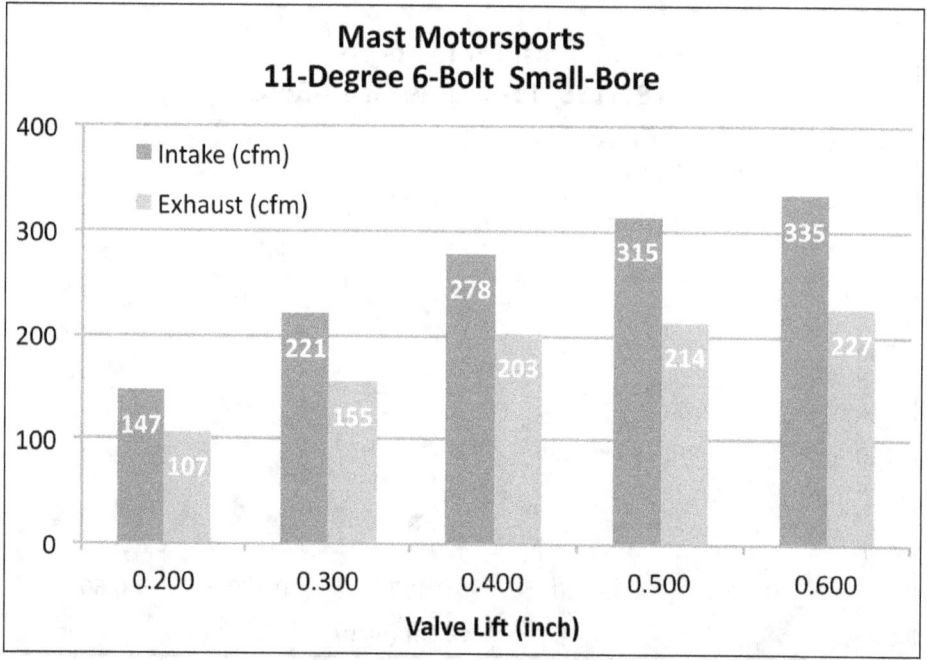

Valves: 2.080-inch intake, 1.60-inch exhaust
Combustion Chamber: 70 cc

Intake Runner: 235 cc
Intake (tested on a 4.00-inch bore):

Lift (inch)	.200	.300	.400	.500	.600
Flow (cfm)	147	221	278	315	335

Exhaust Runner: N/A cc
Exhaust:

Lift (inch)	.200	.300	.400	.500	.600
Flow (cfm)	107	155	203	214	227

Recommended Use: 364 to 416 ci, forced induction or naturally aspirated
Additional Features: 11-degree valve angle, .750-inch-thick deck, LSX 6 head bolts per cylinder, nitrided and microfinished .650-inch-lift valvesprings, lightweight stainless-steel valves, billet aluminum rocker stands, lightweight steel retainers

Mast Motorsports
12-Degree 6-Bolt Large-Bore

The flagship of Mast's cathedral port designs boasts excellent flow all the way to .750 inch of lift. Though cathedral ports are usually not the preferred choice for large-cubic-inch builds, these heads could change all that. Hitting 373 cfm at .750 inch of lift, these heads are on par with many good rectangular ports while boasting much better velocity and exhaust flow. With massive valves for a cathedral, it is no surprise that these heads use LS7-style rocker arms and are appropriate for a 4.125-inch- or-larger bore. Retail price is $1,599 each.

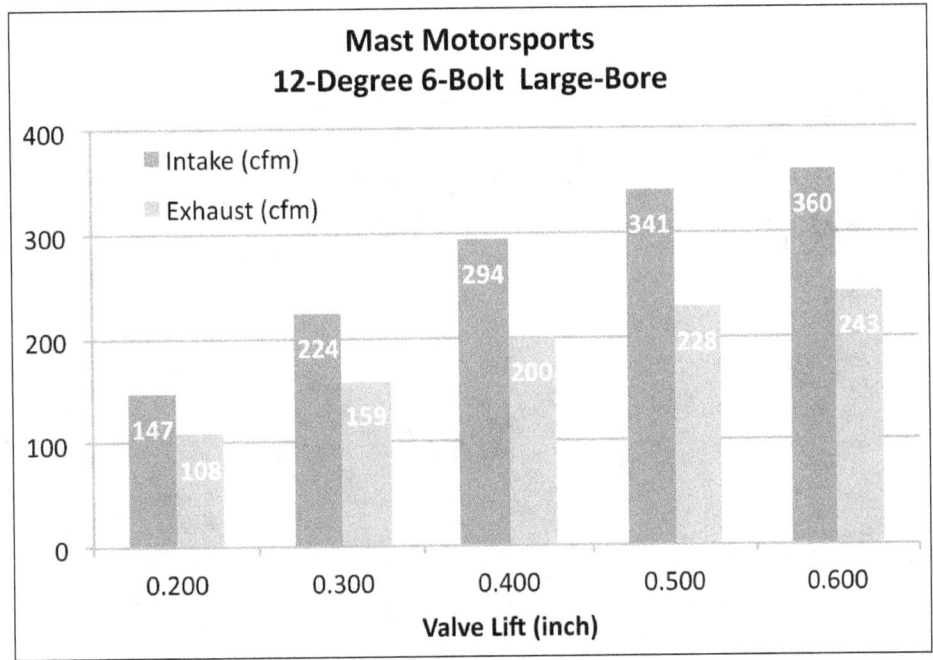

Valves: 2.200-inch intake, 1.600-inch exhaust
Combustion Chamber: 70 cc

Intake Runner: 275 cc
Intake:
Lift (inch)	.200	.300	.400	.500	.600
Flow (cfm)	147	224	294	341	360

Exhaust Runner: N/A cc
Exhaust:
Lift (inch)	.200	.300	.400	.500	.600
Flow (cfm)	108	159	200	228	243

Recommended Use: 427 to 496 ci, forced induction or naturally aspirated
Additional Features: 12-degree valve angle, .750-inch-thick deck, LSX 6 head bolts per cylinder, nitrided and microfinished .650-inch-lift valvesprings, lightweight stainless-steel valves, billet aluminum rocker stands, lightweight steel retainers

CHAPTER 2

Patriot Performance

Includes:

LS6/LS2 & LQ9, Stage II

LS6/LS2 & LQ9, Stage III

LS1, Stage II, 5.3-Liter

Patriot is known for producing a high-quality product at an affordable price, among several different platforms. Maximum air and fuel flow are achieved by in-house CNC designs altering the chamber, bowl, and runners. While itstarted with CNC programs for OEM casting heads, Patriot has branched out into clean-sheet designs while still at an affordable price. The Alabama shop recently opened a new facility to better serve its customers.

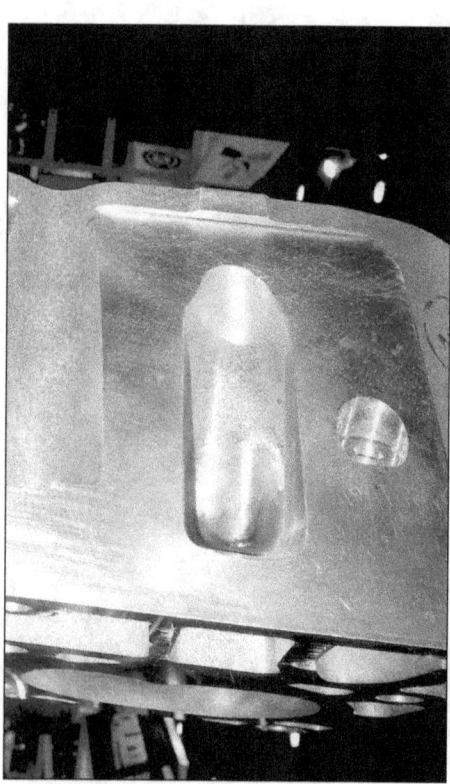

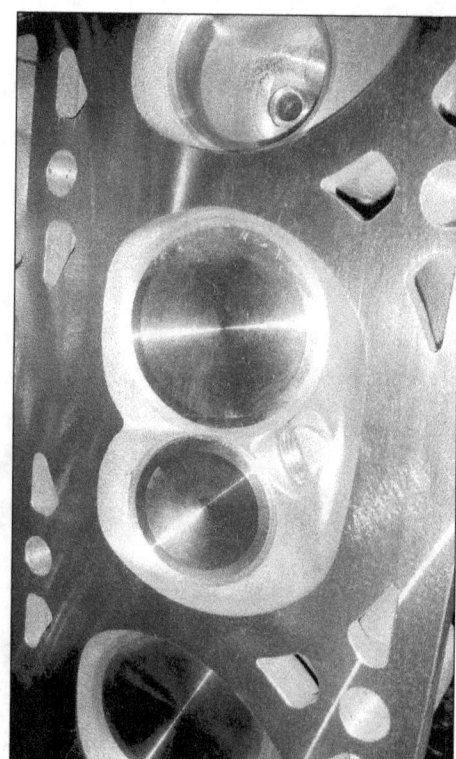

Patriot Performance
LS6/LS2 and LQ9, Stage II

At a very reasonable price, the Stage II CNC porting increases flow by 65 cfm on OEM castings. The LS6/LS2 casting is best suited for higher-compression, naturally aspirated engines and 75- to 150-hp shots of nitrous. The larger chambers on the LQ9 casting make it better suited for mild-boost applications. Both are available with 2.02- or 2.055-inch intake valves and are machined on a 5-axis CNC. Fully assembled, these heads sell for a wallet-friendly $1,335 and compatible with all factory parts and a 3.90-inch bore.

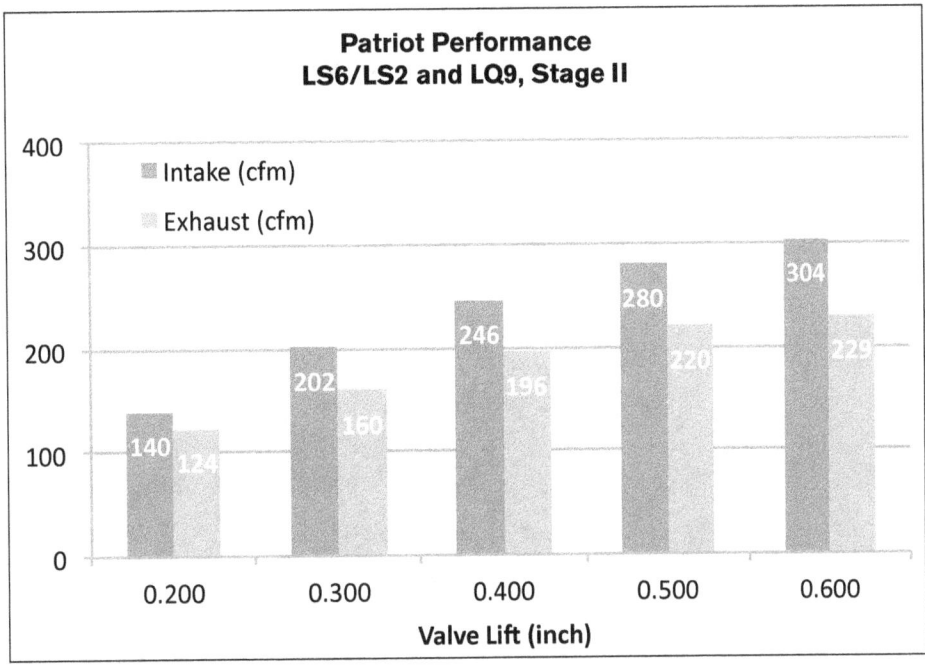

Valves: 2.02/2.055-inch intake, 1.57-inch exhaust
Combustion Chamber: 59, 64, or 72 cc

Intake Runner: 227 cc
Intake:
Lift (inch)	.200	.300	.400	.500	.600
Flow (cfm)	140	202	246	280	304

Exhaust Runner: 70 cc
Exhaust:
Lift (inch)	.200	.300	.400	.500	.600
Flow (cfm)	124	160	196	220	229

Recommended Use: 346 to 370 ci, forced induction or naturally aspirated
Additional Features: Patriot Gold dual .650-inch-lift valvesprings, titanium retainers, Super 7 machined locks, custom-honed manganese bronze guides, machined spring base, Viton seals, 5-angle valve job

Patriot Performance
LS6/LS2 and LQ9, Stage III

The Stage III is also a reasonably priced CNC-ported OEM casting, which boosts flow by 80 cfm. The LS6/LS2 casting is best suited for higher-compression, naturally aspirated or nitrous engines. And again the larger chambers on the LQ9 casting make it better for boost. Both are machined on a 5-axis CNC, and ideal for a 4-inch bore given the large valves and chambers (but do fit a 3.90-inch bore). Thankfully, the added flow does not come at a premium, and the Stage III costs the same $1,335 as the Stage II.

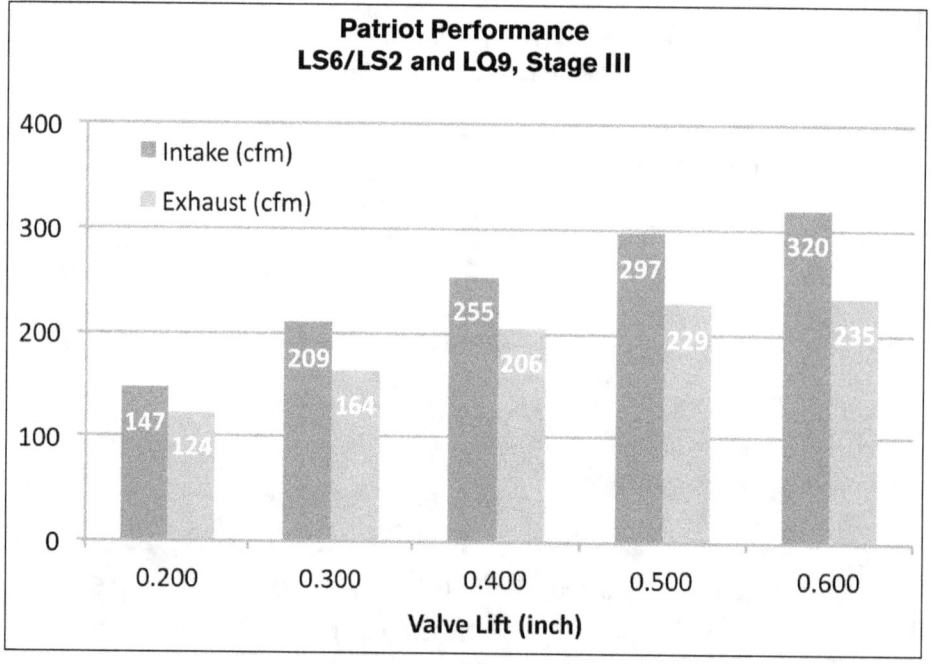

Valves: 2.08-inch intake, 1.60-inch exhaust
Combustion Chamber: 64 or 72 cc

Intake Runner: 227 cc
Intake:

Lift (inch)	.200	.300	.400	.500	.600
Flow (cfm)	147	209	255	297	320

Exhaust Runner: 70 cc
Exhaust:

Lift (inch)	.200	.300	.400	.500	.600
Flow (cfm)	124	164	206	229	235

Recommended Use: 364 to 408 ci, forced induction or naturally aspirated
Additional Features: Patriot Gold dual .650-inch-lift valvesprings, titanium retainers, Super 7 machined locks, custom-honed manganese bronze guides, machined spring base, Viton seals, 5-angle valve job

Patriot Performance
LS1, Stage II, 5.3-Liter

The most economical of the bunch, CNC programs for either the 5.3-liter truck casting or perimeter bolt 1997–1998 LS1 castings offer a 60-cfm jump in flow over stock. The LS1 casting saves the expense of converting the valve covers, coil brackets, and other associated parts. The only catch is the larger 67-cc combustion chamber, as opposed to the 5.3's smaller chamber, which can bump compression to 10.8:1 on a stock bottom-end LS1. Both are machined on a 5-axis CNC, work well in naturally aspirated engines, and with a 75- to 150-hp shot of nitrous. The smaller valves and chamber make these heads compatible with most any bore, and cost a mere $1,230 ($1,095 for early LS1 castings).

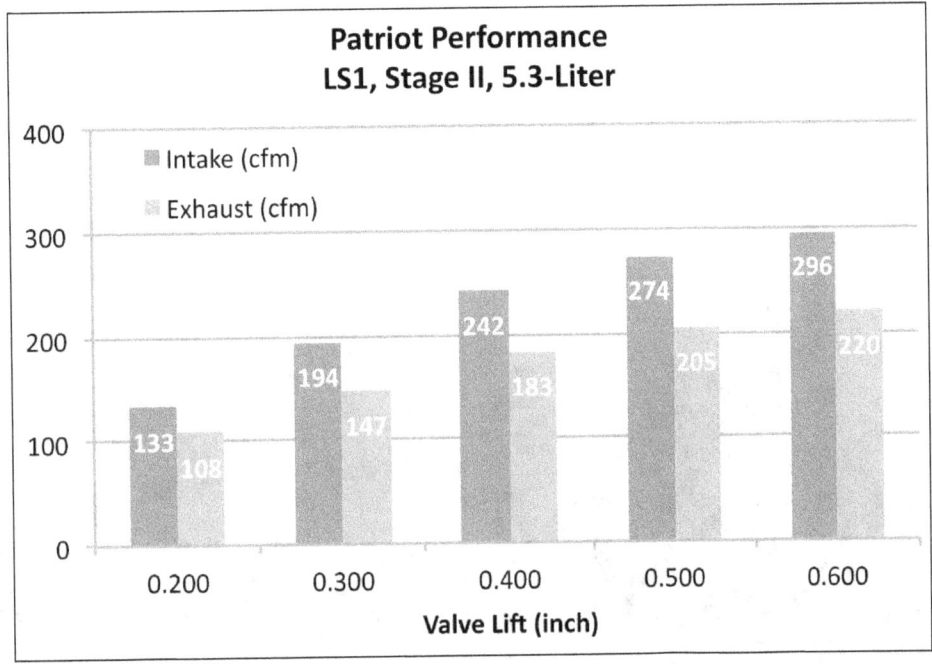

Valves: 2.02-inch intake, 1.57-inch exhaust
Combustion Chamber: 63 or 67 cc

Intake Runner: 220 cc
Intake:

Lift (inch)	.200	.300	.400	.500	.600
Flow (cfm)	133	194	242	274	296

Exhaust Runner: 67 cc
Exhaust:

Lift (inch)	.200	.300	.400	.500	.600
Flow (cfm)	108	147	183	205	220

Recommended Use: 327 to 346 ci, forced induction or naturally aspirated
Additional Features: Patriot Gold dual .650-inch-lift valvesprings, titanium retainers, Super 7 machined locks, custom-honed manganese bronze guides, machined spring base, Viton seals, 5-angle valve job

CHAPTER 2

Precision Race Components

Includes:

Stage 2.5, 5.3-Liter

LS6 Stage 1, 6.0-Liter

LS6 Stage 2.5, 6.0-Liter

LS6 Stage 3, 6.0-Liter

215 cc

227 cc

237 cc

PRC is the R&D and production arm of Texas Speed, developing cylinder head programs for the LS market, including its own aftermarket casting. PRC is known for extensive flow and dyno testing of all its heads as well as affordability. In terms of quality and performance per dollar, PRC is hard to beat. It is no wonder PRC cylinder heads have a few long-standing records in the LS drag race community. (Photos Courtesy Precision Race Components)

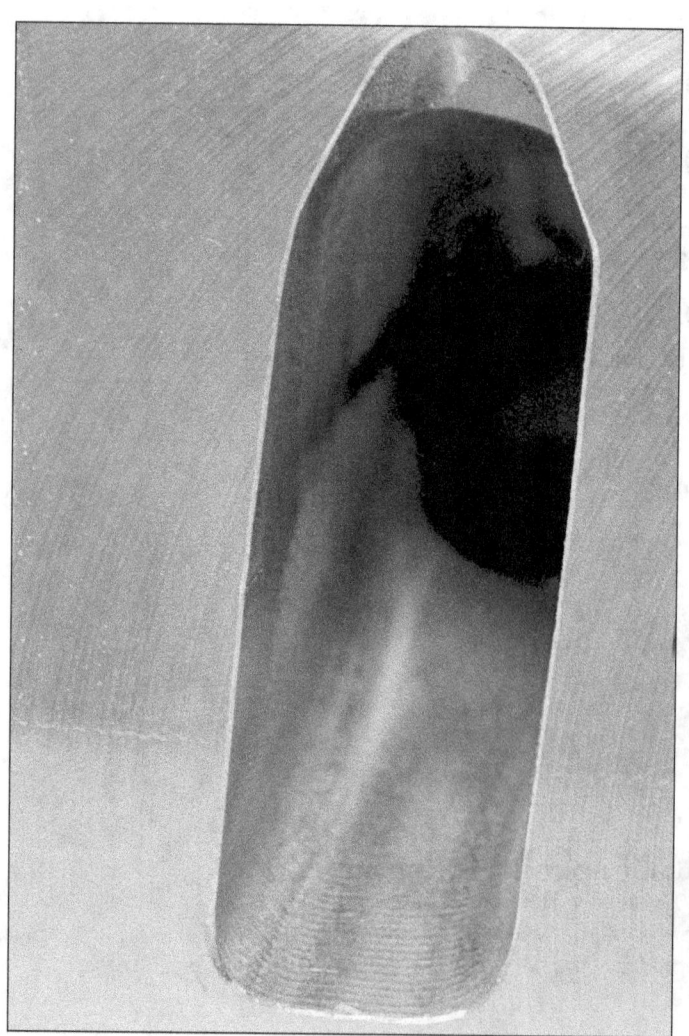
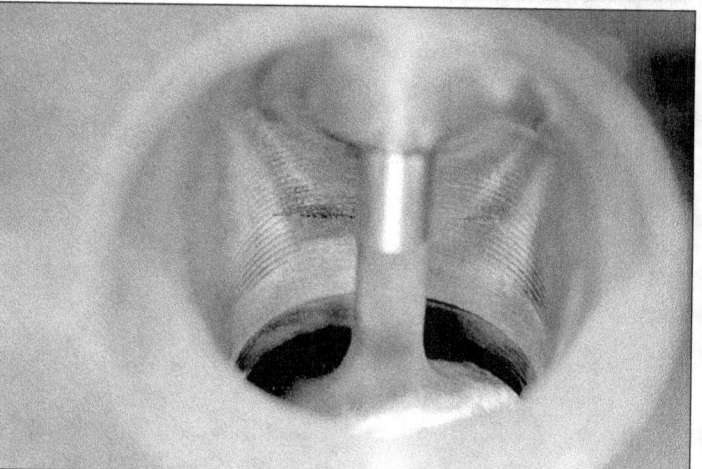
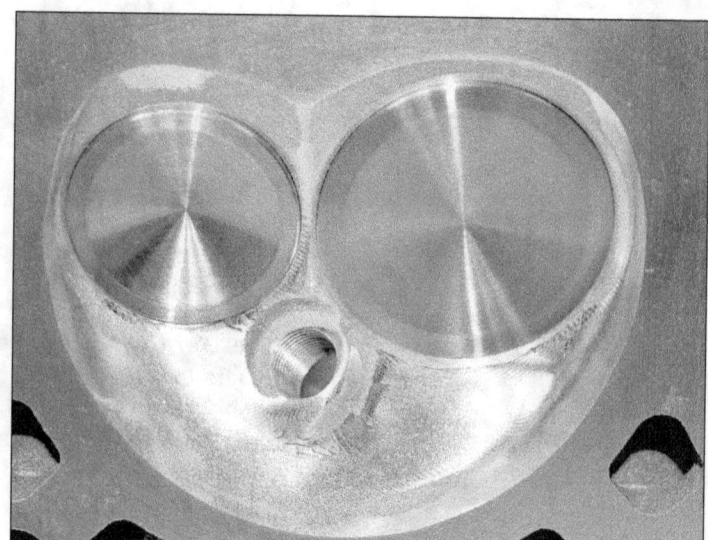

5.3-Liter Stage 2.5

CATHEDRAL PORT CYLINDER HEADS

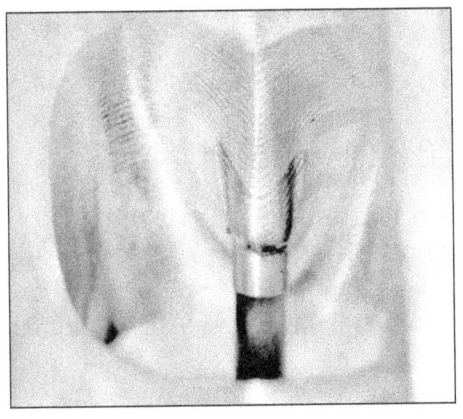  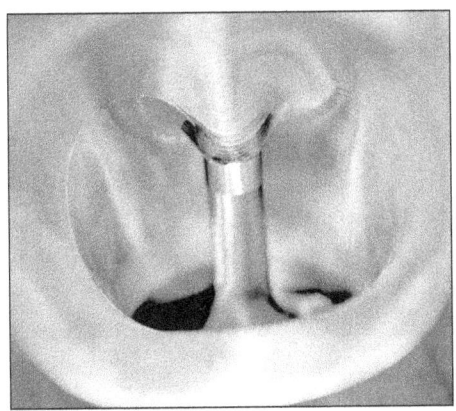

6.0-Liter/LS6 Stage 1, 6.0-Liter/LS6 Stage 2.5, 6.0-Liter/LS6 Stage 3

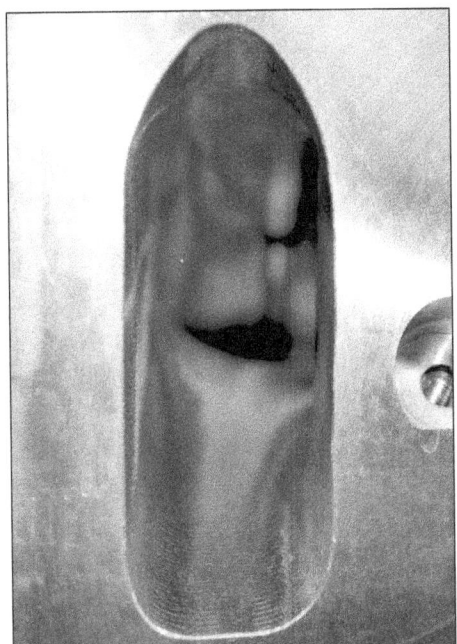 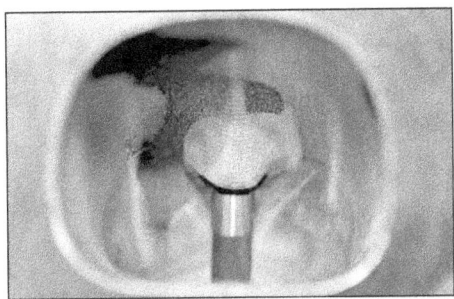 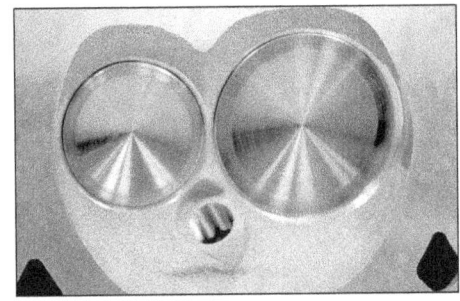

237 cc

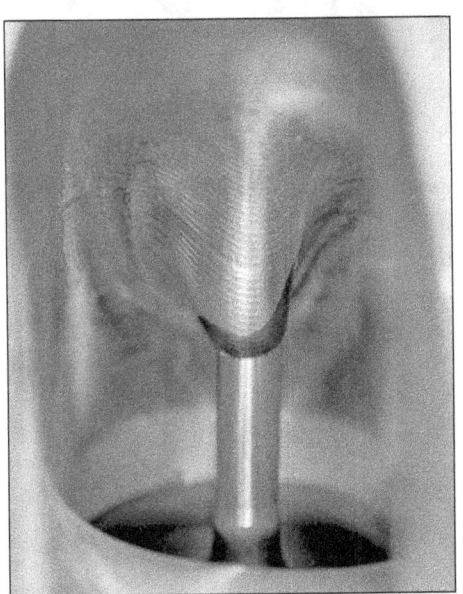 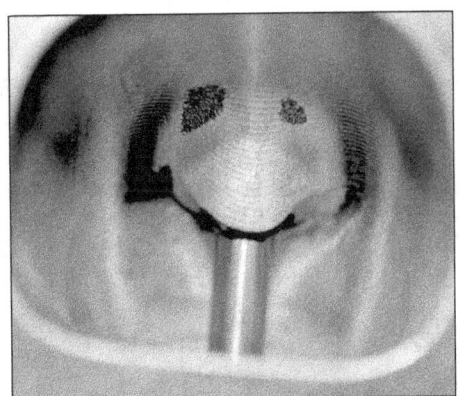 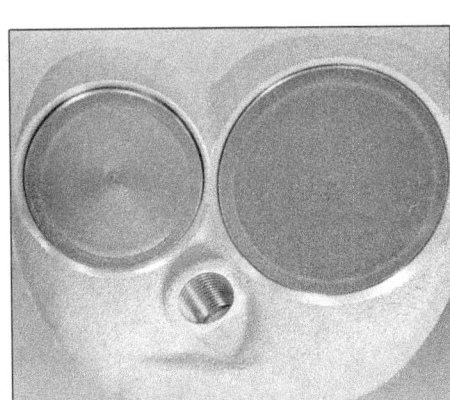

215 cc and 227 cc

Precision Race Components
Stage 2.5, 5.3-Liter

Don't be fooled by the price tag, these cylinder heads have excellent capabilities, which have been exploited on many potent head/cam combos. New "862" or "706" casting cores are CNC-ported and machined to specifications dictated by extensive research and testing. Each set of heads is milled and assembled to the owner's specifications and utilizes stainless-steel valves. Prices start at a budget-friendly $1,235 (assembled), with no core charge. Because these heads are a factory casting, they are compatible with all factory components. The upgraded valves are still friendly to smaller-bore combinations (such as 4.8-liter and 5.3-liter blocks).

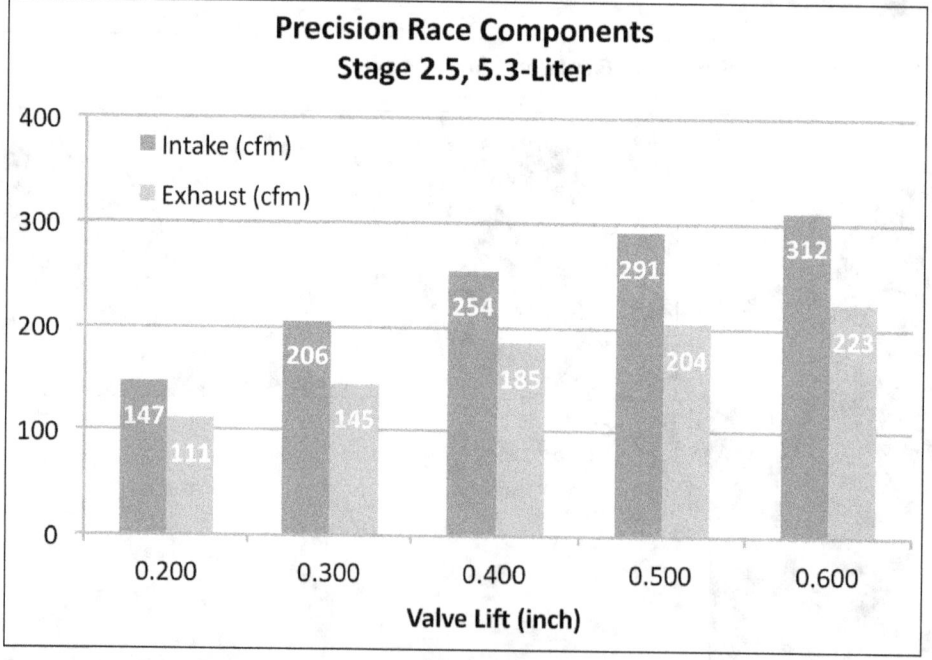

Valves: 2.02-inch intake, 1.575-inch exhaust
Combustion Chamber: 58 to 63 cc

Intake Runner: 220 cc
Intake (tested with a 3.910-inch flow plate):

Lift (inch)	.200	.300	.400	.500	.600
Flow (cfm)	147	206	254	291	312

Exhaust Runner: 76 cc
Exhaust (tested with no exhaust pipe):

Lift (inch)	.200	.300	.400	.500	.600
Flow (cfm)	111	145	185	204	223

Recommended Use: 327 to 346 ci, forced induction or naturally aspirated
Additional Features: PRC .650-inch-lift dual valvespring kit with titanim retainers, optional .675-inch-lift dual valvesprings, Viton valve seals

CATHEDRAL PORT CYLINDER HEADS

Precision Race Components
LS6 Stage 1, 6.0-Liter

PRC's least expensive cylinder head is no slouch, as evidenced by the flow numbers. The base heads come with factory valvesprings, with three different upgrade options. All Stage 1 heads have factory valves and are milled and assembled according to owner specifications. Only new "317" cores are used for the larger chambered 6.0-liter casting, and "243" or "799" cores are used for the LS6. No special components are necessary to use these heads, which are already easy on the wallet with a mere $1,125 price tag (with stock springs). The stock-size valves pose no limitations on bore size.

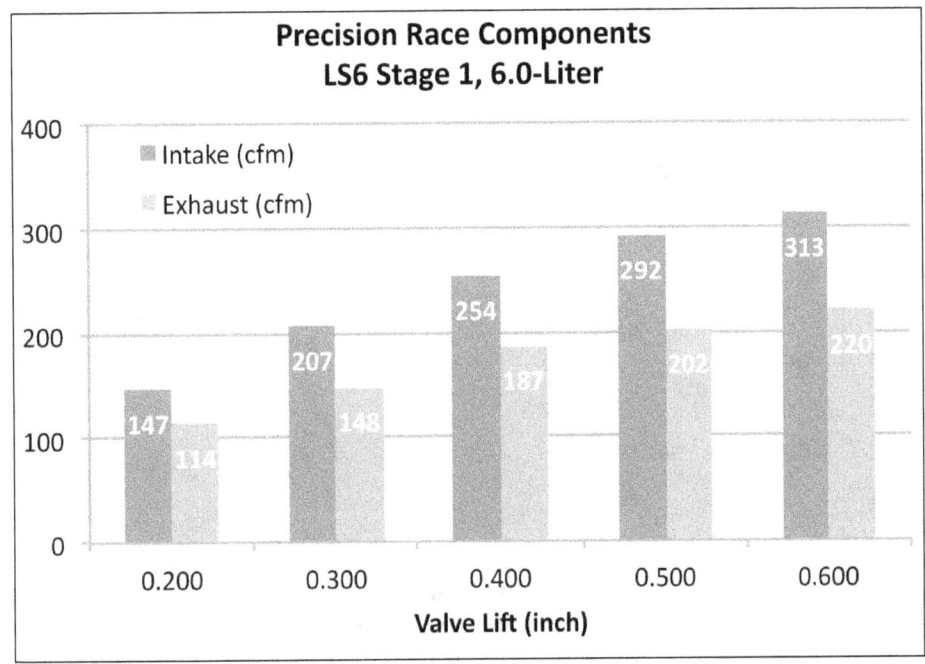

Valves: 2.00-inch intake, 1.55-inch exhaust
Combustion Chamber: 58 to 64 or 65 to 72 cc

Intake Runner: 227 cc
Intake (tested with a 3.910-inch flow plate):

Lift (inch)	.200	.300	.400	.500	.600
Flow (cfm)	147	207	254	292	313

Exhaust Runner: 78 cc
Exhaust (tested with no exhaust pipe):

Lift (inch)	.200	.300	.400	.500	.600
Flow (cfm)	114	148	187	202	220

Recommended Use: 327 to 364 ci, forced induction or naturally aspirated
Additional Features: optional Comp 918, PRC .650- or .675-inch-lift dual valvespring kit with titanium retainers, Viton valve seals

Precision Race Components
LS6 Stage 2.5, 6.0-Liter

Larger stainless-steel valves help unlock even more flow from the OEM castings, which flow enough air for any smaller-cube build and even some stroker applications though the valves pose no issues with shrouding and bore size. Again, the larger chambers on the 6.0-liter heads are suited for boost, but PRC can mill them down as far as 65 cc. If a smaller chamber is desired, such as for a high-compression head/cam setup, the LS6 can be milled down to 58 cc. Pricing starts at $1,525 with PRC's double springs.

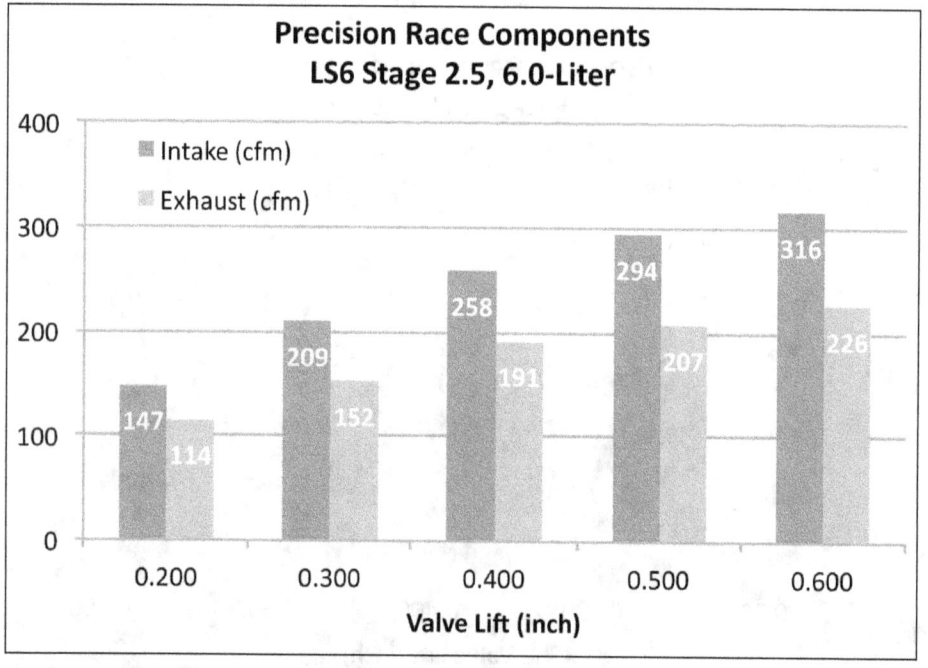

Valves: 2.02-inch intake, 1.575-inch exhaust
Combustion Chamber: 58 to 64 or 65 to 72 cc

Intake Runner: 227 cc
Intake (tested with a 3.910-inch flow plate):

Lift (inch)	.200	.300	.400	.500	.600
Flow (cfm)	147	209	258	294	316

Exhaust Runner: 78 cc
Exhaust (tested with no exhaust pipe):

Lift (inch)	.200	.300	.400	.500	.600
Flow (cfm)	114	152	191	207	226

Recommended Use: 346 to 396 ci, forced induction or naturally aspirated
Additional Features: PRC .650-inch-lift dual valvespring kit, with titanim retainers, Viton valve seals, optional PRC .675-inch-lift valvesprings

Precision Race Components
LS6 Stage 3, 6.0-Liter

The 6.0-liter "317" and LS6 "243" (or "799") castings are pushed to their limit with the largest stainless-steel valves possible, which are ideal for 4-inch bores. The larger chambers on the 6.0-liter heads are ideal for strokers and boost, meanwhile the LS6 heads are best suited for naturally aspirated and nitrous setups. The large valves make a 3.90-inch-or-larger (emphasis on the larger) bore a requirement. With so many upgrades it is no wonder these heads command a price tag of $1,925 (including PRC double valvesprings).

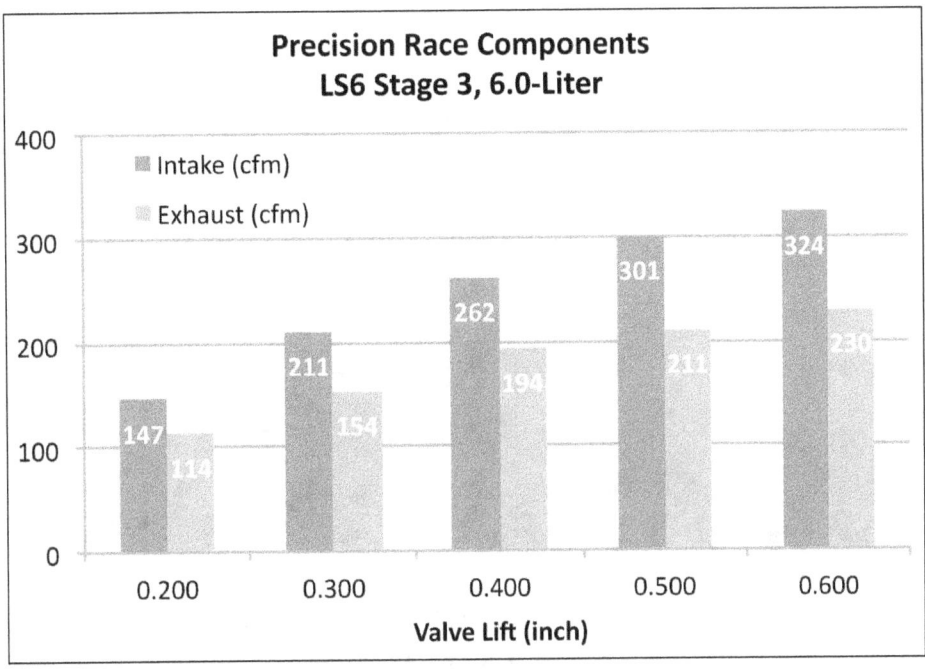

Valves: 2.08-inch intake, 1.60-inch exhaust
Combustion Chamber: 58 to 64 or 65 to 72 cc

Intake Runner: 227 cc
Intake (tested with a 4.030-inch flow plate):
Lift (inch)	.200	.300	.400	.500	.600
Flow (cfm)	147	211	262	301	324

Exhaust Runner: 78 cc
Exhaust (tested with no exhaust pipe):
Lift (inch)	.200	.300	.400	.500	.600
Flow (cfm)	114	154	194	211	230

Recommended Use: 364 to 408 ci, forced induction or naturally aspirated
Additional Features: optional PRC .675-inch-lift dual valvespring kit with titanium retainers, Viton valve seals

CHAPTER 2

Precision Race Components
215 cc

Don't be deceived by the small runner sizes, these heads flow serious air. Whether a stump-puller 408 is your objective, or a stock bottom-end race car that will surpass Texas Speed's record of 9.82 (using these heads), these aftermarket heads can support it. The conservative valve sizes are intended to accommodate small bores (and stock cubic inches) without inhibiting flow. These heads are compatible with factory rockers and other equipment. However, roller rockers are recommended to reduce wear with bronze valveguides (powder metal guides are also available). With PRC's standard .650-inch-lift springs, these heads start at $2,200.

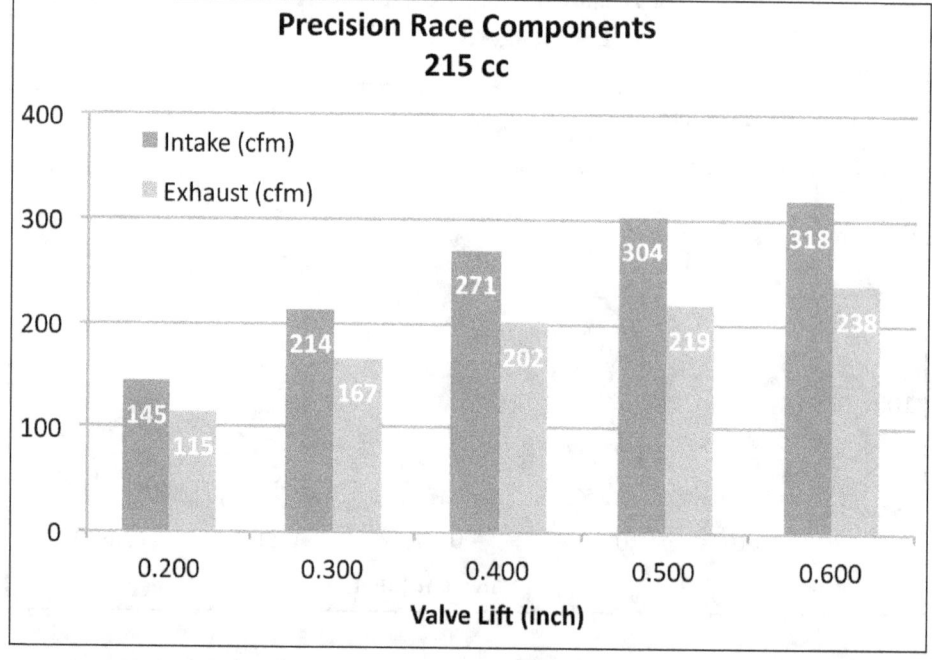

Valves: 2.04-inch intake, 1.60-inch exhaust
Combustion Chamber: 57 to 62 cc

Intake Runner: 215 cc
Intake (tested with a 4.00-inch flow plate):

Lift (inch)	.200	.300	.400	.500	.600
Flow (cfm)	145	214	271	304	318

Exhaust Runner: 84 cc
Exhaust (tested with no exhaust pipe):

Lift (inch)	.200	.300	.400	.500	.600
Flow (cfm)	115	167	202	219	238

Recommended Use: 346-396 ci, forced induction or naturally aspirated
Additional Features: PRC Platinum .660-inch-lift valvespring kit, optional PRC .675- or .700-inch-lift dual valvesprings, titanium retainers, Viton valve seals, bronze valveguides with optional powder metal

Precision Race Components
227 cc

This head was specifically designed for maximum-effort smaller-cube combinations. The larger intake runner doesn't hit its stride until high lift, considerably surpassing the 215-cc head at .650-inch lift (going all the way to 330 cfm). The 227 is designed for a 3.90- to 4.00-inch bore and is compatible with stock rockers and other components (just like the 215-cc); an upgrade to powder metal valveguides is recommended with stock rocker arms. Base price for the 227-cc head is $2,200, which comes assembled with .650-inch-lift PRC valvesprings.

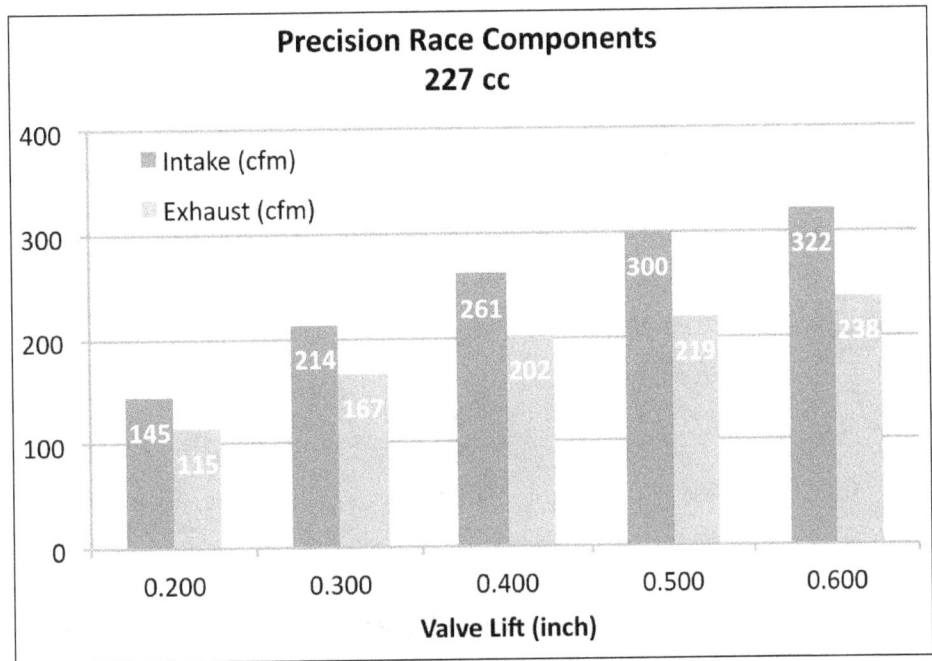

Valves: 2.06-inch intake, 1.60-inch exhaust
Combustion Chamber: 57 to 62 cc

Intake Runner: 227 cc
Intake (tested with a 4.00-inch flow plate)
Lift (inch)	.200	.300	.400	.500	.600
Flow (cfm)	145	214	261	300	322

Exhaust Runner: 84 cc
Exhaust (tested with no exhaust pipe):
Lift (inch)	.200	.300	.400	.500	.600
Flow (cfm)	115	167	202	219	238

Recommended Use: 346 to 402 ci, forced induction or naturally aspirated
Additional Features: PRC .650-inch-lift valvespring kit, optional PRC .675- or .700-inch-lift dual valvesprings, titanium retainers, Viton valve seals, bronze valveguides with optional powder metal

Precision Race Components
237 cc

Based on the same aftermarket casting as the 215- and 227-cc heads, the 237-cc version is made for 4-inch-and-larger bores. From radical 370- to 376-ci combos to strokers, PRC's highest flowing cathedral port handles them all in stride. The massive 2.10-inch intake valves provide incredible high-end capabilities that few other cathedral ports can offer, perfect for big cubic inches and boost. Just like the other versions, the 237-cc is compatible with factory rockers and other equipment. Despite its flow capabilities, the price tag is still a mere $2,200 with the standard .650-inch-lift PRC springs.

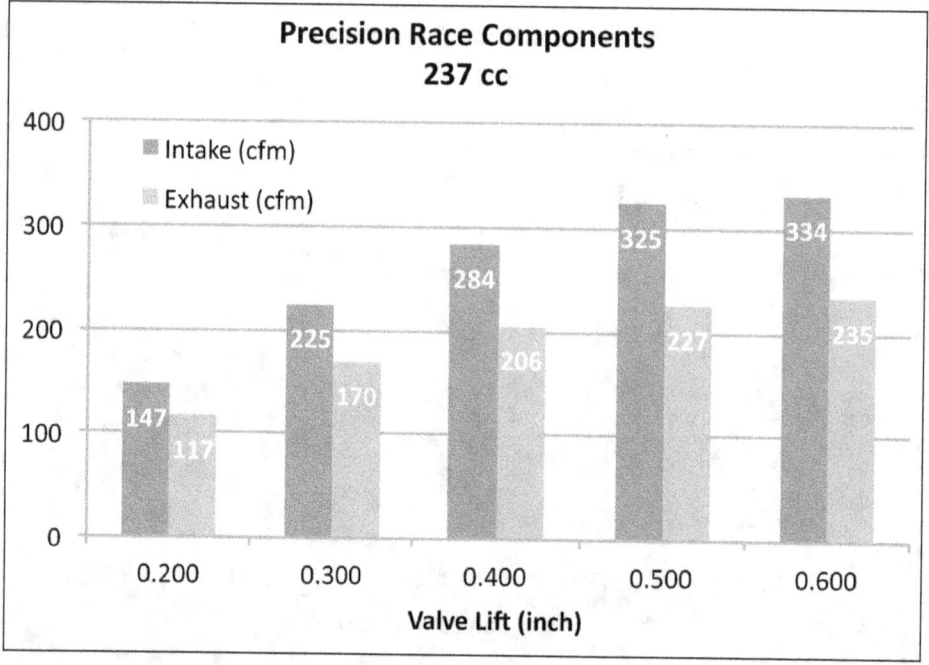

Valves: 2.100-inch intake, 1.600-inch exhaust
Combustion Chamber: 68 cc

Intake Runner: 237 cc
Intake (tested with a 4.030-inch flow plate):
Lift (inch)	.200	.300	.400	.500	.600
Flow (cfm)	147	225	284	325	334

Exhaust Runner: 84 cc
Exhaust (tested with no exhaust pipe):
Lift (inch)	.200	.300	.400	.500	.600
Flow (cfm)	117	170	206	227	235

Recommended Use: 370 to 427 ci, forced induction or naturally aspirated
Additional Features: PRC .650-inch-lift valvespring kit, optional PRC .675- or .700-inch-lift dual valvesprings, titanium retainers, Viton valve seals, bronze valveguides with optional powder metal

CATHEDRAL PORT CYLINDER HEADS

Includes:

LS2/LS6 Stage 1

LS2/LS6 Stage 2

Total Engine AirFlow

Total Engine Airflow (TEA) began in the early 1990s in Bowling Green, Kentucky, and established itself as a premiere center for cylinder head research and development. The company has since been moved to Ohio, working closely with sister company Trick Flow. Years of flow bench and dyno testing have helped shape the CNC-machining design of cylinder heads and manifolds. In addition to its regular line of CNC-ported LS heads, TEA also offers custom porting options including factory castings such as the L92/LS3 and various cathedral port heads. Customized performance airflow solutions are also available. (Photos Courtesy Total Engine Airflow)

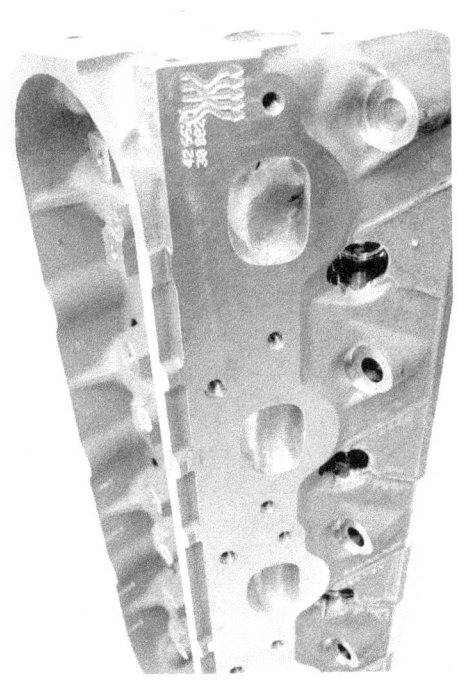
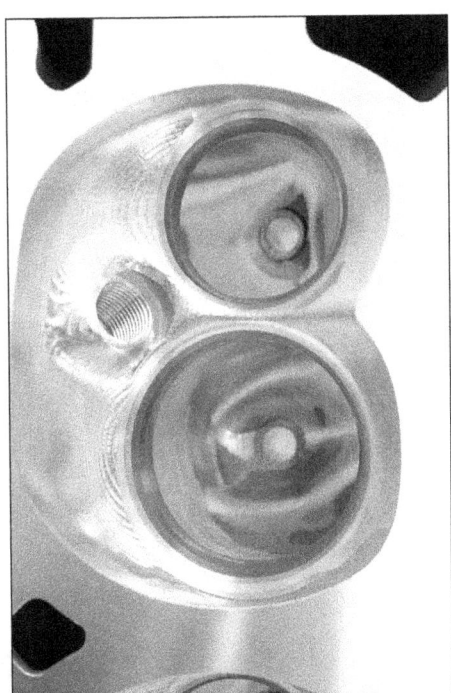

Total Engine AirFlow
LS2/LS6 Stage 1

TEA's Stage 1 program takes the customer-supplied "243" or "799" casting to the next level with a custom four-angle valve job, CNC porting, hand blending of the port and valve job, and back-cut intake valves. Stock valves keep cost down and low- to mid-lift flow up, with the added benefit of small-bore (4.8 and 5.3-liter) compatibility. Because these are stock castings, there are no special components necessary. Many options are available, such as milling to decrease the size of the combustion chambers. Fully assembled with .650-inch-lift dual valvesprings, the Stage 1 heads cost only $1,199 (with a customer-supplied core).

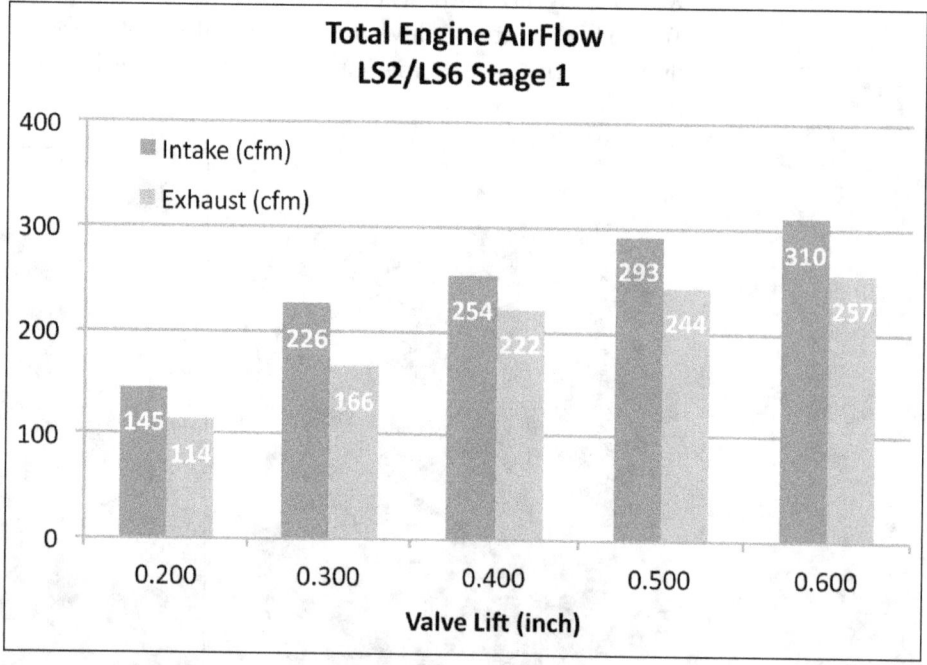

Valves: 2.00-inch intake, 1.55-inch exhaust
Combustion Chamber: 65 cc

Intake Runner: 225 cc
Intake (tested with a 3.90-inch bore):

Lift (inch)	.200	.300	.400	.500	.600
Flow (cfm)	145	226	254	293	310

Exhaust Runner: N/A cc
Exhaust: (tested with a 1.875-inch exhaust pipe):

Lift (inch)	.200	.300	.400	.500	.600
Flow (cfm)	114	166	222	244	257

Recommended Use: 346 to 402 ci, forced induction or naturally aspirated
Additional Features: .650-inch-lift dual valvesprings, titanium retainers

Total Engine AirFlow
LS2/LS6 Stage 2

The Stage 2 program is TEA's most powerful stock-casting cathedral port. The biggest difference between the Stage 1 and the Stage 2 is the use of larger Ferrea valves and accompanying valve job, which was developed on the Trick Flow Specialties (TFS) 215-cc head. Just like the Stage 1, the 243 or 799 casting receives full CNC porting of the runners and hand blending of the port and valve job. A 3.90-inch-or-larger bore is recommended, and no other special requirements or components are necessary with Stage 2 heads. $1,399 buys you the CNC porting, valve job, and assembly with custom PAC dual .650-inch springs and titanium retainers.

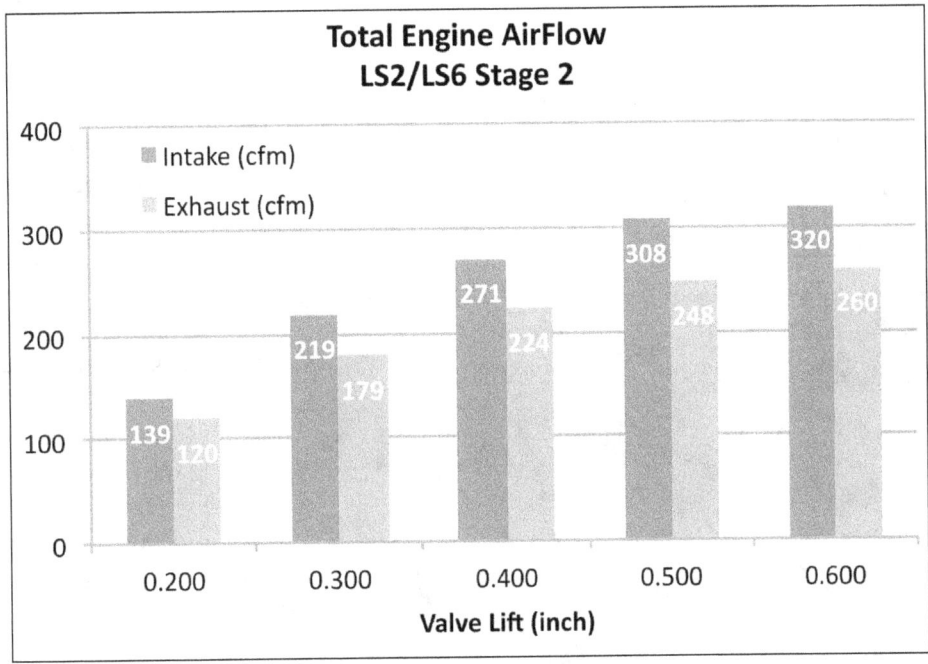

Valves: 2.04-inch intake, 1.57-inch exhaust
Combustion Chamber: 65 cc

Intake Runner: 225 cc
Intake (tested with a 3.90-inch bore):

Lift (inch)	.200	.300	.400	.500	.600
Flow (cfm)	139	219	271	308	320

Exhaust Runner: N/A cc
Exhaust (tested with a 1.875-inch exhaust pipe):

Lift (inch)	.200	.300	.400	.500	.600
Flow (cfm)	120	179	224	248	260

Recommended Use: 346 to 402 ci, forced induction or naturally aspirated
Additional Features: .650-inch-lift dual valvesprings, titanium retainers, milling

CHAPTER 2

Trick Flow Specialties

Includes:	
GenX 205	GenX 225
GenX 215	GenX 235
GenX 220 for LS1	GenX 245
GenX 220 for LS2	265 cc

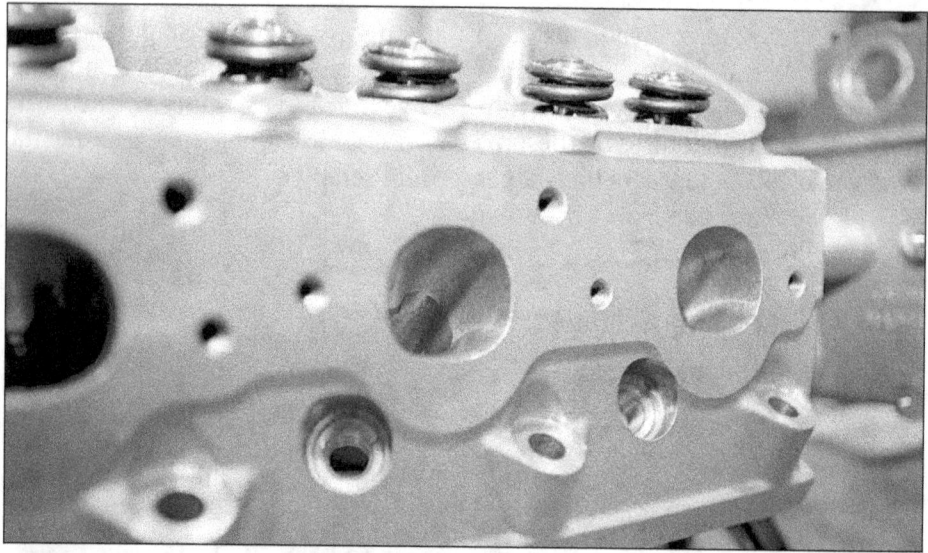

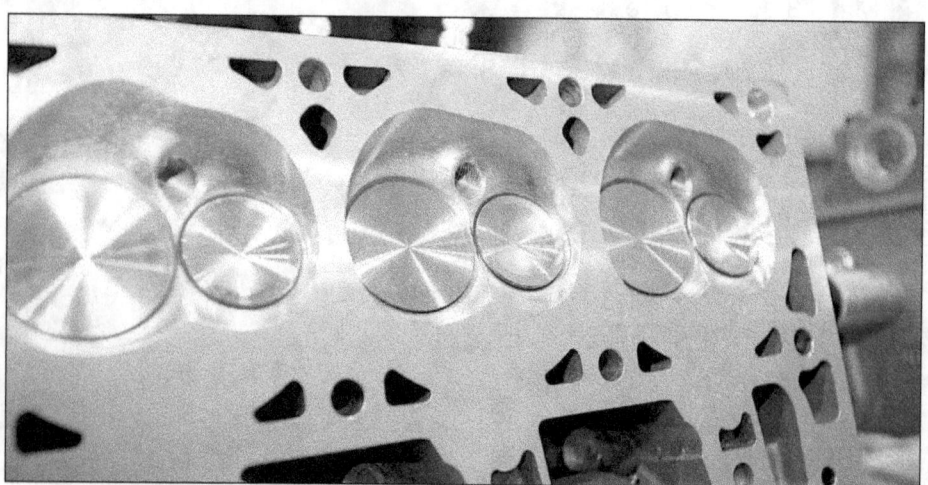

TFS began in 1983 in Ohio, making big-block Ford cylinder heads, but has since branched out to many Chevy applications and even camshafts, intake manifolds, and other engine components. While it were not the first on the scene with an aftermarket LS head, its cathedral offering is considered to be one of the best and was influential on designs thereafter. This well-thought-out design also carries into various packages, with carefully selected camshaft profiles and quality components to make installations trouble-free. Look for TFS to continue to push the envelope with its designs, including an LS3 casting.

GenX 205 and GenX 215

CATHEDRAL PORT CYLINDER HEADS

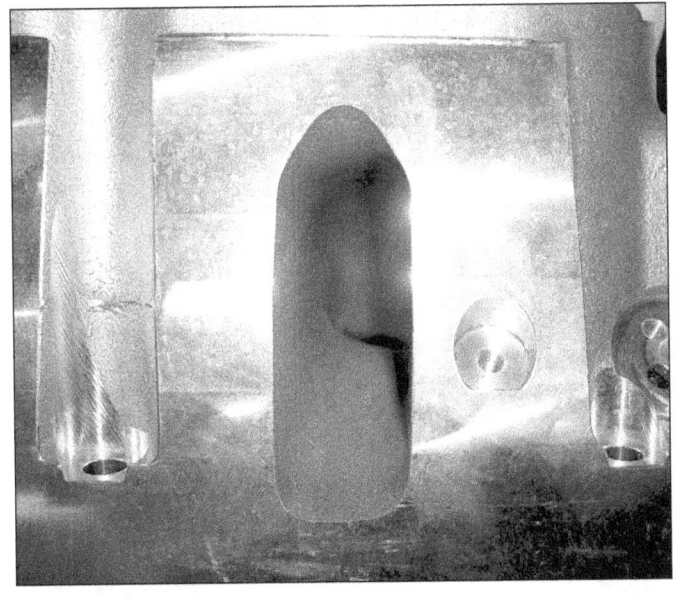

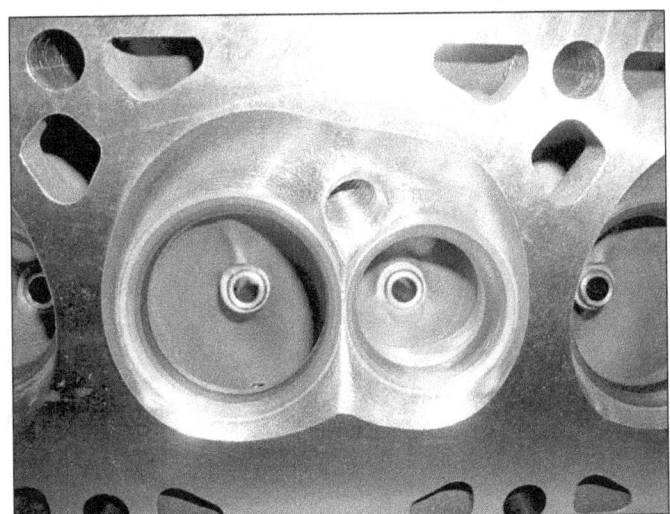

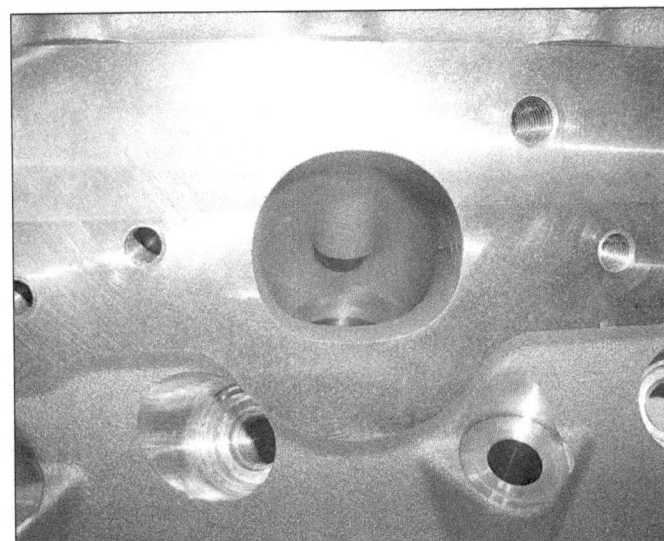
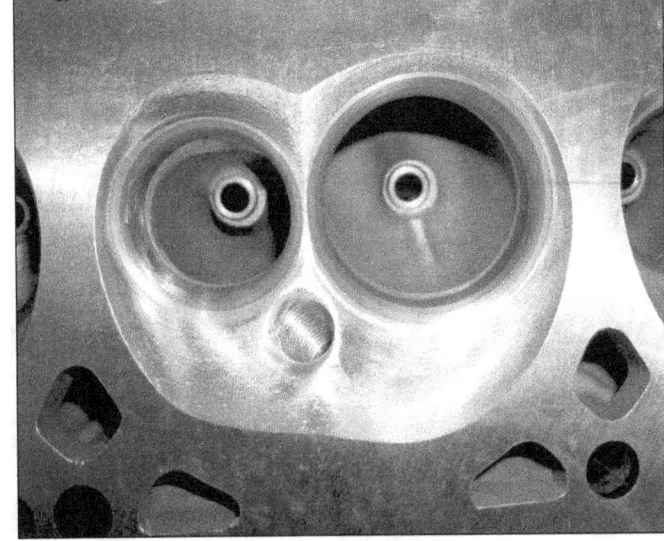

GenX 220 for LS1

GenX 220 for LS2

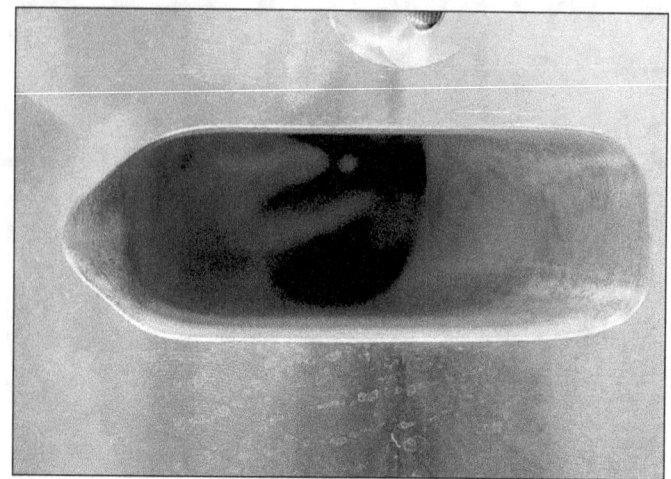

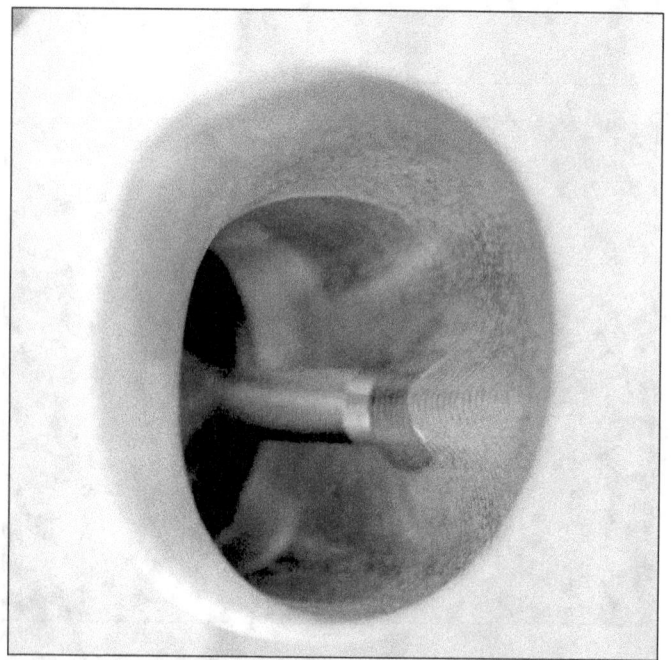
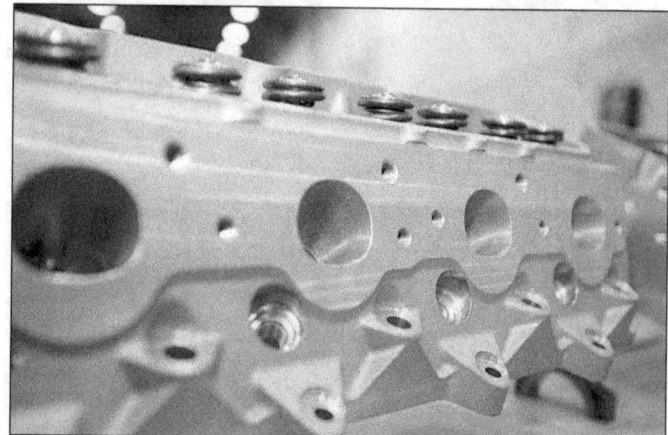
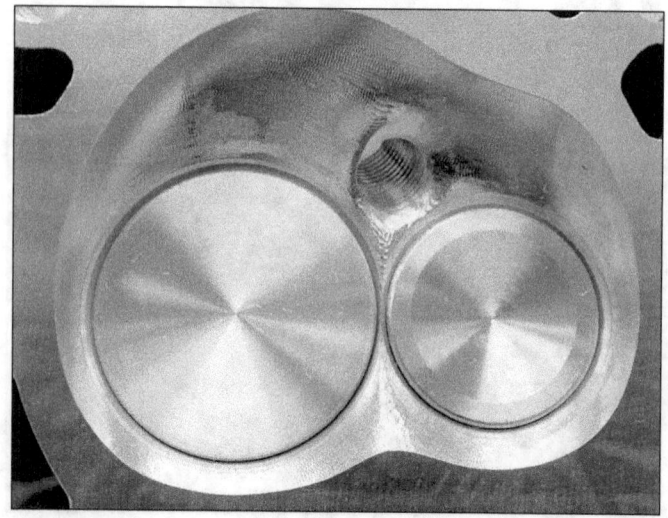

GenX 225

GenX 235, GenX 245, 265 cc (Photos Courtesy Vengeance Racing)

CATHEDRAL PORT CYLINDER HEADS

Trick Flow Specialties GenX 205

These heads are designed specifically for truck engines such as the small-bore 4.8- and 5.3-liter, though they could also be useful in a 5.7-liter looking for maximum torque. The 2.00-inch valves accommodate the smaller bores; however, the rest of the head is CNC-ported to facilitate great flow. The chambers are CNC-machined and bowl-blended to refine the shape, yet are stock size to maintain compression. Unlike their larger cousins, these heads have powdered metal valveguides to make them friendly to factory rocker arms. To further help cut costs, the GenX heads are compatible with factory valve covers, sensors, etc. Fully assembled this fresh casting goes for $1,995 (a pair) through Summit Racing and other dealers.

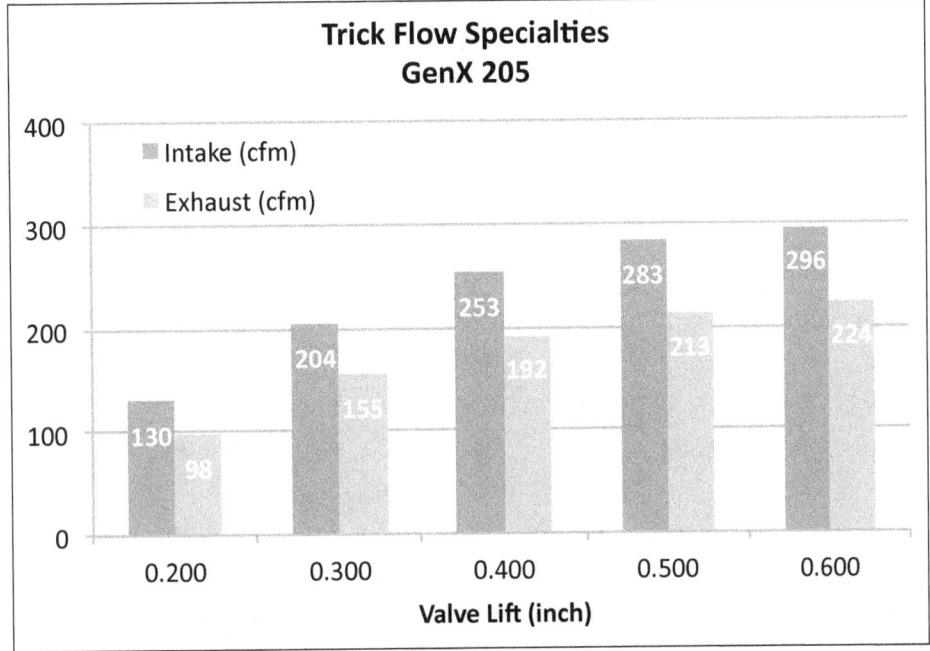

Valves: 2.00-inch intake, 1.575-inch exhaust
Combustion Chamber: 58 cc

Intake Runner: 205 cc
Intake (tested on a 3.90-inch bore):

Lift (inch)	.200	.300	.400	.500	.600
Flow (cfm)	130	204	253	283	296

Exhaust Runner: 80 cc
Exhaust (tested with a 1.75 x 4-inch pipe):

Lift (inch)	.200	.300	.400	.500	.600
Flow (cfm)	98	155	192	213	224

Recommended Use: 293 to 346 ci, forced induction or naturally aspirated
Additional Features: 1.300-inch-diameter valvesprings, chrome-moly or titanium retainers available, ductile iron valve seats, powdered metal valveguides

Trick Flow Specialties
GenX 215

For your typical head/cam LS1 the TFS 215 is hard to beat, with great top-end flow and torque. This is a smart choice for any 3.90-inch bore from mild to wild. The 13.5-degree valve angle means increased piston-to-valve clearance, decreased shrouding, and great mid-lift flow. CNC-ported intake and exhaust runners with CNC-machined and bowl-blended chambers make this a high-performing head. Roller rockers are a must with the bronze valveguides. All other OEM components bolt right on, including center-bolt valve covers. Fully assembled, the 215s cost $2,396 per set from Summit Racing.

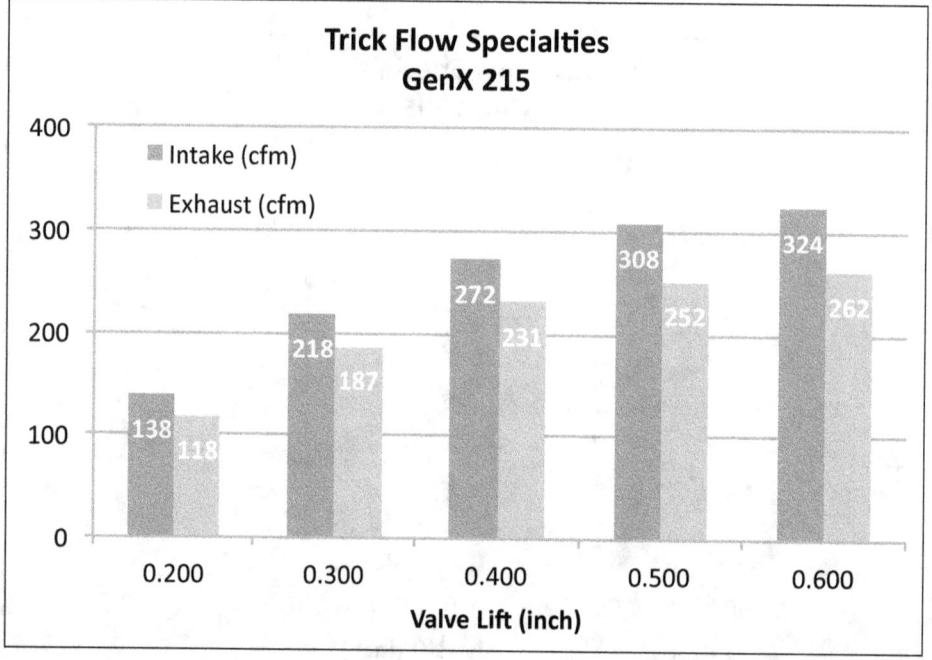

Valves: 2.040-inch intake, 1.575-inch exhaust
Combustion Chamber: 64 cc

Intake Runner: 215 cc
Intake (tested on a 3.900-inch bore):

Lift (inch)	.200	.300	.400	.500	.600
Flow (cfm)	138	218	272	308	324

Exhaust Runner: 80 cc
Exhaust (tested with a 1.875-inch exhaust pipe):

Lift (inch)	.200	.300	.400	.500	.600
Flow (cfm)	118	187	231	252	262

Recommended Use: 346 to 396 ci, forced induction or naturally aspirated
Additional Features: 1.300-inch-diameter (.600-inch maximum lift) valvesprings, titanium retainers, ductile iron valve seats, bronze valveguides

Trick Flow Specialties
GenX 220 for LS1

These as-cast heads offer all the great features and nearly the performance of the CNC-ported heads, but at a better price. From the 13.5-degree valve angle to the raised valve cover rail, relocated spark plugs, and rigid casting design, these heads have it all. Like the 215s, roller rockers are required. A 3.90-inch bore is also a requirement, with no other special considerations. Fully assembled, a pair of GenX 220s go for $1,700 through Summit Racing.

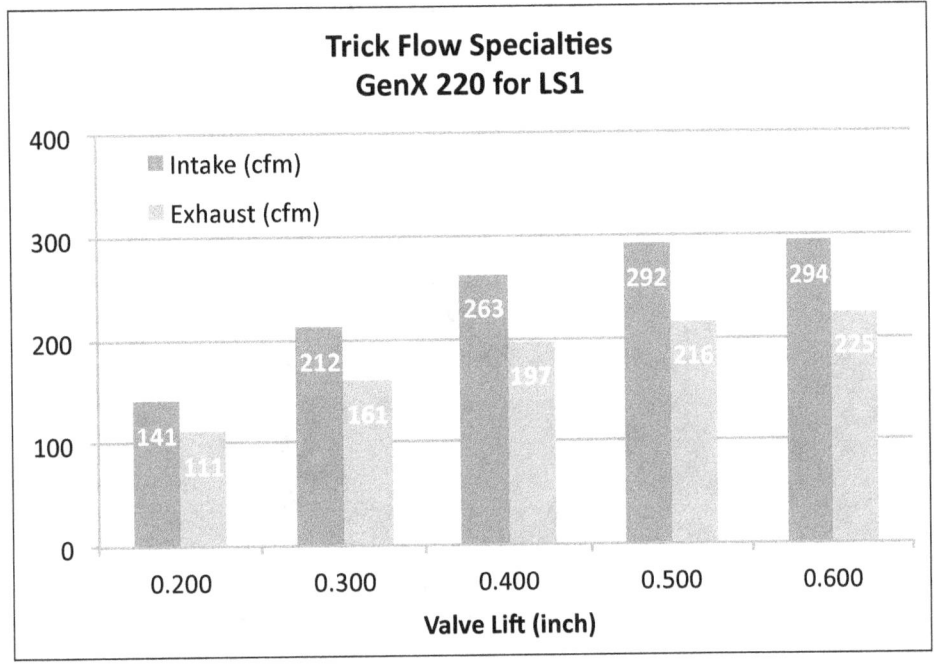

Valves: 2.04-inch intake, 1.575-inch exhaust
Combustion Chamber: 64 cc

Intake Runner: 220 cc
Intake (tested with a 4.00-inch flow plate)

Lift (inch)	.200	.300	.400	.500	.600
Flow (cfm)	141	212	263	292	294

Exhaust Runner: 80 cc
Exhaust (tested with a 1.75 x 4-inch exhaust pipe):

Lift (inch)	.200	.300	.400	.500	.600
Flow (cfm)	111	161	197	216	225

Recommended Use: 346 to 396 ci, forced induction or naturally aspirated
Additional Features: 1.300-inch-diameter (.600-inch maximum lift) valvesprings, titanium retainers, ductile iron valve seats, bronze valveguides

Trick Flow Specialties GenX 220 for LS2

Just like the LS1 version these Fast As Cast heads offer all of the great features of the 13.5-degree casting, but in an affordable package. The LS2 version boasts larger intake valves for the 4.00-inch bore and a slightly larger chamber. Roller rockers are required, with no other special needs. Just like the LS1 version, these heads cost $1,700 per pair, fully assembled.

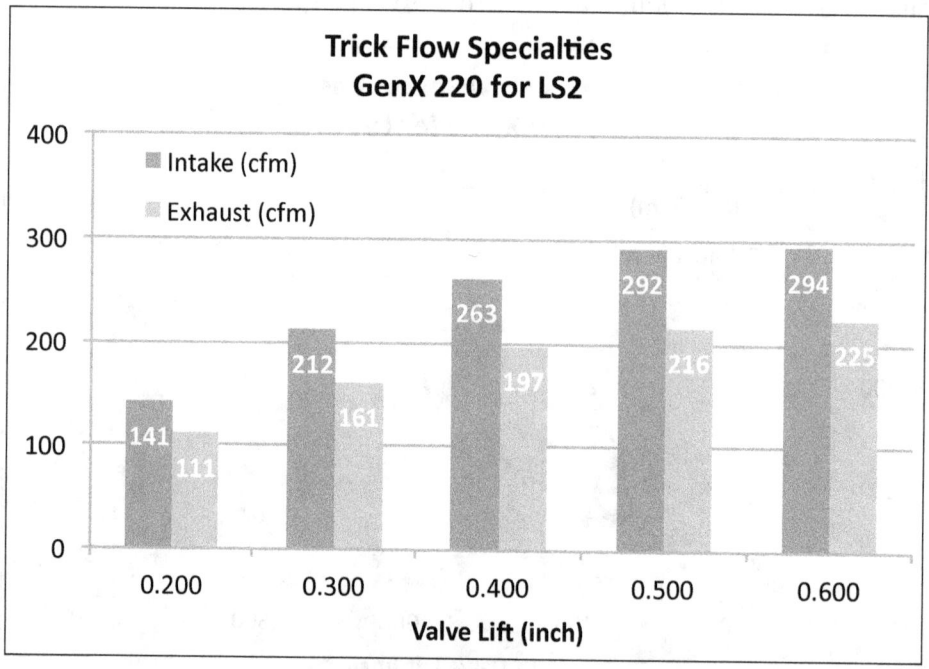

Valves: 2.055-inch intake, 1.575-inch exhaust
Combustion Chamber: 65 cc

Intake Runner: 220 cc
Intake (tested on a 4.00-inch bore):
Lift (inch)	.200	.300	.400	.500	.600
Flow (cfm)	141	212	263	292	294

Exhaust Runner: 80 cc
Exhaust (tested with a 1.75 x 4-inch exhaust pipe):
Lift (inch)	.200	.300	.400	.500	.600
Flow (cfm)	111	161	197	216	225

Recommended Use: 364 to 416 ci, forced induction or naturally aspirated
Additional Features: 1.300-inch-diameter (.600-inch maximum lift) valvesprings, titanium retainers, ductile iron valve seats, bronze valveguides

Trick Flow Specialties GenX 225

The GenX 225 picks up where the 215 head left off, adding greater volume and flow; best suited for 4-inch-or-larger bores (though it can fit a 3.90-inch bore):. The substantial capabilities of this fully CNC-ported head can keep up with strokers and forced induction, while also working for some stock cubic-inch combos. Again, this casting sports a 13.5-degree valve angle, raised valve cover rails, and optimized spark plug location. Just as with the 215, roller rockers are required. For $2,396, these heads come fully assembled and ready to bolt onto any Gen III or IV with factory components and fasteners.

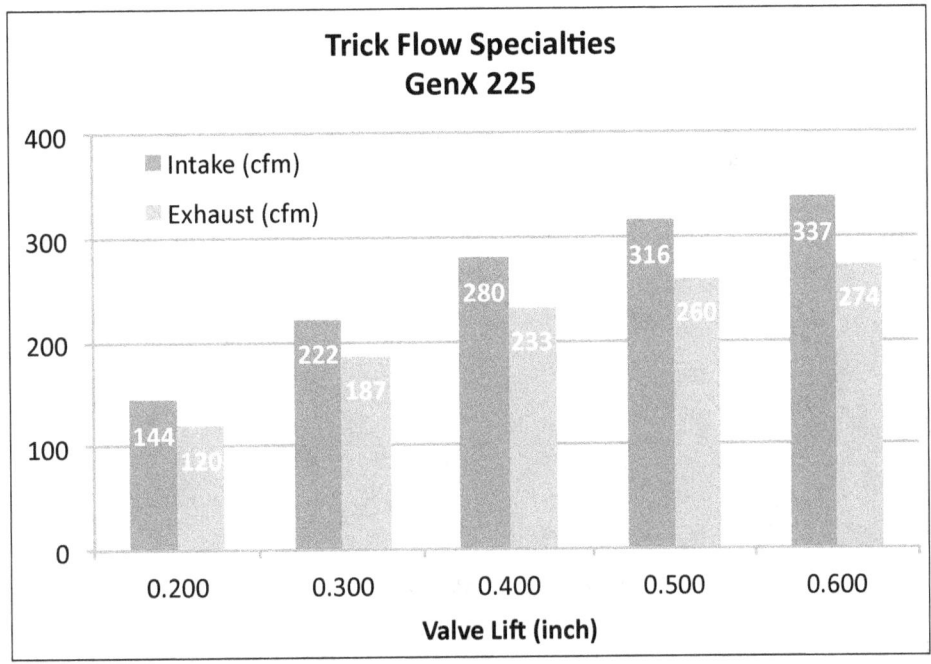

Valves: 2.055-inch intake, 1.575-inch exhaust
Combustion Chamber: 65 cc

Intake Runner: 225 cc
Intake (tested on a 4.030-inch bore):
Lift (inch)	.200	.300	.400	.500	.600
Flow (cfm)	144	222	280	316	337

Exhaust Runner: 80 cc
Exhaust (tested with a 1.875-inch exhaust pipe):
Lift (inch)	.200	.300	.400	.500	.600
Flow (cfm)	120	187	233	260	274

Recommended Use: 364 to 416 ci, forced induction or naturally aspirated
Additional Features: 1.300-inch-diameter (.600-inch maximum lift) valvesprings with optional upgrades, titanium retainers, ductile iron valve seats, bronze valveguides

Trick Flow Specialties
GenX 235

The TFS 235s come in several varieties, from fully CNC-ported to bare and as-cast. The large valves and chambers are designed for 4.030-inch-and-larger bore, which makes them appropriate on high-boost LQ9- and LS3-based combos or for larger-cube street engines. Built with these applications in mind, TFS offers a 6-head-bolt option for LSX blocks. Since the 235s come from the same casting as the smaller versions, they also have a 13.5-degree valve angle, raised valve cover rails, and revised spark plug location. Factor in a set of roller rockers when budgeting for the $2,450 (fully assembled) price tag.

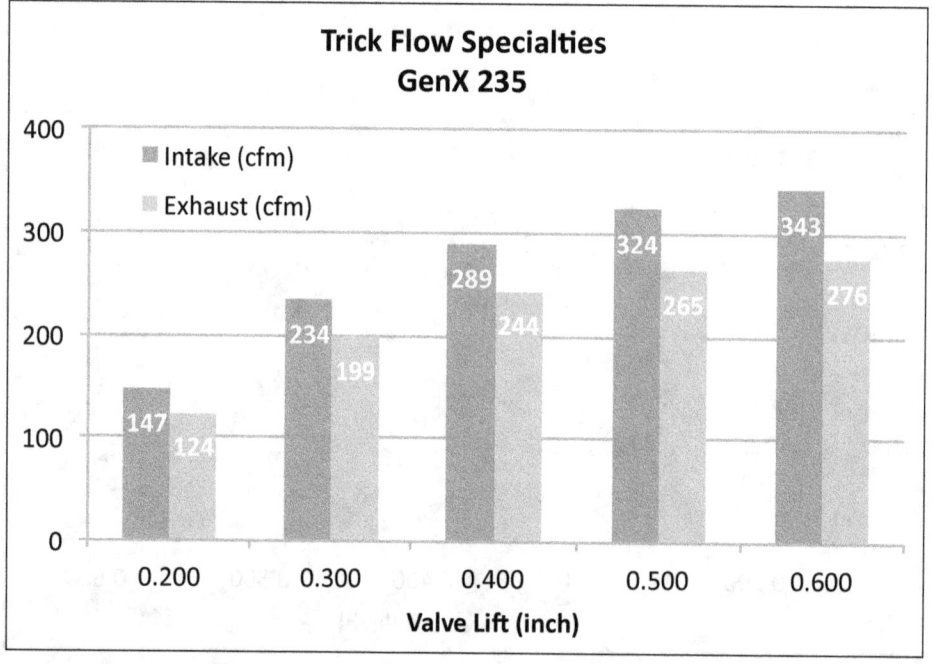

Valves: 2.080-inch intake, 1.60-inch exhaust
Combustion Chamber: 70 cc

Intake Runner: 235 cc
Intake (tested on a 4.030-inch bore):
    Lift (inch)   .200   .300   .400   .500   .600
    Flow (cfm) 147   234   289   324   343

Exhaust Runner: 80 cc
Exhaust (tested with a 1.875-inch exhaust pipe):
    Lift (inch)   .200   .300   .400   .500   .600
    Flow (cfm) 124   199   244   265   276

Recommended Use: 370 to 434 ci, forced induction or naturally aspirated
Additional Features: 1.300-inch-diameter (.600-inch maximum lift) valvesprings with optional upgrades, titanium retainers, ductile iron valve seats, bronze valve-guides

Trick Flow Specialties GenX 245

The 245-cc GenX head pushes the limits of the cathedral port casting, utilizing massive intake valves that rival rectangular ports, making it suitable for large-bore applications only (though it fits a 4.030-inch). CNC-ported runners and CNC-machined chambers (with bowl-blending) facilitate massive flow, and the 6-bolts-per-cylinder head bolt provision is standard for better clamping with aftermarket blocks. Just like the others, the 245s feature a 13.5-degree valve angle and raised valve cover rails to accommodate the required aftermarket roller rockers. An optional nitrous exhaust port can increase flow to 290 cfm at .600-inch lift. The added machine work puts this head at a starting price of $1,326 (each) when fully assembled with the standard 1.300-inch-diameter dual valvesprings, though Total Engine AirFlow sells this head with other spring options.

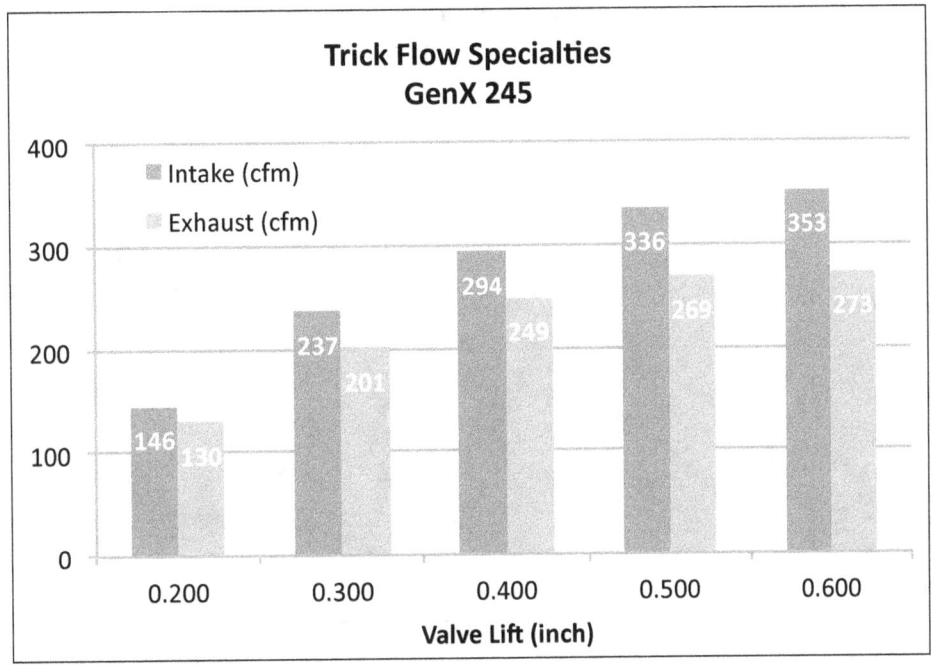

Valves: 2.100-inch intake, 1.600-inch exhaust
Combustion Chamber: 70 cc

Intake Runner: 245 cc
Intake (tested on a 4.155-inch bore):

Lift (inch)	.200	.300	.400	.500	.600
Flow (cfm)	146	237	294	336	353

Exhaust Runner: 80 cc
Exhaust (tested with a 1.875-inch exhaust pipe):

Lift (inch)	.200	.300	.400	.500	.600
Flow (cfm)	130	201	249	269	273

Recommended Use: 427 to 502 ci, forced induction or naturally aspirated
Additional Features: 1.300-inch-diameter (.600-inch maximum lift) valvesprings with optional upgrades, titanium retainers, ductile iron valve seats, bronze valveguides, optional nitrous exhaust port

Trick Flow Specialties/Total Engine AirFlow
265 cc

TEA CNC-ports the Trick Flow casting to a massive 265 cc to make it an all-out drag head, taking the already impressive 245-cc head and injecting it with steroids. Built for large-lift camshafts and high RPM, this head comes with massive PAC valvesprings, competition 55-degree valve job, and titanium intake valves. Titanium or inconel exhaust valves are optional upgrades to the standard stainless-steel valves from Victory-1. Optional nitrous exhaust ports hit an unbelievable 306 cfm at 1.00 inch of lift. This head comes only with LSX-style 6-bolts-per-cylinder head bolt provisions for aftermarket blocks because a 4.155-inch bore is required. The TFS casting, of course, has a 13.5-degree valve angle and raised valve cover rails to accommodate the required aftermarket roller rockers. These heads start at $3,950 for the pair (assembled).

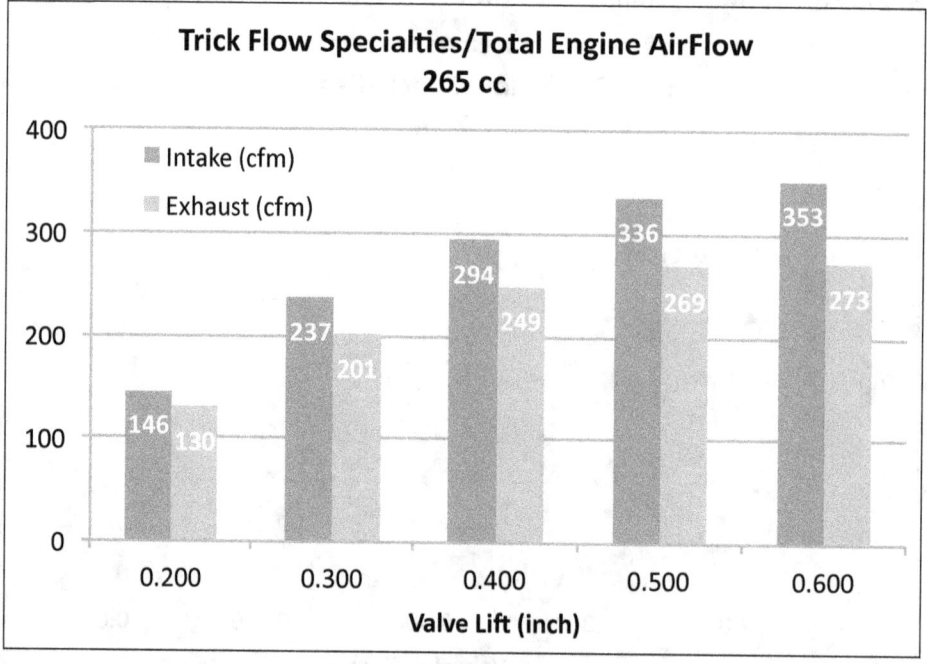

Valves: 2.100-inch intake, 1.600-inch exhaust
Combustion Chamber: 64 cc

Intake Runner: 265 cc
Intake (tested on a 4.155-inch bore):
Lift (inch)	.200	.300	.400	.500	.600
Flow (cfm)	146	237	294	336	353

Exhaust Runner: 85 cc
Exhaust (tested with a 1.875-inch exhaust pipe):
Lift (inch)	.200	.300	.400	.500	.600
Flow (cfm)	130	201	249	269	273

Recommended Use: 434 to 502 ci, forced induction or naturally aspirated
Additional Features: .850-inch-lift PAC valvesprings with optional upgrades, titanium retainers, ductile iron valve seats with optional beryllium copper, bronze valveguides, optional nitrous exhaust port

CATHEDRAL PORT CYLINDER HEADS

West Coast Cylinder Heads

Includes:

Edelbrock 4.8/5.3-Liter

Edelbrock LS1, 215 cc

Warhawk, 15-Degree, CNC

Edelbrock LS2, 245 cc

WCCH is quickly becoming one of the foremost designers of CNC programs for aftermarket LS castings, though it has its roots in programs for OEM castings. Both the street and race crowd are well satisfied with WCCH's All Pro, Brodix, Edelbrock, and factory designs. Though West Coast has been machining heads for more than 23 years in Southern California, with various small- and big-block applications in all forms of motorsports and street performance, the LS market is quickly taking over the business. (Photos Courtesy West Coast Cylinder Heads)

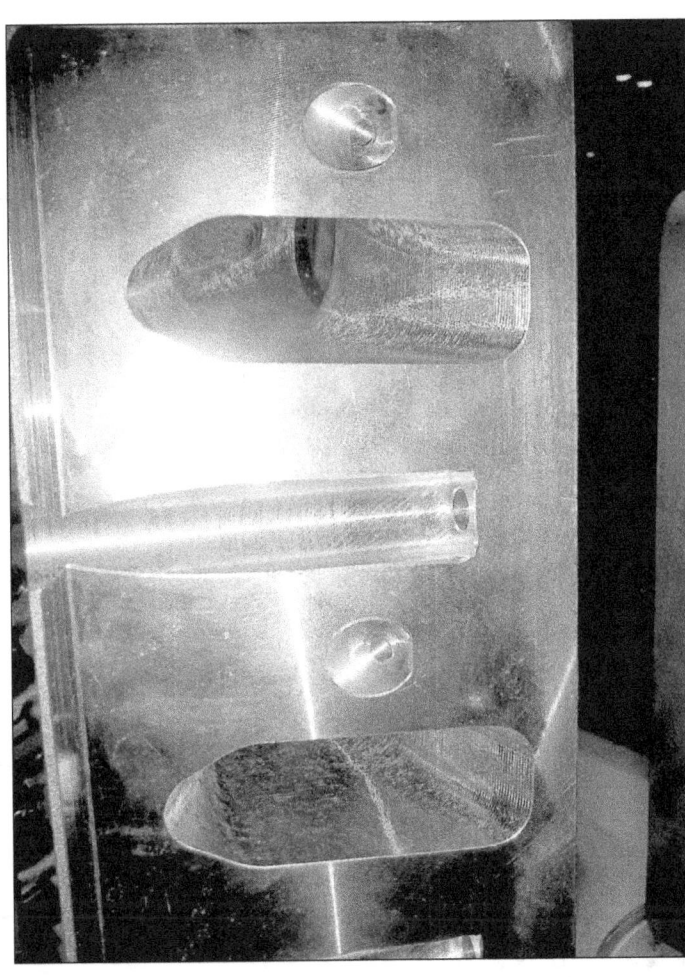

CHAPTER 2

West Coast Cylinder Heads
Edelbrock 4.8/5.3-Liter

Built for the popular 4.8- or 5.3-liter truck engines, WCCH uses a custom CNC program on Edelbrock's Pro Port casting to create a torquey, small-runner design with great low- and mid-lift flow numbers. The Edelbrock casting is compatible with factory rockers and other equipment, and utilizes the stock LS1 valve angle. As you'd expect from a CNC-ported aftermarket casting these heads go for $2,340 fully assembled.

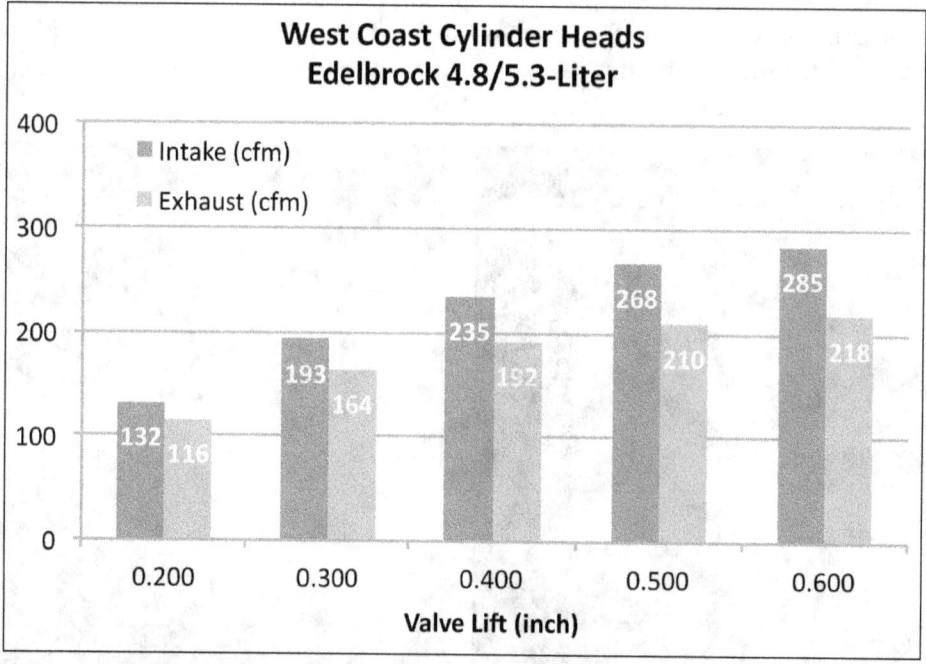

Valves: 2.00-inch intake, 1.57-inch exhaust
Combustion Chamber: 58 cc

Intake Runner: 201 cc
Intake (tested on a 3.780-inch bore):

Lift (inch)	.200	.300	.400	.500	.600
Flow (cfm)	132	193	235	268	285

Exhaust Runner: 81 cc
Exhaust:

Lift (inch)	.200	.300	.400	.500	.600
Flow (cfm)	116	164	192	210	218

Recommended Use: 292 to 327 ci, forced induction or naturally aspirated
Additional Features: 15-degree valve angle, 5/8-inch-thick deck

West Coast Cylinder Heads
Edelbrock LS1, 215 cc

Starting with Edelbrock's Pro Port casting, WCCH's CNC program opens the intake runners up to 212 cc, perfect for a stock cubic-inch combo, or even a larger-cube combo where torque is at a premium. The flow numbers are exceptionally high for the runner sizes, which make these heads so versatile. These heads are compatible with all OEM equipment and require a 3.90-inch bore. Just like the smaller truck heads, the 215s come fully assembled for $2,340.

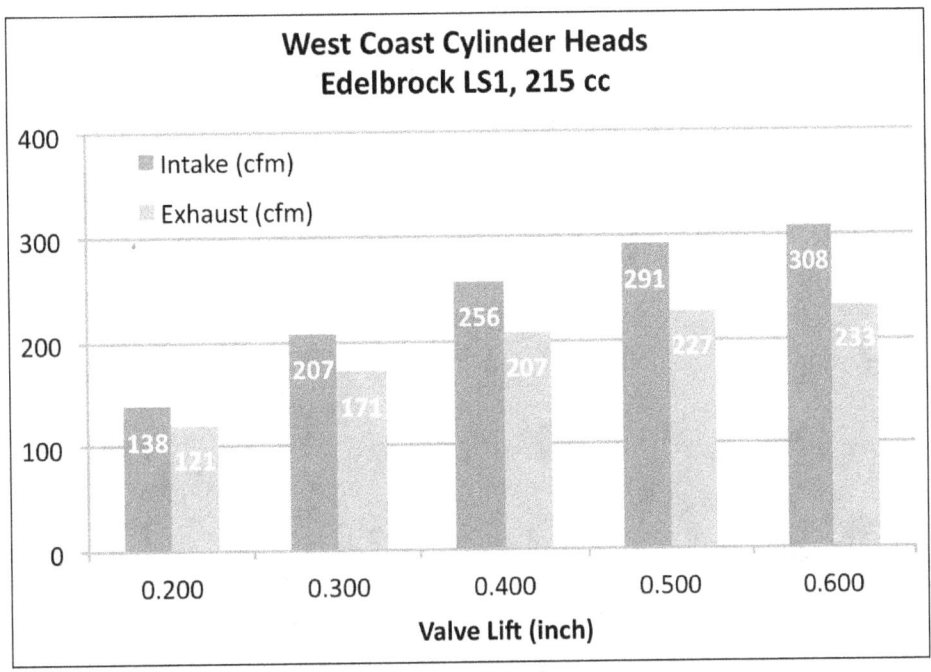

Valves: 2.055-inch intake, 1.600-inch exhaust
Combustion Chamber: 66 cc

Intake Runner: 212 cc
Intake (tested on a 4.030-inch bore):

Lift (inch)	.200	.300	.400	.500	.600
Flow (cfm)	138	207	256	291	308

Exhaust Runner: 82 cc
Exhaust (tested with a stub pipe):

Lift (inch)	.200	.300	.400	.500	.600
Flow (cfm)	121	171	207	227	233

Recommended Use: 346 to 396 ci, forced induction or naturally aspirated
Additional Features: 15-degree valve angle, 5/8-inch-thick deck, variety of valvespring options

West Coast Cylinder Heads
Edelbrock LS2, 245 cc

On the largest version of the Edelbrock-based trio from WCCH, the large 245-cc intake runners are extremely peaky and benefit large-lift camshafts. Flow continues to rise as it hits .700-inch lift at 337.2 cfm. Though these heads work well with a high-boost 370-ci engine, without forced induction substantial cubes are needed to properly match the large runners. Just like the others, these heads are also compatible with OEM fasteners, sensors, and rocker arms. Despite the added time on the CNC machine, these heads also start at $2,340 with premium upgrades available.

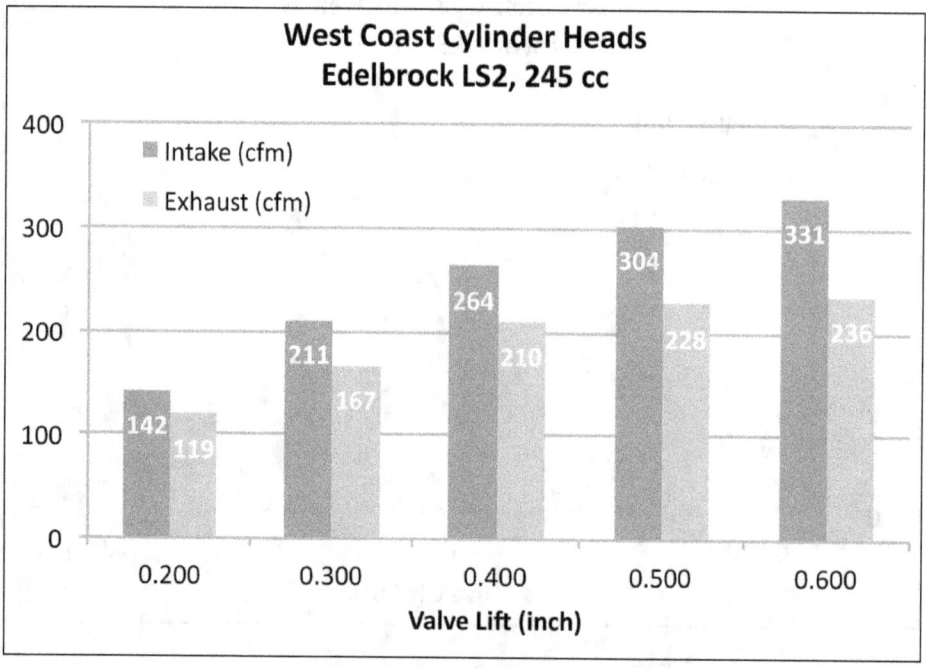

Valves: 2.055-inch intake, 1.600-inch exhaust
Combustion Chamber: 66 or 74 cc

Intake Runner: 245 cc
Intake (tested on a 4.030-inch bore):
Lift (inch)	.200	.300	.400	.500	.600
Flow (cfm)	142	211	264	304	331

Exhaust Runner: 88 cc
Exhaust (tested with a stub pipe):
Lift (inch)	.200	.300	.400	.500	.600
Flow (cfm)	119	167	210	228	236

Recommended Use: 370 to 440 ci, forced induction or naturally aspirated
Additional Features: 15-degree angle, 5/8-inch-thick deck, variety of valvespring options

World Products
Warhawk, 15-Degree, CNC

Just like its as-cast cousin, the CNC version flows better as the lift increases past .600 inch and actually hits 330 cfm at .800 inch. On a large-cubic-inch or race application this head has plenty of potential, yet still is completely compatible with factory rockers and other components. However, most likely a solid roller and shaft-mount rockers is the chosen pairing with these heads. An unported version is also available that flows 289 and 204 cfm at .600-inch lift using 235- and 87-cc runners. A 3.90-inch-or-larger bore is required, and most retailers list these heads at $876 each (fully assembled).

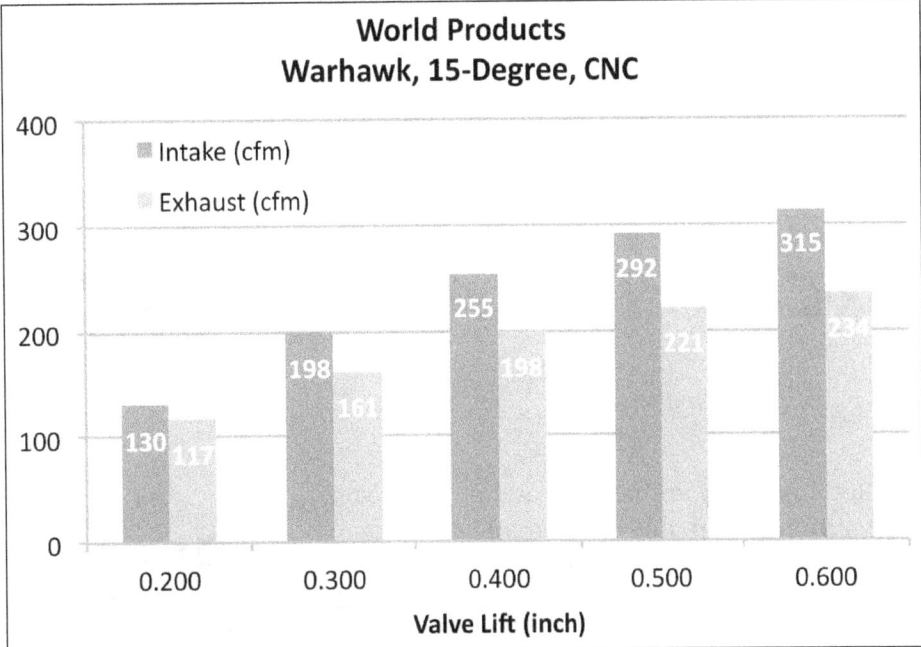

Valves: 2.08-inch intake, 1.60-inch exhaust
Combustion Chamber: 64 or 72 cc

Intake Runner: 235 cc
Intake (tested on a SF-1020 flow bench)
Lift (inch)	.200	.300	.400	.500	.600
Flow (cfm)	130	198	255	292	315

Exhaust Runner: 90 cc
Exhaust (tested with no exhaust pipe):
Lift (inch)	.200	.300	.400	.500	.600
Flow (cfm)	117	161	198	221	234

Recommended Use: 370 to 440 ci, forced induction or naturally aspirated
Additional Features: .300-inch raised valve cover rail, hardened valve seats, manganese bronze valveguides, .600- or .700-inch maximum lift valvesprings

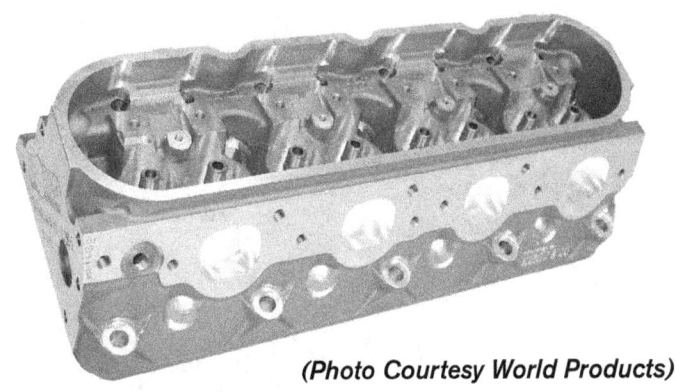

(Photo Courtesy World Products)

CHAPTER 3

Rectangular Port Cylinder Heads

Rectangular port heads boast a clear advantage in the flow department and are ideal for high-RPM, big-cubic-inch, and purpose-built drag racing applications.

Factory castings are capable of 360 to 400 cfm when ported properly, which can make it difficult to justify an aftermarket casting. However, aftermarket castings boast designs more suitable for both more extreme applications and street cars looking for better torque. Factory heads have design compromises for emissions and cost (obviously missing from aftermarket designs) and are optimized for low-lift camshafts and other OEM components. However, the aftermarket can achieve the performance potential of a race head that is compatible with factory intake and exhaust patterns.

RECTANGULAR PORT CYLINDER HEADS

Factory Heads

LS7

These were the first heads to bring race car quality and technology to the OEM side. Although common in the aftermarket, CNC-porting of the intake and exhaust runners is usually too costly for a factory head. Titanium intake valves and sodium-filled exhaust valves were previously unheard of in a domestic factory engine, which revved to 7,200 rpm, another anomaly for a pushrod V-8. Right out of the box, these heads have supported more than 600 hp naturally aspirated and substantially more with forced induction. The large, raised runners and 12-degree valve angle enable substantial flow that supports large cubic inches. And the large valves necessitate a 4.125-inch or larger bore, and otherwise bolt right up with LS7-specific intake manifold bolts. These heads are available at any Chevrolet Performance dealer for around $1,500. (Photos Courtesy General Motors)

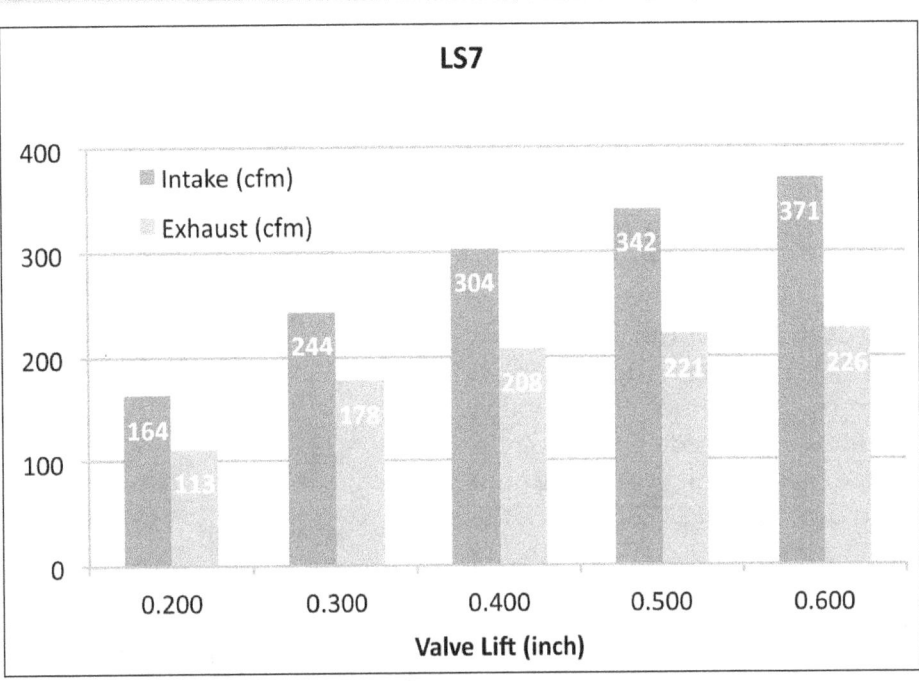

Valves: 2.200-inch intake, 1.61-inch exhaust
Combustion Chamber: 70 cc

Intake Runner: 259 cc
Intake (tested on a 4.125-inch bore):

Lift (inch)	.200	.300	.400	.500	.600
Flow (cfm)	164	244	304	342	371

Exhaust Runner: 85 cc
Exhaust (tested with no exhaust pipe):

Lift (inch)	.200	.300	.400	.500	.600
Flow (cfm)	113	178	208	221	226

Recommended Use: 427 to 502 ci, forced induction or naturally aspirated
Additional Features: 12-degree valve angle, Del West titanium intake valves, sodium-filled exhaust valves

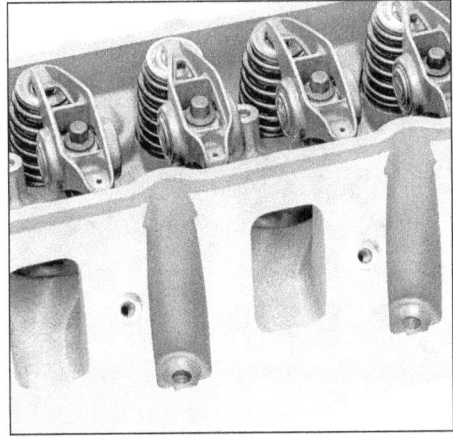
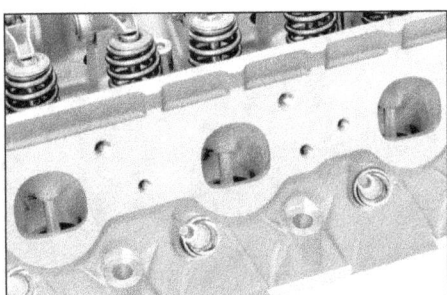
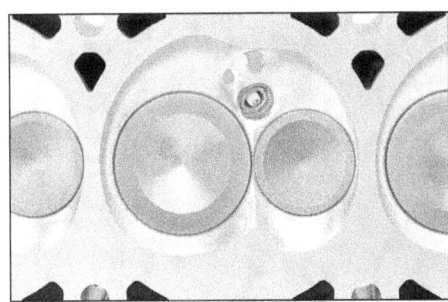

L92/LS3/LSA

These mini-LS7 heads debuted in Australia first in the 2006 Holden Commodore (among others) as the L76 and L98, but are most commonly known for their debut on the 2007 Escalade's L92. Only one significant change was made for use on the LS3 engine in the Corvette, Camaro, and G8 GXP–hollow-stem valves. A better casting was used for added strength on the supercharged LSA, but it is also mostly unchanged since its original inception. Though sacrifices were made for emissions, you won't find a higher-flowing head for the money. The L92 head was the first to boast 330 cfm while being dirt cheap, which started the craze. The massive intake valves necessitate a 4-inch-or-larger bore with no other special consideration needed. These heads are available for a scant $375 from Chevrolet Performance dealers, making them an excellent bang for the buck. (Photos Courtesy General Motors)

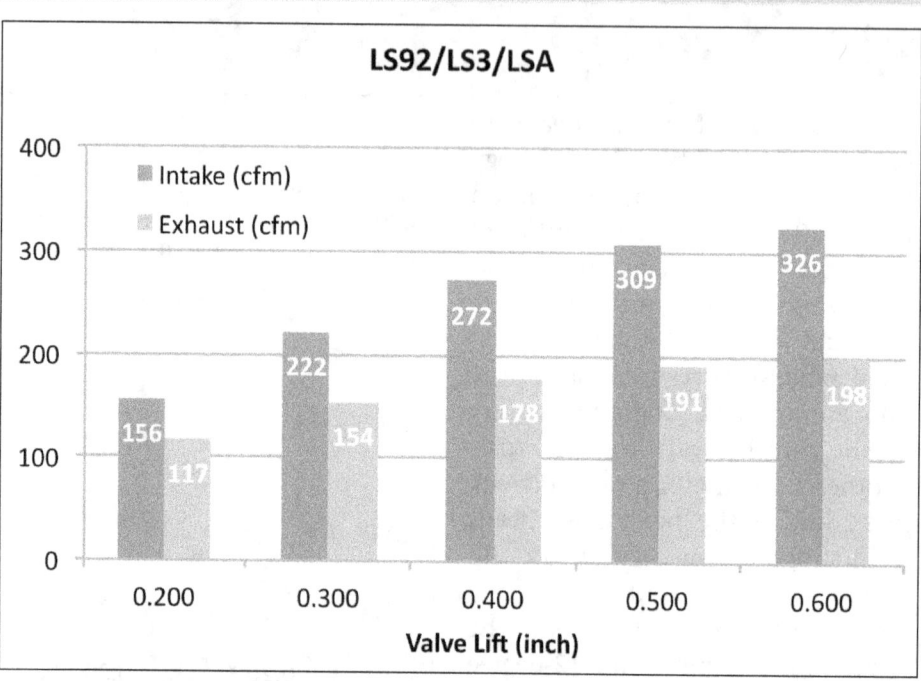

Valves: 2.165-inch intake, 1.59-inch exhaust
Combustion Chamber: 68 cc

Intake Runner: 261 cc
Intake (tested on a 4.155-inch bore):

Lift (inch)	.200	.300	.400	.500	.600
Flow (cfm)	156	222	272	309	326

Exhaust Runner: 89 cc
Exhaust (tested with no exhaust pipe):

Lift (inch)	.200	.300	.400	.500	.600
Flow (cfm)	117	154	178	191	198

Recommended Use: 364 to 427 cc, forced induction or naturally aspirated
Additional Features: 15-degree valve angle

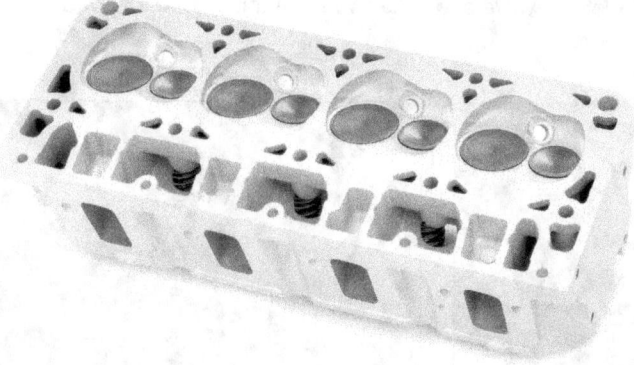

LS9

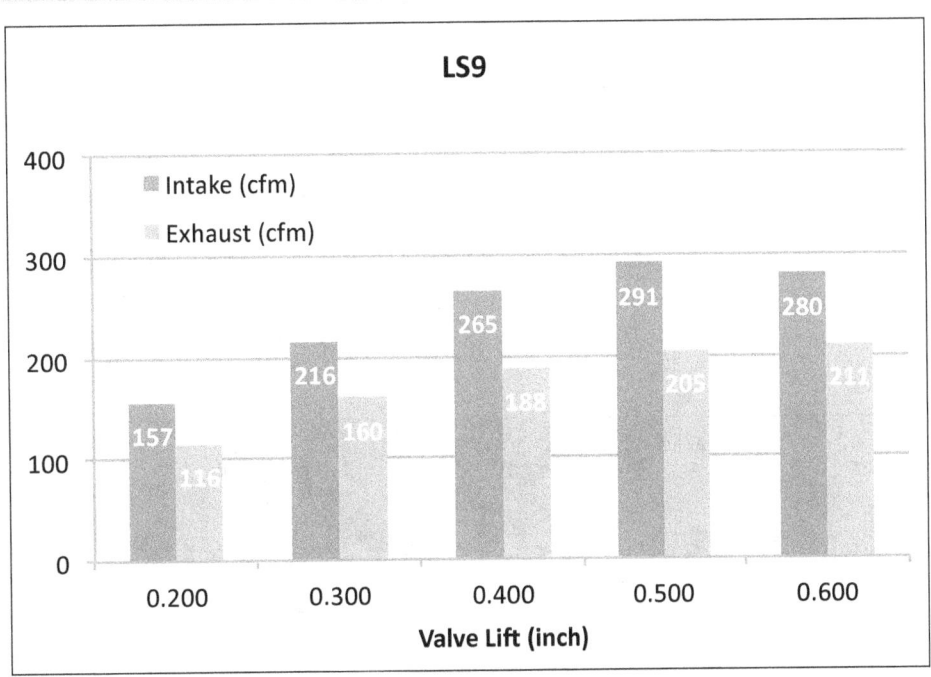

The formula for building the most powerful factory GM engine ever was fairly simple: Add a supercharger to the LS3 and beef it up considerably. Though they bare plenty of resemblance to the LS3, the LS9 head has a number of features that make them more suitable for boosted applications. The rotocast method (also used on the LSA) and the use of A356T6 alloy make this a stronger casting that is better at handling the added heat generated from a supercharger. The factory CNC porting would seemingly increase flow, but a few changes to the port shape were made to improve swirl that actually decreases flow (but improves overall performance in a supercharged application). Titanium intake valves and sodium-filled exhaust valves keep it on par with the LS7 and allow the engine to peak at 6,500 rpm. Just like the LS3, the large valves require a 4-inch bore, and the LS9 also has a thicker deck and larger head bolts for better clamping with boost. If you are not using an LS9 block, you need ARP head studs to rectify. The intake manifold locating bosses also need to be machined for use with an LS3 or L92 manifold. Any Chevrolet Performance dealer sells these heads for around $1,120.

Valves: 2.165-inch intake, 1.59-inch exhaust
Combustion Chamber: 68 cc

Intake Runner: 261 cc
Intake (tested on a 4.06-inch bore):

Lift (inch)	.200	.300	.400	.500	.600
Flow (cfm)	157	216	265	291	280

Exhaust Runner: 89 cc
Exhaust (tested with no exhaust pipe):

Lift (inch)	.200	.300	.400	.500	.600
Flow (cfm)	116	160	188	205	211

Recommended Use: 364 to 427 ci, positive displacement supercharger
Additional Features: 15-degree valve angle, Del West titanium intake valves, sodium-filled exhaust valves

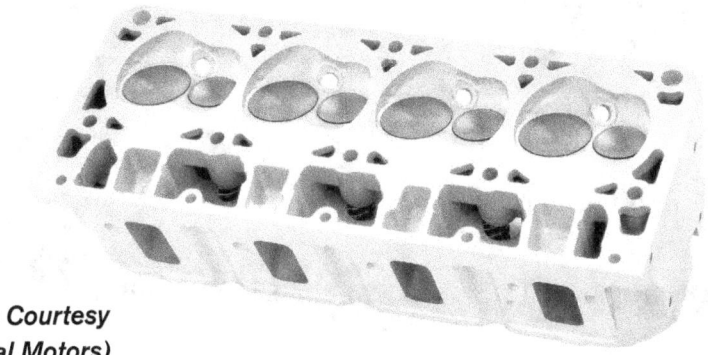

(Photo Courtesy General Motors)

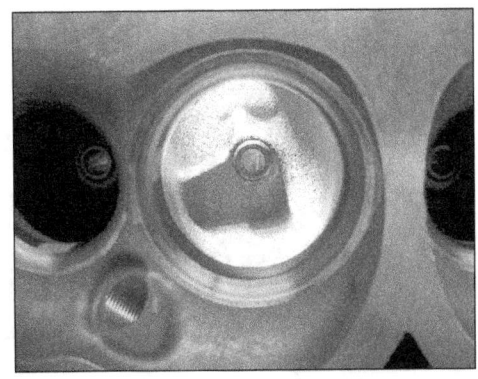

CHAPTER 3

Aftermarket Heads

Includes:

L92, 267 cc

LS3, 275 cc

LS7, 280 cc

Advanced Induction

North Carolina–based Advanced Inductions is widely known for CNC head porting, with programs for the Gen II, III, and IV small-block only. Specializing in such a finite area makes AI particularly knowledgable, precise, and efficient. Advanced Inductions offers a plethora of heads with aftermarket and factory castings. It also offers intake manifold porting and valvetrain kits with a specially designed camshaft. (Photos Courtesy Advanced Induction)

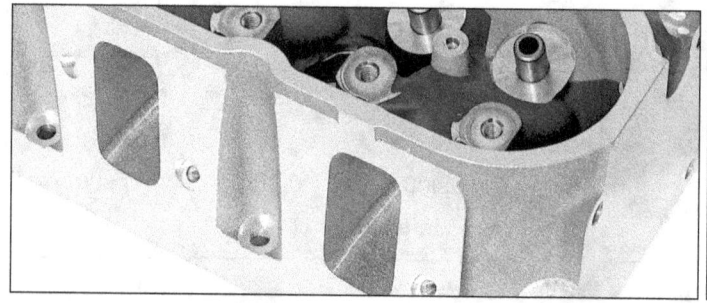

L92 267 cc

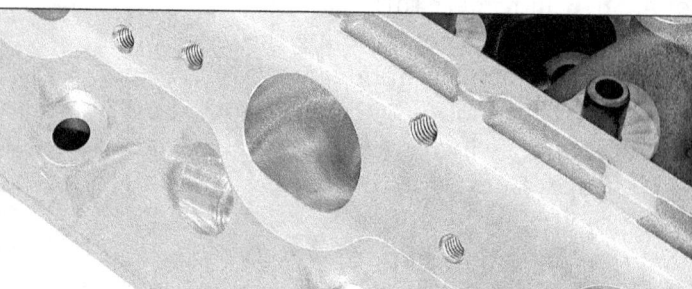

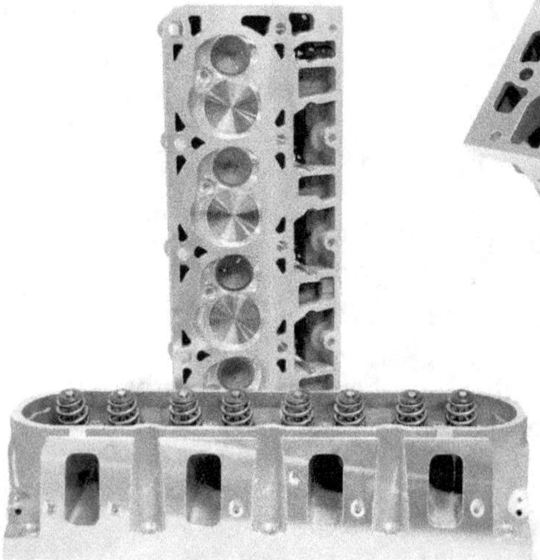

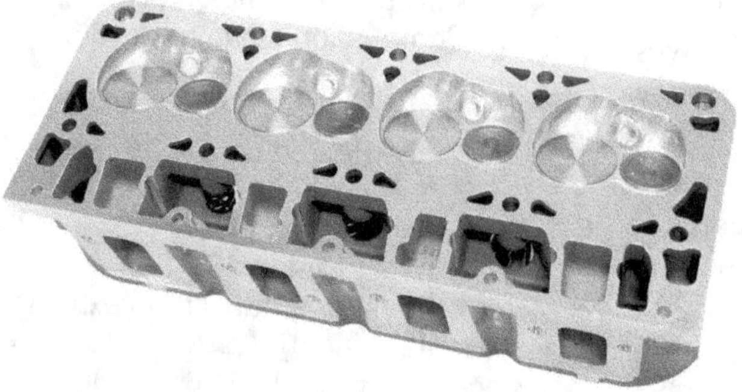

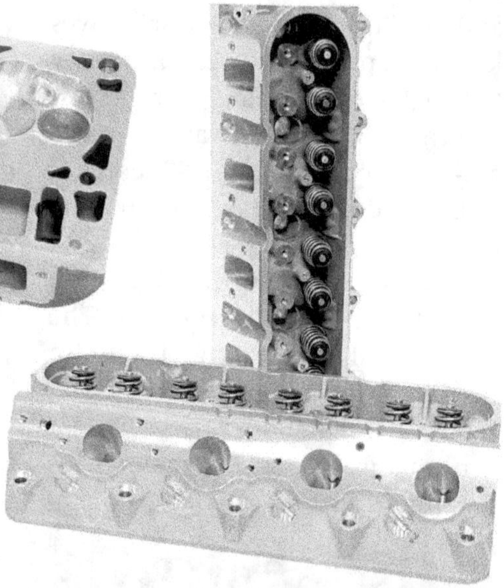

LS3 275 cc

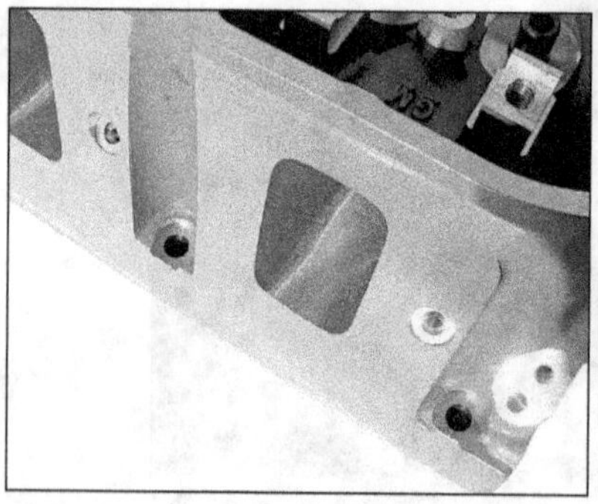

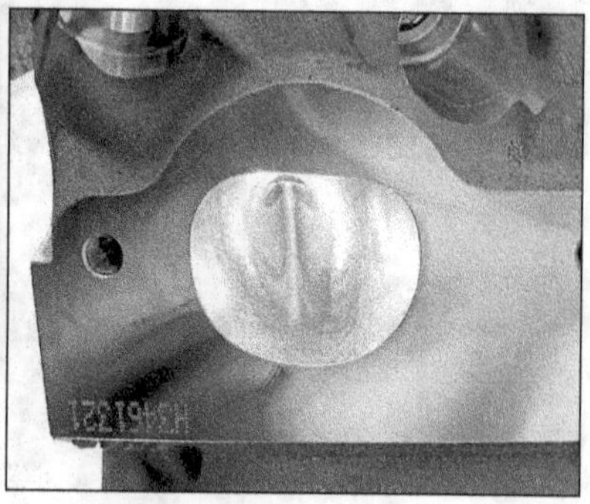

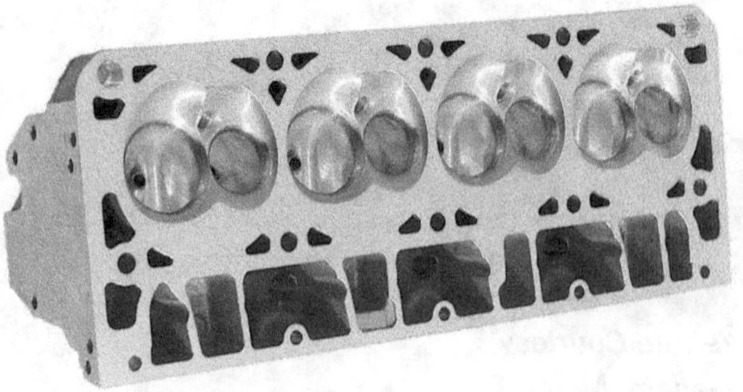

LS7 280 cc

RECTANGULAR PORT CYLINDER HEADS

Advanced Induction
L92, 267 cc

Because the "823" casting already comes with such a large port, Advanced Induction focuses on simply increasing the efficiency and shape of the intake runners. A large portion of the gains, though, come from opening up the exhaust ports. In fact, AI offers a more budget-friendly version with stock intake runners (and ported exhaust) that it claims is good for 20 to 35 rwhp. The pricier 267-cc head is known for its torque and throttle response. Flow (cfm) increases 43.2 on the intake side and 15.5 on the exhaust while still using factory valves (note baseline flow numbers are considerably lower than the prior stock heads). Flow continues to rise at .700-inch lift making these a great pairing with a large camshaft. The only requirement for installing these heads is a 4-inch-or-larger bore. $995 covers the machining and labor cost for AI's 267-cc program, with additional charges for upgraded valvesprings, retainers, valveguides, etc.

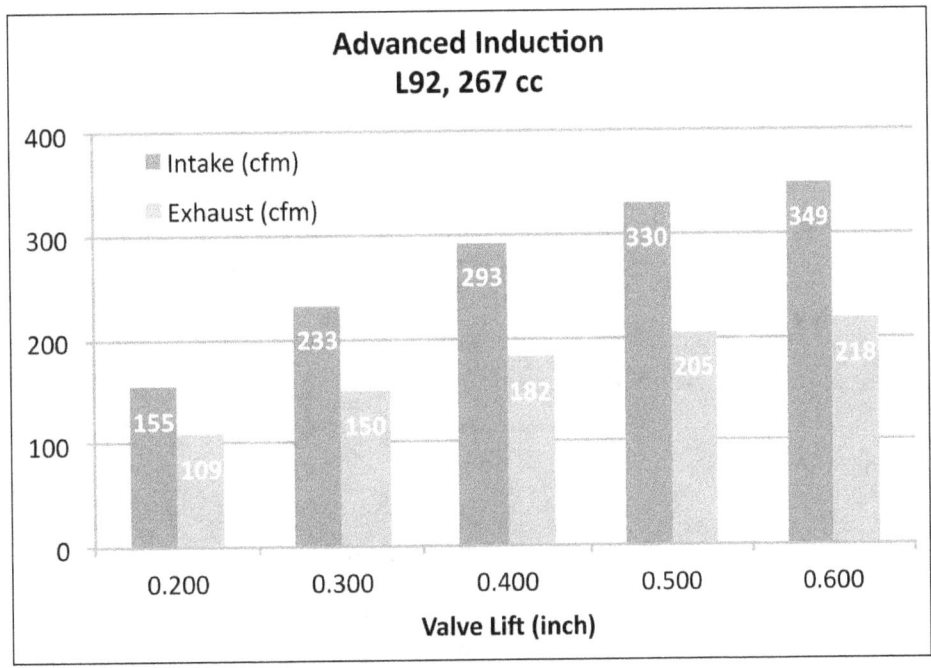

Valves: 2.165-inch intake, 1.59-inch exhaust
Combustion Chamber: 62 to 73 cc

Intake Runner: 267 cc
Intake (tested on a 4.03-inch bore):
  Lift (inch)   .200   .300   .400   .500   .600
  Flow (cfm)   155   233   293   330   349

Exhaust Runner: 90+ cc
Exhaust (tested with no exhaust pipe):
  Lift (inch)   .200   .300   .400   .500   .600
  Flow (cfm)   109   150   182   205   218

Recommended Use: 364 to 427 ci, forced induction or naturally aspirated
Additional Features: CNC-ported runners, CNC competition valve job, factory valves cleaned and precision ground, PCD-milled deck and flanges, several valvespring and retainer options

CHAPTER 3

Advanced Induction
LS3, 275 cc

Three different sizes are offered in AI's "821" casting, starting at 270 cc and then going up to 280 cc. The largest of the three is recommended for high-RPM and large-displacement applications, and the smallest works well in the 600- to 700-hp combinations that stay below 7,000 rpm. The 275-cc version, though, splits the difference and offers substantial port cleanup. AI says significant core shift among the GM castings causes large area to remain as cast, which does not affect function. The largest of the three CNC programs eliminates most of these areas. No special parts are required for installation. AI charges $995 for machining and labor, plus additional amounts for various valvespring and other upgrades.

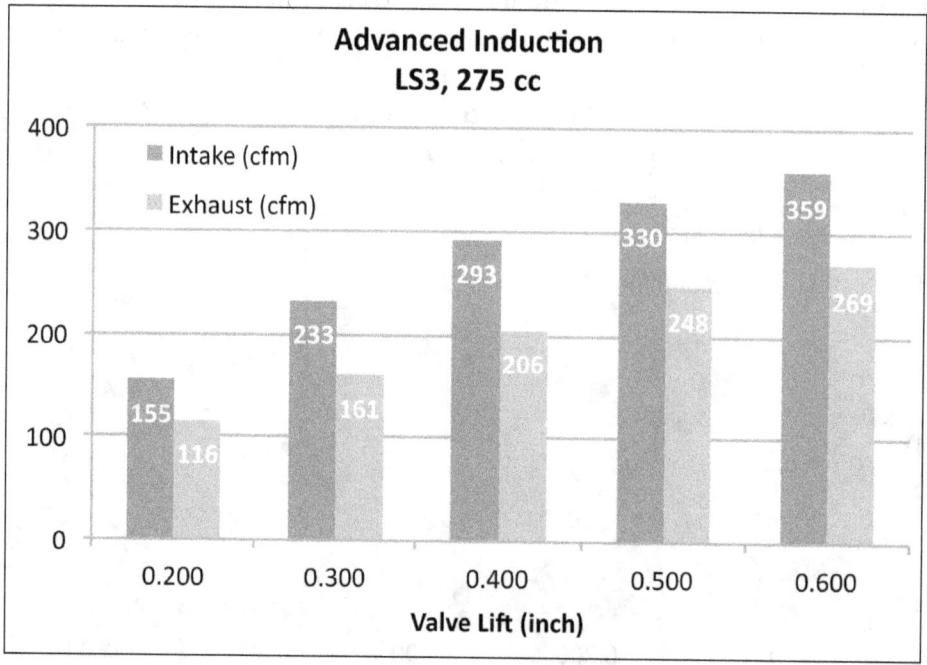

Valves: 2.165-inch intake, 1.59-inch exhaust
Combustion Chamber: 62-73 cc

Intake Runner: 275 cc
Intake (tested on a 4.065-inch bore):

Lift (inch)	.200	.300	.400	.500	.600
Flow (cfm)	155	233	293	330	359

Exhaust Runner: 90+ cc
Exhaust (tested with no exhaust pipe):

Lift (inch)	.200	.300	.400	.500	.600
Flow (cfm)	116	161	206	248	269

Recommended Use: 416 to 454 ci, forced induction or naturally aspirated
Additional Features: CNC-ported runners, CNC competition valve job, factory valves cleaned and precision ground, PCD-milled deck and flanges, several valvespring and retainer options

RECTANGULAR PORT CYLINDER HEADS

Advanced Induction
LS7, 280 cc

The 280-cc LS7 heads represent the baddest of the factory castings, but only scratch the surface of AI's capabilities. While subject to the same inconsistency of any factory head, a superior port design and finish make these a very attractive option for larger-cube builds whether road racing, daily driving, or drag racing. These heads have proven to be capable of 680 rwhp in a naturally aspirated, hydraulic roller, street engine. At .700-inch lift the raised intake runners peak at a staggering 391.7 cfm. As you'd expect from a factory casting, no extra requirements are needed for installation, just a 4.125-inch-or-larger bore. Machining and labor cost $1,195, additional charges apply for bronze valveguides, Manley exhaust valves, AI custom DLC-coated titanium intake valves, and various valvespring options.

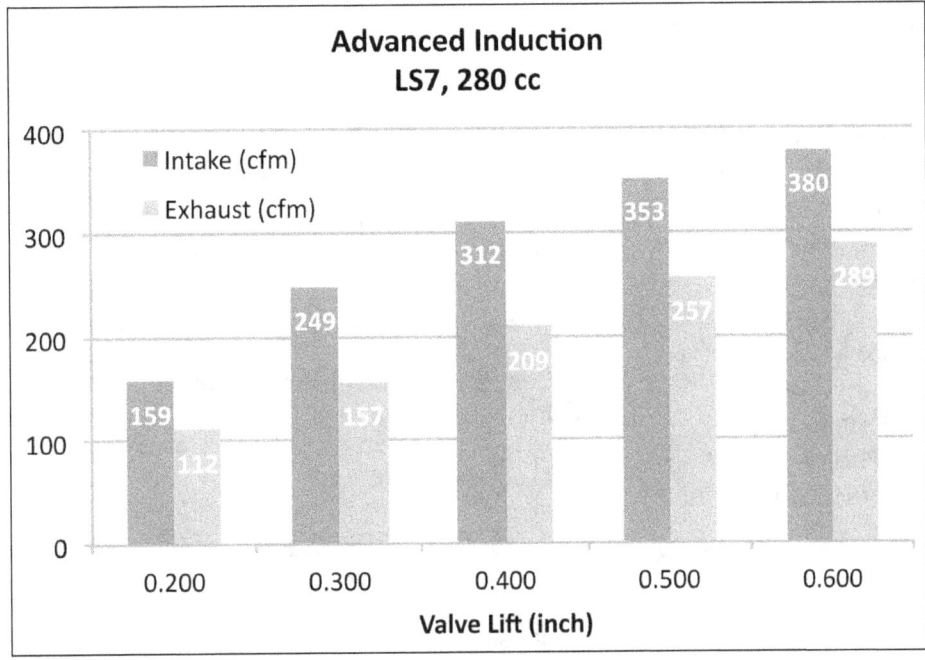

Valves: 2.20-inch intake, 1.61-inch exhaust
Combustion Chamber: 62 to 73 cc

Intake Runner: 280 cc
Intake (tested on a 4.125-inch bore):

Lift (inch)	.200	.300	.400	.500	.600
Flow (cfm)	159	249	312	353	380

Exhaust Runner: 90+ cc
Exhaust (tested with no exhaust pipe):

Lift (inch)	.200	.300	.400	.500	.600
Flow (cfm)	112	157	209	257	289

Recommended Use: 427 to 502 ci, forced induction or naturally aspirated
Additional Features: CNC-ported runners, CNC competition valve job, factory valves cleaned and precision ground, PCD-milled deck and flanges, several valvespring and retainer options

CHAPTER 3

All Pro/West Coast Cylinder Heads
LS7

Designed as a direct replacement for the factory LS7 head, the All Pro head uses stock rocker arms and intake manifold. However, with the West Coast's two programs, neither is recommended. The smaller 267-cc intake flows 395 cfm at .650-inch lift; meanwhile, the larger 277-cc version exceeds 400 cfm at higher lift numbers. Both require a 4.125-inch-or-larger bore, and the 277-cc is intended for 440-plus-ci. Plenty of clearance for 7/16-inch-diameter pushrods is provided. As you'd expect from an aftermarket casting with this much potential, prices start at $3,300 (bare). Stainless-steel valves are a mere $288, and valvesprings for a hydraulic roller are $515. Titanium and inconel valves, solid-roller valvesprings, and Jesel shaft-mount rockers are available. (Photos Courtesy West Coast Cylinder Heads)

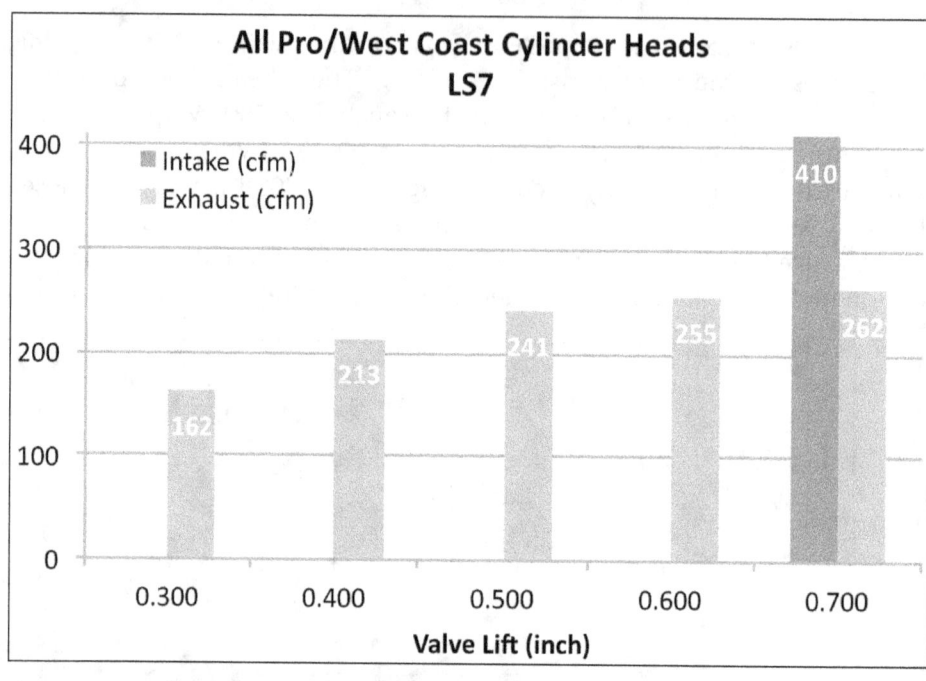

Valves: 2.205-inch intake, 1.60-inch exhaust
Combustion Chamber: 70 cc

Intake Runner: 267 cc
Intake:
Lift (inch)	.300	.400	.500	.600	.700
Flow (cfm)	N/A	N/A	N/A	N/A	410

Exhaust Runner: 108 cc
Exhaust:
Lift (inch)	.300	.400	.500	.600	.700
Flow (cfm)	162	213	241	255	262

Recommended Use: 427 to 502 ci, forced induction or naturally aspirated
Additional Features: ARP rocker arm bolts and stands provided, hollow-stem stainless-steel or titanium intake valves, stainless-steel or Inconel exhaust valves, several valvespring options

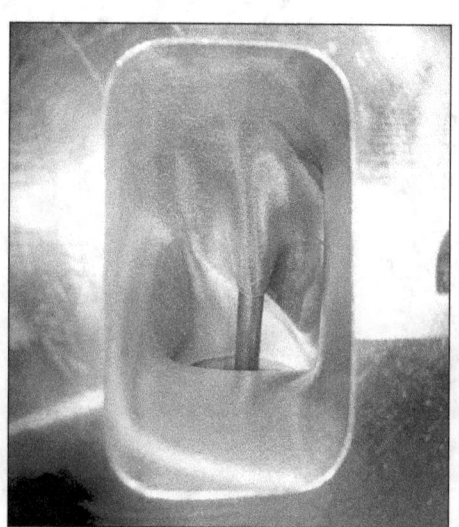
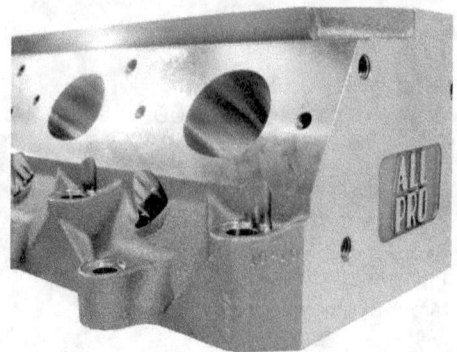
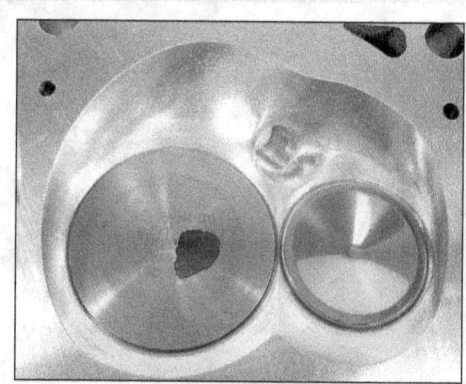

Arao Engineering
LS7 Stage II, 32-Valve

The Arao (pronounced "arrow") LS7 heads boast some of the best exhaust numbers in the business making them ideal for forced induction. The revolutionary 32-valve head uses a unique rocker system that uses pushrods to activate four valves per cylinder and make better use of the chamber. These heads are perhaps the most exotic and least tested; however, the potential is obvious when you consider how much power 32-valve Ferrari V-8 engines make per cubic inch. Arao says the dual intake valves are equivalent to a 3.3-inch intake valve, and the exhaust valves equal a single 2.8-inch valve in terms of curtain flow area. The chamber is a fast-burn, low-detonation design that requires less spark advance at peak power levels. These heads are compatible with standard LS pistons and camshafts, though Arao says less lift is needed due to the high flow "under the curve." A cathedral port version is also near production. These revolutionary heads command a hefty price, commensurate with the tremendous R&D required. Prices start at $7,499, and the heads come fully assembled with valve covers and rocker system (required for installation). Custom pistons are recommended for high-compression engines that need valve reliefs for adequate piston-to-valve clearance. (Photos Courtesy Arao Engineering)

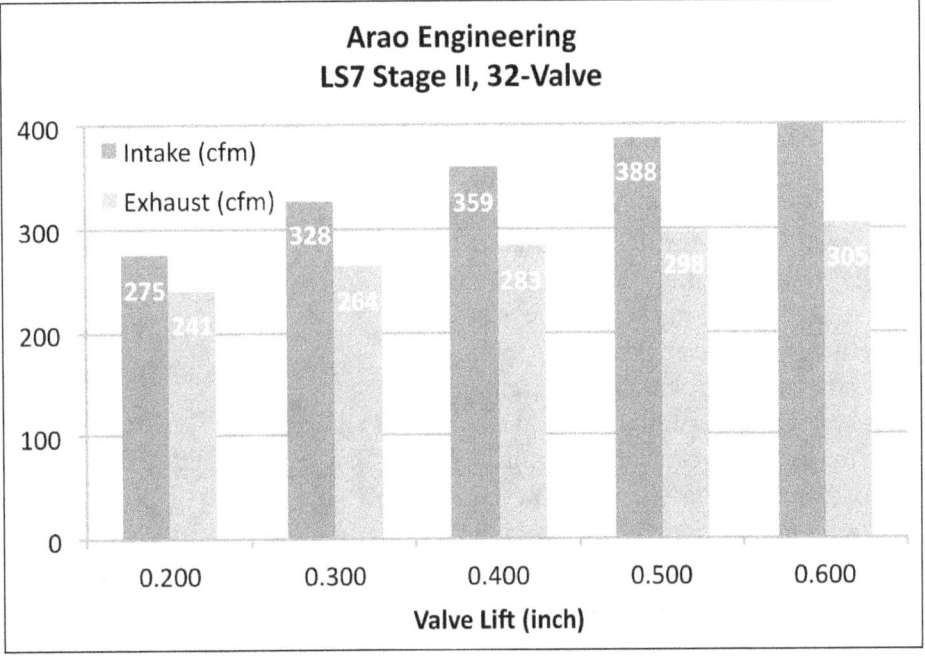

Valves: dual 1.72-inch intake, 1.4-inch exhaust
Combustion Chamber: 54-61 cc

Intake Runner: N/A cc
Intake:

Lift (inch)	.300	.400	.500	.600	.700
Flow (cfm)	275	328	359	388	405

Exhaust Runner: N/A cc
Exhaust:

Lift (inch)	.300	.400	.500	.600	.700
Flow (cfm)	241	264	283	298	305

Recommended Use: 427 to 502 ci, forced induction
Additional Features: LSX 6 bolts per cylinder; .600-inch conical valvesprings (available .700-inch dual springs), rockers, pushrods, and valve covers included

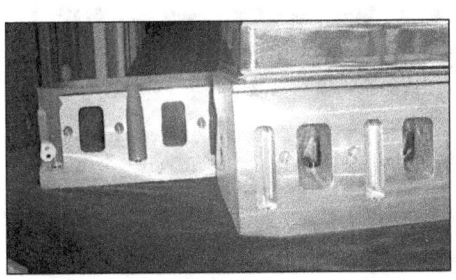
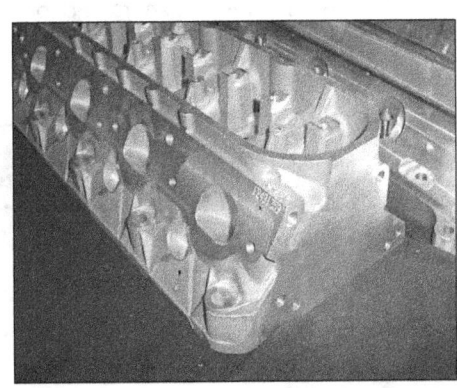

Brodix STS BR 7 273

Brodix is no stranger to building high-quality cylinder heads (dating back to the 1970s), but the company is a newcomer to the LS market. These LS7-style heads make up its first offering, boasting excellent flow numbers for the runner size thanks to the straight runners with excellent line of sight. The largest CNC version uses huge valves to achieve more than 416 cfm at .700-inch lift. A smaller (264 cc) CNC version is also available for lower-lift cam, street applications that flow 376 cfm at .650-inch lift, and an un-ported version that hits 364 cfm. All heads are made of A-356 virgin alloy, use the standard 12-degree valve angle, and are compatible with LS7 components such as intake manifolds, rocker arms, and exhaust manifolds (or headers).

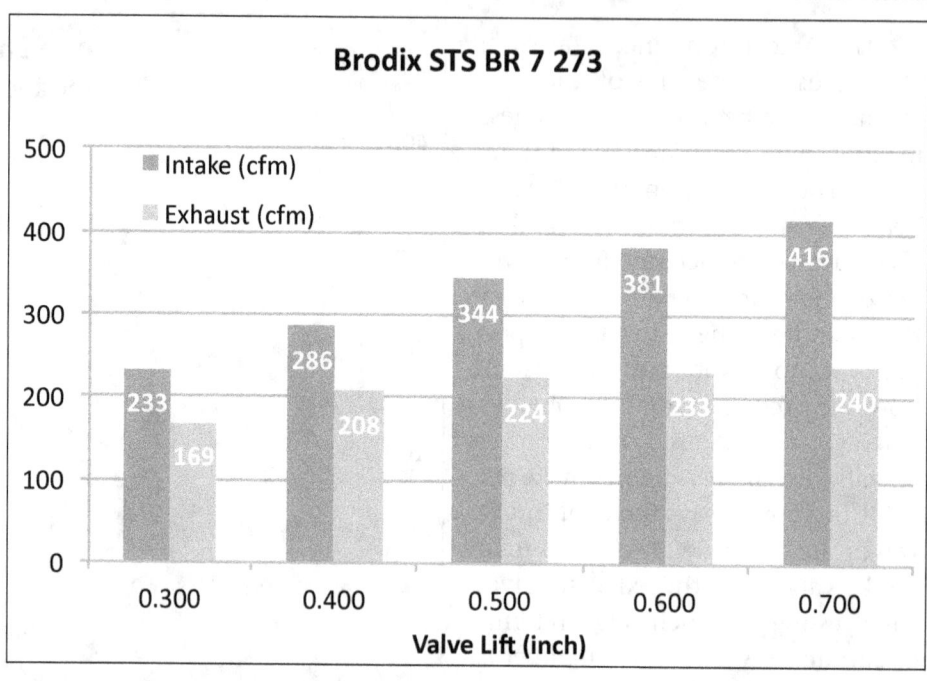

Valves: 2.250 intake, 1.614-inch exhaust
Combustion Chamber Size: 71 cc

Intake Runner: 273 cc
Intake:

Inch Lift	.300	.400	.500	.600	.700
CFM	233	286	344	381	416

Exhaust Runner: 85 cc
Exhaust:

Inch Lift	.300	.400	.500	.600	.675
CFM	169	208	224	233	240

Recommended Use: 427 to 502 ci, forced induction or naturally aspirated
Additional Features: 50-degree intake and 45-degree exhaust valve job, 12-degree valve angle; available with 1.295-inch OD springs (.600-inch max lift), 7-degree steel retainers and locks, bowl blended, matched intake ports (to gasket), and competition valve job

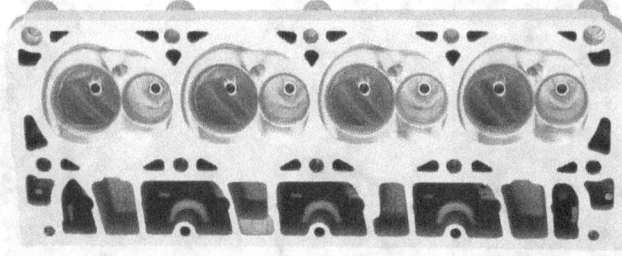
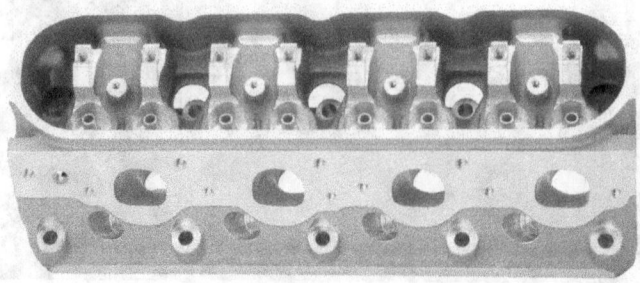

RECTANGULAR PORT CYLINDER HEADS

Includes:

LS3, CNC

LS9, CNC

LS7, CNC

Lingenfelter Performance Engineering

John Lingenfelter was not only a racing legend, but he spent more than 30 years reinventing cars and trucks for world-class performance. Today that tradition is carried on by current owner Ken Lingenfelter and a talented crew of builders and engineers. Extensive research and development has been poured into the LS market, as LPE's sole concern outside of servicing its past small-block LT5 and LT1 customers. LPE has programs for stock and aftermarket castings as well as custom porting and a variety of other services (such as engine building) and products for the street, drag race, road race, and top-speed crowd. (Photos Courtesy Lingenfelter Performance Engineering)

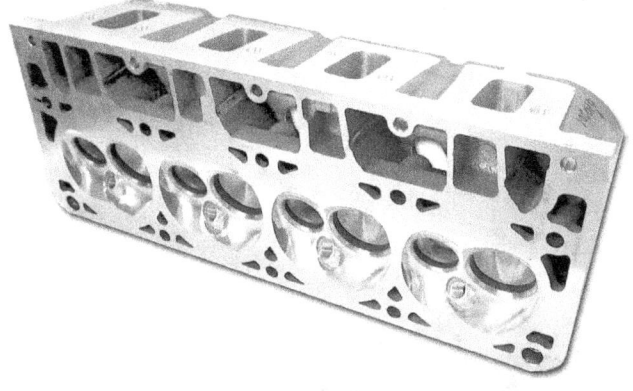

CNC LS3

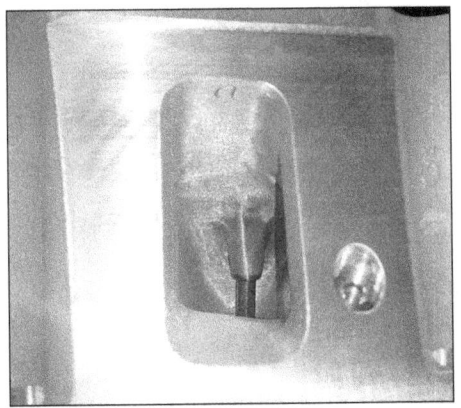
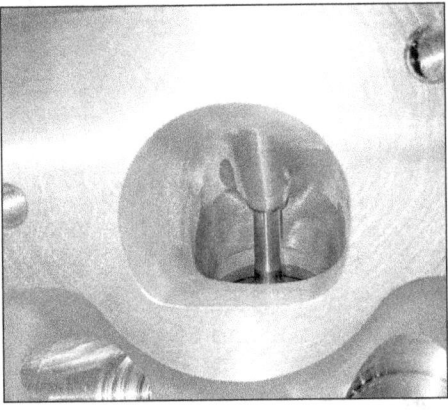
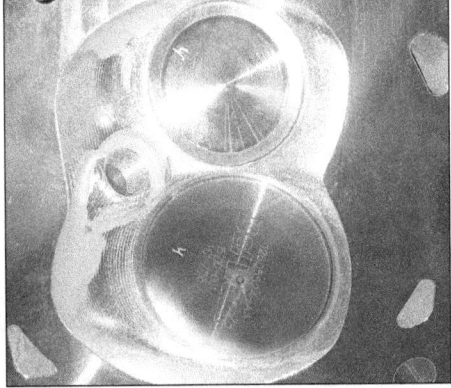

CNC LS9

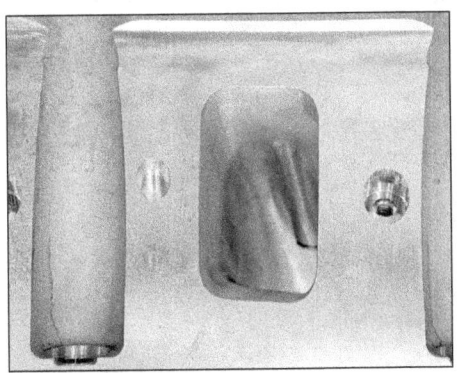
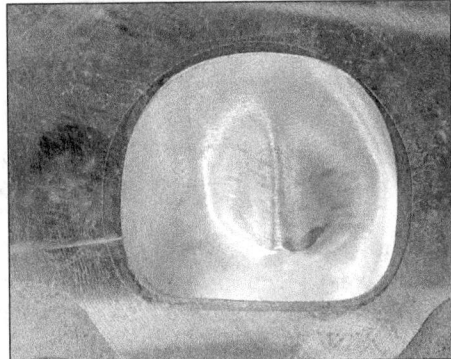
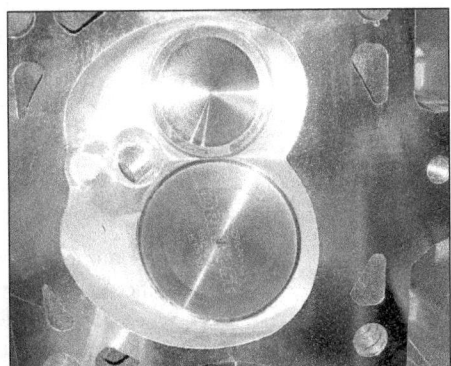

CNC LS7

HIGH-PERFORMANCE GM LS-SERIES CYLINDER HEAD GUIDE

Lingenfelter Performance Engineering LS3, CNC

Lingenfelter Performance Engineering (LPE) is one of the oldest and most prestigious names in the LS industry. Countless hours have been spent developing the program for LS3 heads, which is carried out on an in-house 5-axis CNC machine. These heads are clearly built with its supercharged and turbocharged customers in mind, using Inconel exhaust valves to handle the added heat while also keeping valvetrain weight to a minimum. These were engineered with more street-based engines in mind as flow tapers off after .650-inch lift where it hits 352 cfm. These heads are available for 10:1 or 11:1 compression (with stock bottom-end LS3s). As with all L92 heads, a 4-inch or larger bore is required. Fully assembled with Comp Cams 918 springs and titanium retainers these heads cost only $1,098.

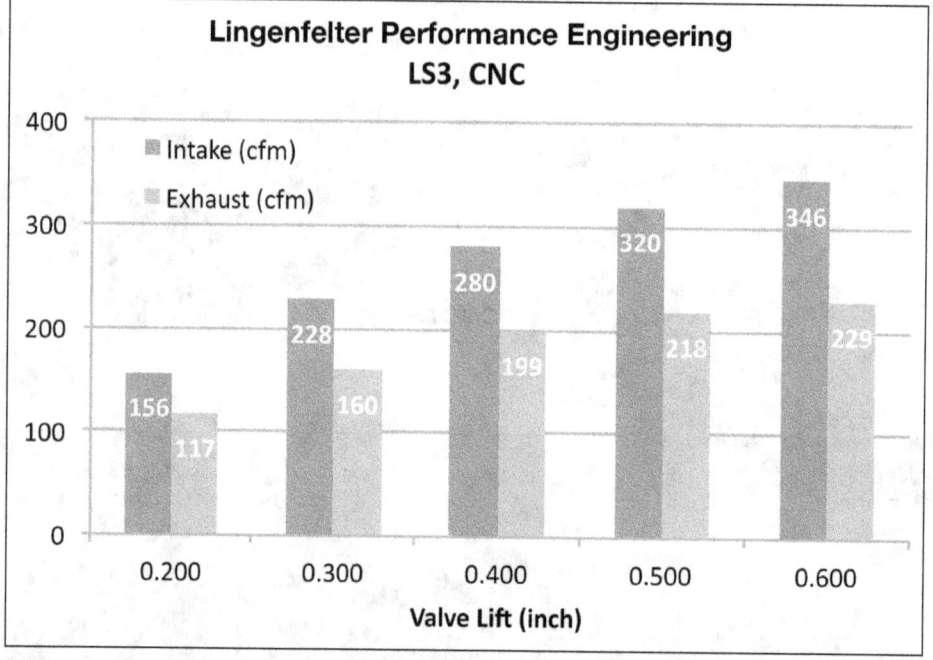

Valves: 2.165-inch intake, 1.59-inch exhaust
Combustion Chamber: 62 and 68 cc

Intake Runner: 275 cc
Intake (tested on a 4.065-inch bore):
   Lift (inch) .200 .300 .400 .500 .600
   Flow (cfm) 156 228 280 320 346

Exhaust Runner: 93 cc
Exhaust (tested with no exhaust pipe):
   Lift (inch) .200 .300 .400 .500 .600
   Flow (cfm) 117 160 199 218 229

Recommended Use: 364 to 427 ci, forced induction
Additional Features: hollow-stem intake valves, Inconel exhaust valves, 3-angle valve job, resurfaced deck, Comp Cams 918 valvesprings, titanium retainers, and 10-degree locks

RECTANGULAR PORT CYLINDER HEADS

Lingenfelter Performance Engineering
LS9, CNC

LPE's LS9 heads are very affordable, yet high-flowing with a lightweight valvetrain. It is a combination that would suit naturally aspirated or forced-induction applications; however, the stronger alloy, thicker deck surface, and better clamping capabilities make them best suited for boost or juice. Like all LPE heads, these were created by sectioning a stock head to measure wall thickness and then countless hours of hand porting were spent before recreating on the 5-axis in-house CNC machine. LPE's LS9 program is virtually identical to that of the LS3, L92, and LSA, as it does away with the "wings" as they impede flow and are believed to cause ignition timing restrictions (that would otherwise cost you power). These heads require a 4-inch- or-larger bore and ARP head studs, but are machined to except an LS3 or L92 intake manifold. LPE's LS9 heads cost $1,489 fully assembled with factory titanium intake valves and sodium-filled exhaust valves, Comp Cams 918 springs, and titanium retainers and locks.

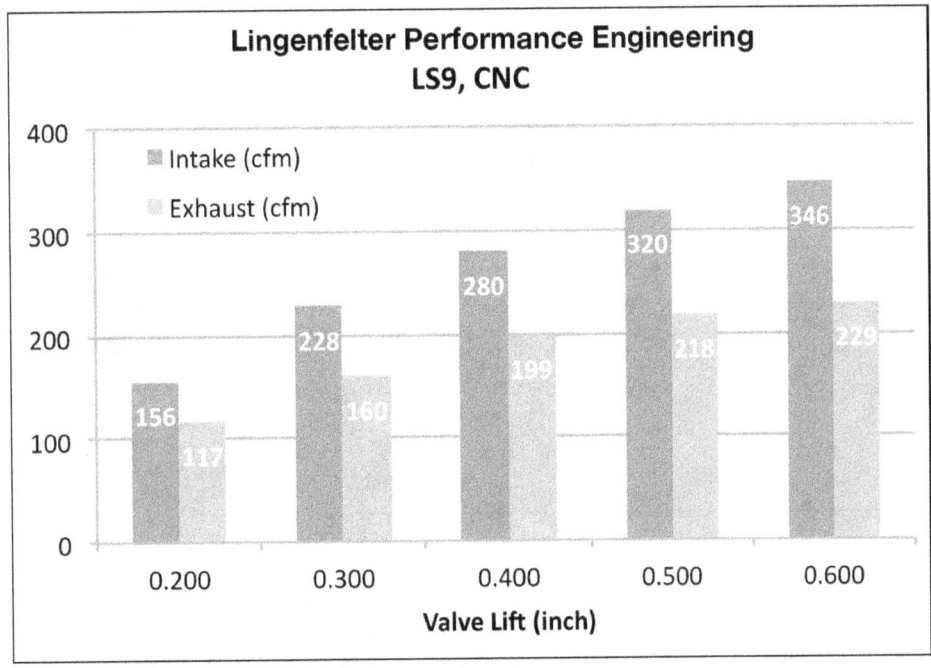

Valves: 2.165-inch intake, 1.59-inch exhaust
Combustion Chamber: 68 cc

Intake Runner: 275 cc
Intake (tested on a 4.065-inch bore):
   Lift (inch) .200   .300   .400   .500   .600
   Flow (cfm) 156   228   280   320   346

Exhaust Runner: 93 cc
Exhaust (tested with no exhaust pipe):
   Lift (inch) .200   .300   .400   .500   .600
   Flow (cfm) 117   160   199   218   229

Recommended Use: 364 to 427 ci, forced induction
Additional Features: titanium intake valves, sodium-filled exhaust valves, 3-angle valve job, resurfaced deck, Comp Cams 918 valvesprings, GM LS9/LS7 retainers

Lingenfelter Performance Engineering LS7, CNC

Despite the heads coming from the factory with a clean CNC porting, there is plenty of room for improvement, as LPE proves with its LS7 program. These heads hit a whopping 395 cfm before falling off at .700-inch lift. LPE uses these heads in its 630- and 660-hp C6 Z06 packages, where maintaining velocity, torque, and street manners is very important. The same program is also offered on Chevrolet Performance's six-bolt version of the LS7 head for those utilizing the extra clamping of an aftermarket block. With a supplied core, prices start at $1,095 depending on valvespring options; the LSX casting starts at $3,595 (no core required).

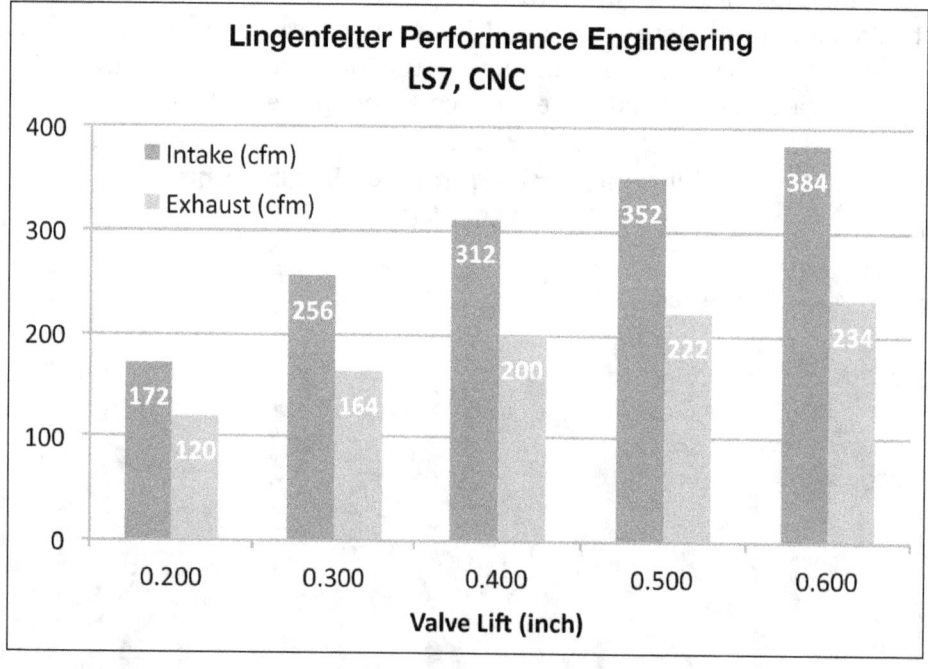

Valves: 2.205-inch intake, 1.615-inch exhaust
Combustion Chamber: 66-74 cc

Intake Runner: 270 cc
Intake (tested on a 4.125-inch bore):
Lift (inch)	.200	.300	.400	.500	.600
Flow (cfm)	172	256	312	352	384

Exhaust Runner: 90 cc
Exhaust (tested with no exhaust pipe):
Lift (inch)	.200	.300	.400	.500	.600
Flow (cfm)	120	164	200	222	234

Recommended Use: 427 to 502 ci, forced induction or naturally aspirated
Additional Features: titanium intake valves, sodium-filled exhaust valves, 3-angle valve job, resurfaced deck, stock valvesprings and retainers with upgrades available, Chevrolet Performance LSX-LS7 6-bolt casting also available

RECTANGULAR PORT CYLINDER HEADS

Includes:

L92 Stage 3, CNC

LS7, CNC

Livernois Motorsports

Livernois was the first to produce aluminum radiators for automotive use as well as the tooling and machines to produce them. Livernois offers CNC programs for OEM and aftermarket castings. In the LS community, Livernois is widely known for its fifth-generation Camaro products and services, and has managed to produce the very first 2012 Camaro ZL1 to run a 9-second quarter-mile—using a Livernois cam and CNC-ported heads. (Photos Courtesy Livernois Motorsports)

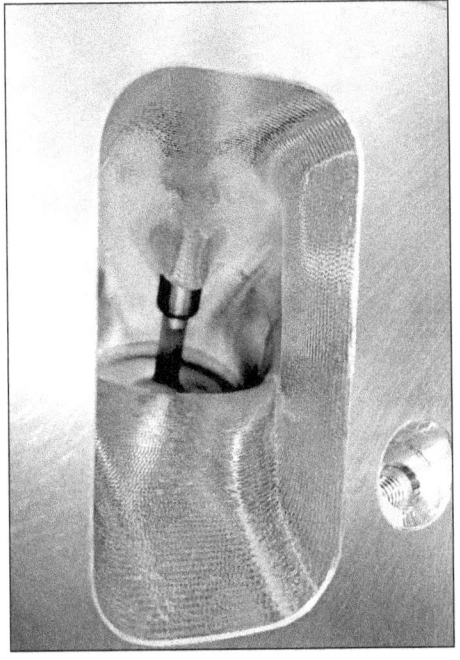
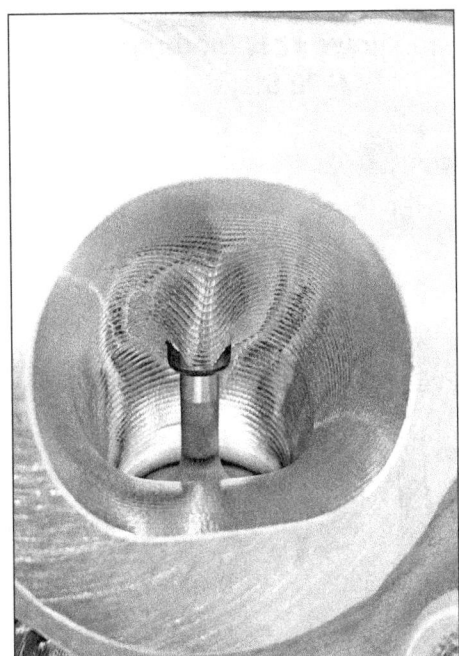
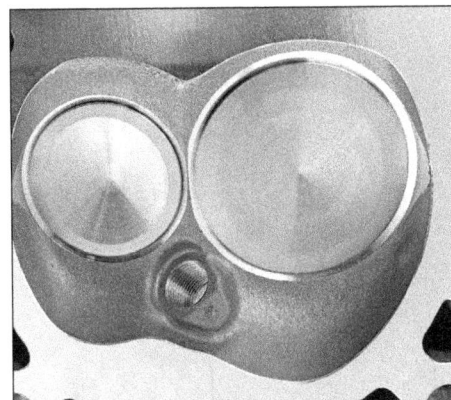

CNC Stage 3 L92

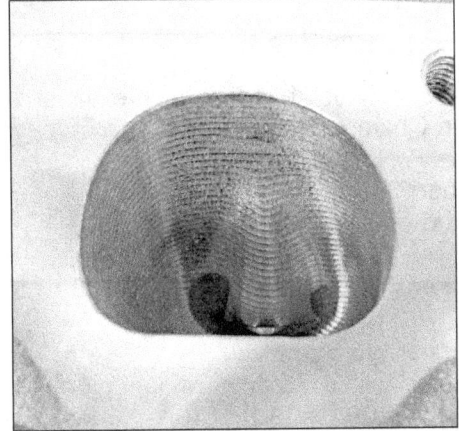

CNC LS7

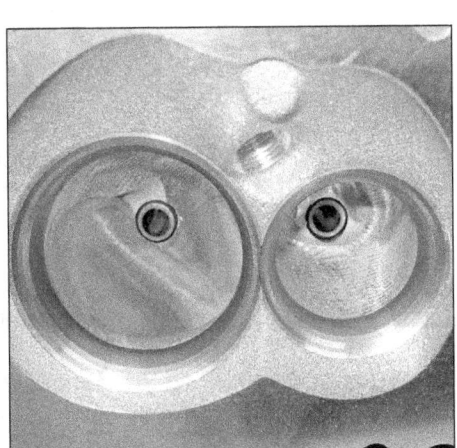

HIGH-PERFORMANCE GM LS-SERIES CYLINDER HEAD GUIDE

Livernois Motorsports
L92 Stage 3, CNC

This Michigan-based engine builder and tuner churns out plenty of potent LS3 Corvettes and 2010 Camaros, so it's no surprise it has several cylinder head packages. Livernois' Stage 3 uses Manley stainless-steel valves with the boost addict in mind, and its own proprietary dual-coil valvesprings and titanium retainers. A Stage 2 package is also available using stock GM valves, using the same carefully shaped port design that is crafted on a 5-axis CNC machine. Flow numbers hit 359.9 cfm at .800-inch lift. No core is required with the $2,099 price tag. As with all L92/LS3 heads, the minimum bore needed is 4.00 inches.

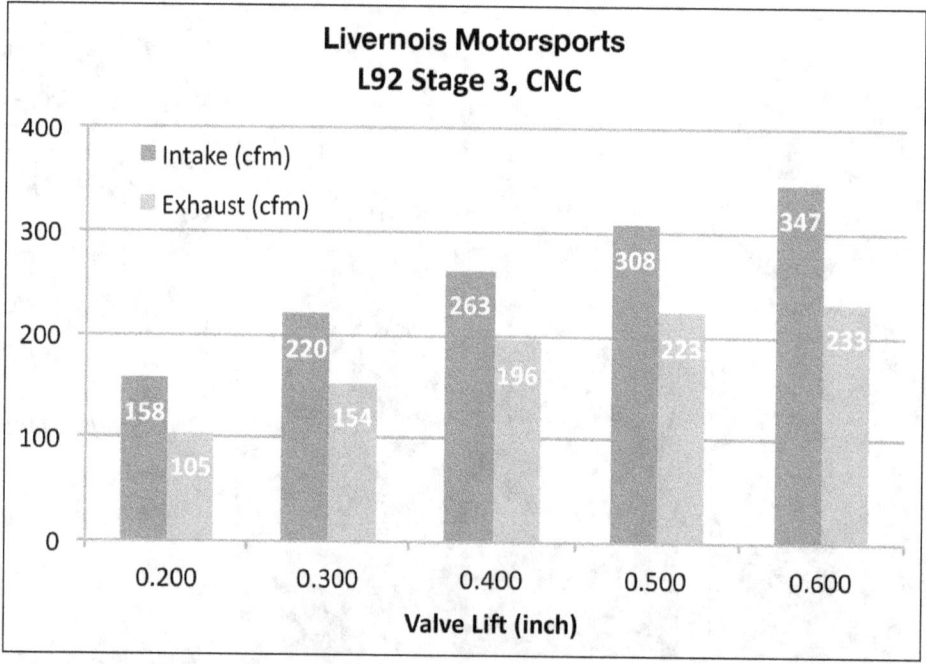

Valves: 2.160-inch intake, 1.590-inch exhaust
Combustion Chamber: 68 cc

Intake Runner: 280 cc
Intake (tested on a 4.06-inch bore):
Lift (inch)	.200	.300	.400	.500	.600
Flow (cfm)	158	220	263	308	347

Exhaust Runner: 95 cc
Exhaust (tested with 1.75-inch exhaust pipe):
Lift (inch)	.200	.300	.400	.500	.600
Flow (cfm)	105	154	196	223	233

Recommended Use: 364 to 427 ci, forced induction or naturally aspirated
Additional Features: Manley stainless-steel valves, Super 7 locks, Livernois dual valvesprings for up to .690-inch lift, titanium retainers

Livernois Motorsports
LS7, CNC

Livernois' program for the OEM LS7 casting or GMPP LSX-LS7 (6-bolt) casting boasts equally impressive flow numbers. Suitable for large-bore street cars; up to 388.5 cfm can support plenty of horsepower whether naturally aspirated or forced induction. Using a Livernois cam and LS7 bottom end, these heads typically make more than 615 rwhp with supporting components (air intake, headers, exhaust, etc.) on a Corvette Z06. Naturally, a 4.125-inch bore is required. With a customer-supplied core, the parts and labor cost $1,430. The 6-bolt, LSX-LS7 Stage 2 heads cost $3,800 (fully assembled). A Stage 3 version is also available, which adds $400 to the price.

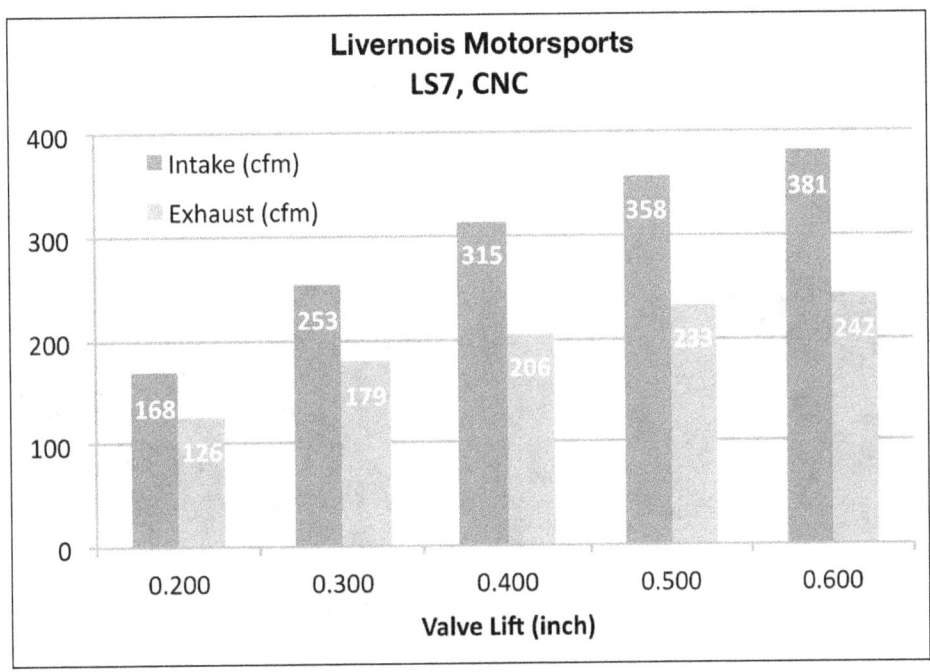

Valves: 2.200-inch intake, 1.610-inch exhaust
Combustion Chamber: 70 cc

Intake Runner: 270 cc
Intake:

Lift (inch)	.200	.300	.400	.500	.600
Flow (cfm)	168	253	315	358	381

Exhaust Runner: 94 cc
Exhaust:

Lift (inch)	.200	.300	.400	.500	.600
Flow (cfm)	126	179	206	233	242

Recommended Use: 427 to 502 ci, forced induction or naturally aspirated
Additional Features: ground stock valves, Super 7 locks, Livernois dual valvesprings for up to .690-inch lift, titanium retainers

CHAPTER 3

Mast Motorsports

The fast-growing Mast Motorsports was founded on the principles of engineering, developing high-quality LS components, and thorough assembly of LS crate engines—embracing new and cutting-edge technology. Mast is constantly developing new products for the LS market that push the design envelope for the highest performance.

> **Includes:**
>
> LS3, 11-Degree Small Bore
>
> LS3, 11-Degree Medium Bore
>
> LS3, 11-Degree Large Bore
>
> LS7, 12-Degree, 305 cc

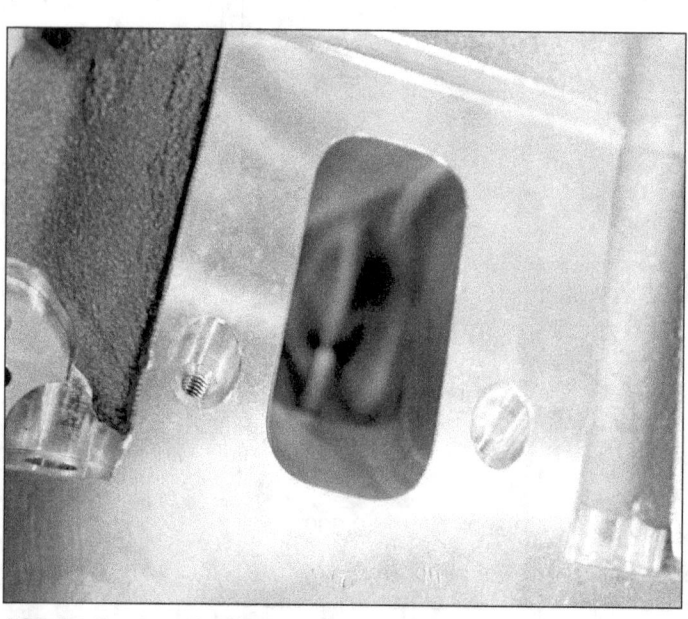

LS3 11-Degree Small Bore

LS3 11-Degree Medium Bore

LS3 11-Degree Large Bore

LS7 305-cc 12-Degree

Mast Motorsports
LS3, 11-Degree Small-Bore

Mast brought the first small-bore rectangular port heads to market a few years ago, and since then there still has not been a higher flowing head for a 3.90-inch bore (up to 353 cfm). An 11-degree valve angle enables the straight runners as well as plenty of piston-to-valve clearance with big cams. The large CNC-ported runners make these heads best suited for high RPM or forced induction. The clean-sheet casting design uses a .750-inch-thick deck, and is compatible with all LS3/L92 valvetrain components (including stock rocker arms) and intake manifolds. These heads retail for $1,300 each, fully assembled.

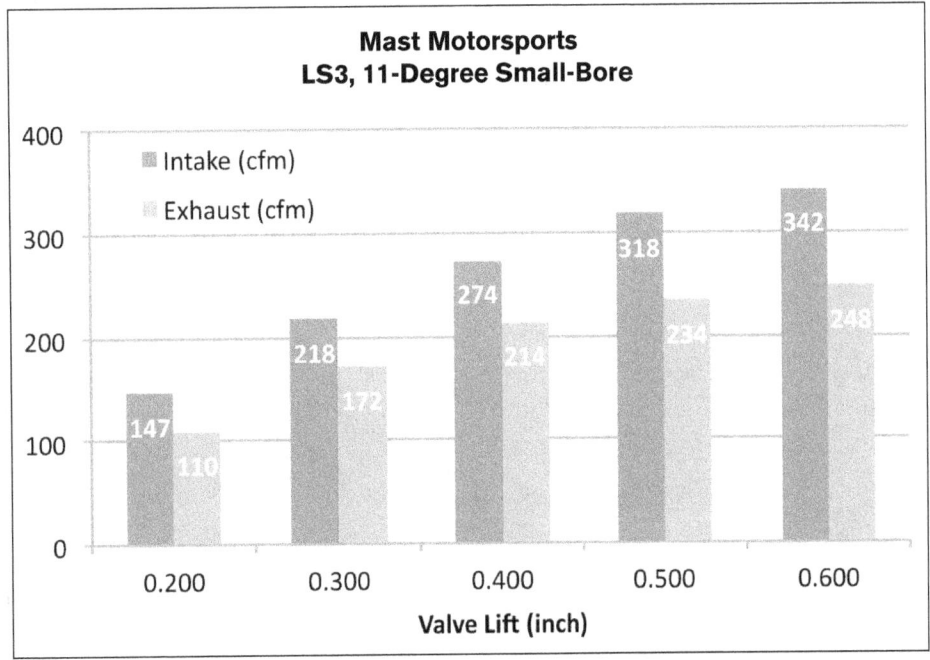

Valves: 2.040-inch intake, 1.57-inch exhaust
Combustion Chamber: 62 cc

Intake Runner: 260 cc
Intake (tested on a 3.90-inch bore):
    Lift (inch) .200 .300 .400 .500 .600
    Flow (cfm) 147 218 274 318 342

Exhaust Runner: 102 cc
Exhaust (tested with no exhaust pipe):
    Lift (inch) .200 .300 .400 .500 .600
    Flow (cfm) 110 172 214 234 248

Recommended Use: 346 to 396 ci, forced induction or naturally aspirated
Additional Features: Mast stainless-steel valves, steel retainers, machined locks, nitrided and microfinished .650-inch-lift valvesprings

Mast Motorsports
LS3, 11-Degree Medium-Bore

The added material, altered port shape, and valve angle of Mast's casting enable some incredible flow capabilities over the factory heads. Flow continues to rise to .700-inch lift, where it hits 372 cfm, making it a good match to a high-lift cam. Stroker and boosted engines can benefit the most from the added flow (cfm); however, the small (compared to stock) runners keep velocity high enough to make good power with stock cubic-inch, naturally aspirated combos with a 4.00- to 4.070-inch bore. If you are using aftermarket blocks you can go with the 6-bolt version to accommodate the extra head bolts. Like the small-bore head, retail price is $1,300 each.

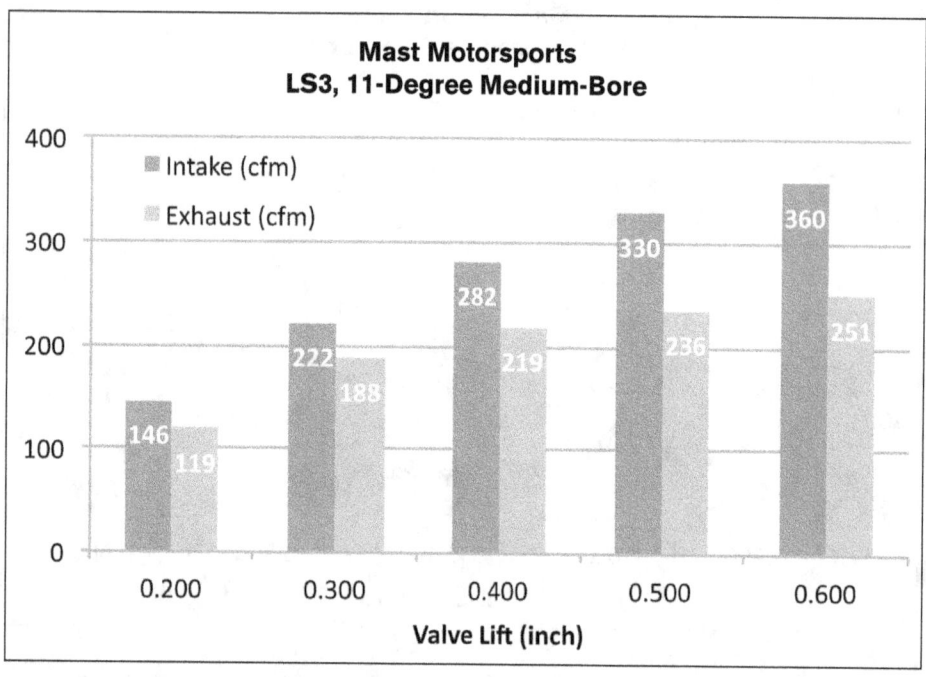

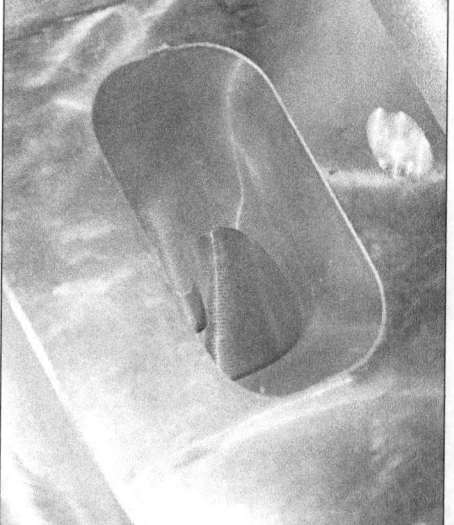

Valves: 2.165-inch intake, 1.60-inch exhaust
Combustion Chamber: 69 cc

Intake Runner: 265 cc
Intake (tested on a 4.00-inch bore):

Lift (inch)	.200	.300	.400	.500	.600
Flow (cfm)	146	222	282	330	360

Exhaust Runner: 102 cc
Exhaust (tested with no exhaust pipe):

Lift (inch)	.200	.300	.400	.500	.600
Flow (cfm)	119	188	219	236	251

Recommended Use: 364 to 427 ci, forced induction or naturally aspirated
Additional Features: Mast stainless-steel valves, steel retainers, machined locks, nitrided and microfinished .650-inch-lift valvesprings, available for 6-bolt aftermarket blocks

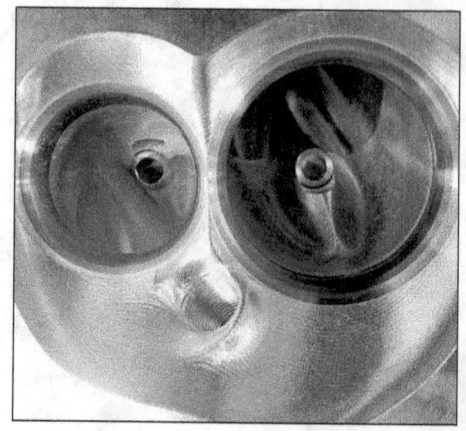

Mast Motorsports
LS3, 11-Degree Large-Bore

Though the runners are not much larger than the medium-bore version, the huge LS7-size valves make all the difference. The flow numbers rival any ported LS7 head as a result, yet it is still compatible with LS3 valvetrain components and intake manifolds. Flow numbers hit an amazing 390 cfm at .700-inch lift, unheard of for an LS3-style port. Six-head-bolt provisions come standard to match aftermarket blocks and provide extra clamping force. Like the other rectangular port heads from Mast, these also boast an 11-degree valve angle and .750-inch deck from their clean-sheet casting design. A 4.125-inch bore is required, as are LS7-style rocker arms (OEM or aftermarket). Retail price is $1,600 each.

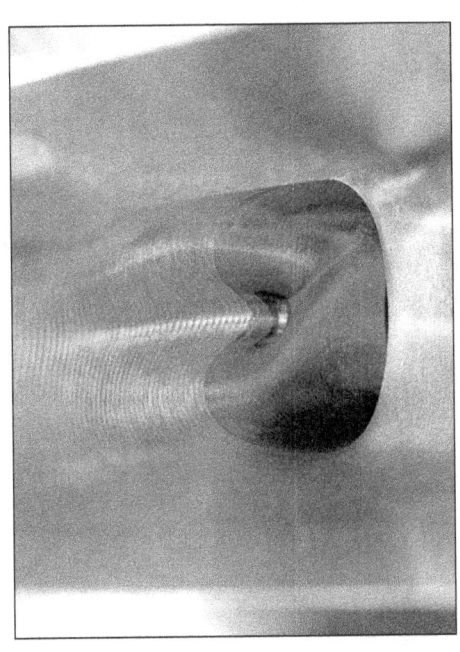

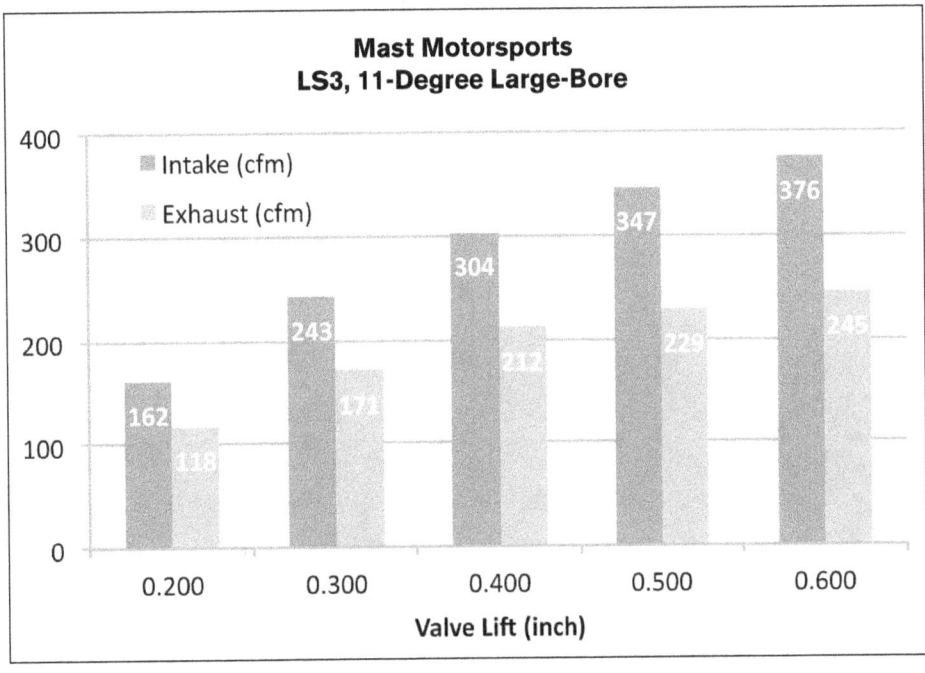

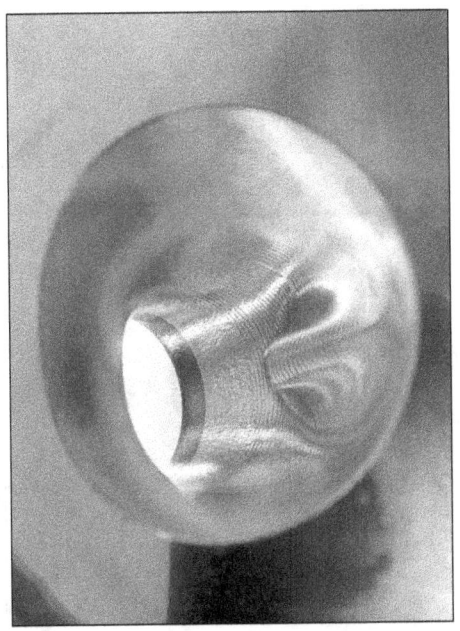

Valves: 2.20-inch intake, 1.60-inch exhaust
Combustion Chamber: 69 cc

Intake Runner: 270 cc
Intake (tested on a 4.125-inch bore):

Lift (inch)	.200	.300	.400	.500	.600
Flow (cfm)	162	243	304	347	376

Exhaust Runner: 102 cc
Exhaust (tested with no exhaust pipe):

Lift (inch)	.200	.300	.400	.500	.600
Flow (cfm)	118	171	212	229	245

Recommended Use: 388 to 502 ci, forced induction or naturally aspirated
Additional Features: Mast stainless-steel valves, steel retainers, machined locks, nitrided and microfinished .650-inch-lift valvesprings, 6-head-bolt provisions for aftermarket blocks

CHAPTER 3

Mast Motorsports
LS7, 12-Degree, 305 cc

Mast also has its own twist on the LS7 head, starting with a higher-flowing version of the original with a more conservative 274-cc intake runner. However, the big bad boy 305-cc is the one racers and 454- to 502-ci stroker builders gravitate toward. This head continues to flow as the flow bench hits 1.00-inch of valve lift and 410 cfm. The large runners are not for the faint of heart, small cams, or average street cars. Six-head-bolt provisions are standard. These heads are compatible with LS7 rockers and other components, and a 4.125-inch (or larger) bore is required. Each head costs $1,600.

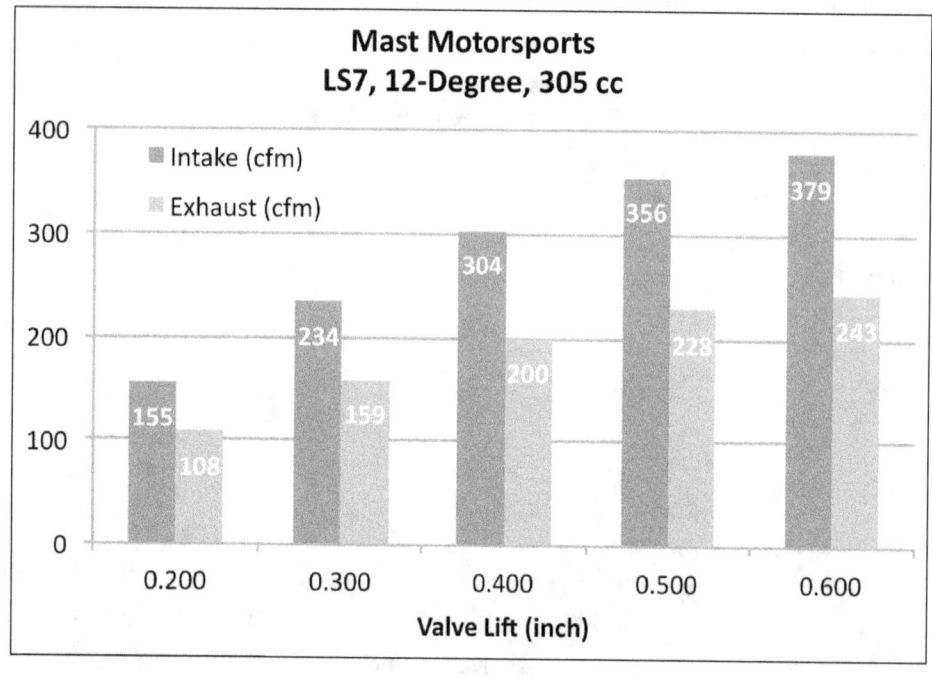

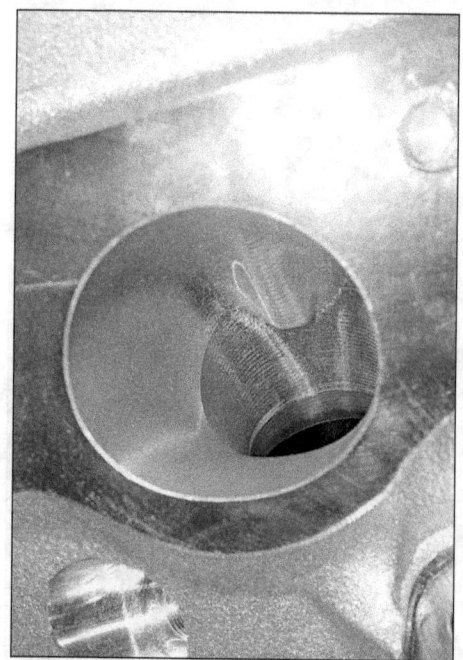

Valves: 2.250-inch intake, 1.60-inch exhaust
Combustion Chamber: 69 cc

Intake Runner: 305 cc
Intake (tested on a 4.125-inch bore):

Lift (inch)	.200	.300	.400	.500	.600
Flow (cfm)	155	234	304	356	379

Exhaust Runner: 102 cc
Exhaust (tested with no exhaust pipe):

Lift (inch)	.200	.300	.400	.500	.600
Flow (cfm)	108	159	200	228	243

Recommended Use: 427 to 502 ci, forced induction or naturally aspirated
Additional Features: Mast stainless-steel valves, steel retainers, machined locks, nitrided and microfinished .650-inch-lift valvesprings, 6-head-bolt provisions for aftermarket blocks

RECTANGULAR PORT CYLINDER HEADS

Procomp Electronics LS3

Another clean-sheet casting comes from Procomp, which uses high-grade aluminum and superior quality control to outdo the factory casting. The advanced port design easily surpasses some of the finest CNC factory heads, and also utilizes a proprietary multi-angle seat design. This head comes fully CNC-machined either bare or fully assembled with stainless valves and dual valvesprings. A 4.00-inch-or-larger bore is needed with stock-size valves; however, upgrades are available for large-bore applications. Retail price is $645 each for a bare head. (Photos Courtesy Procomp Electronics)

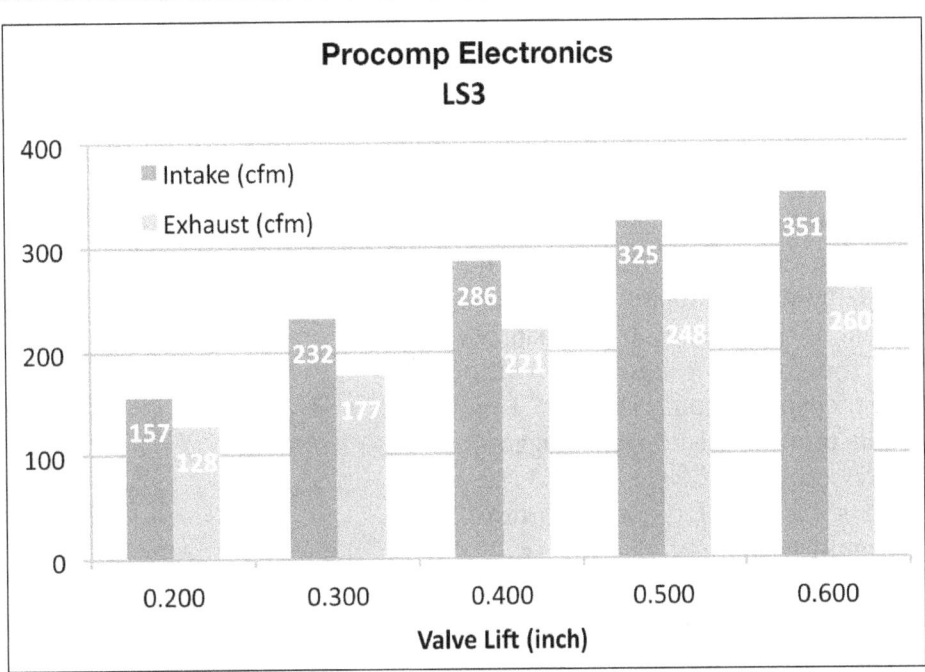

Valves: 2.165-inch intake, 1.59-inch exhaust
Combustion Chamber: 68 cc

Intake Runner: 274 cc
Intake:

Lift (inch)	.200	.300	.400	.500	.600
Flow (cfm)	157	232	286	325	351

Exhaust Runner: 84 cc
Exhaust:

Lift (inch)	.200	.300	.400	.500	.600
Flow (cfm)	128	177	221	248	260

Recommended Use: 364 to 427 ci, forced induction or naturally aspirated
Additional Features: hardened seats, bronze valveguides, dual valvesprings

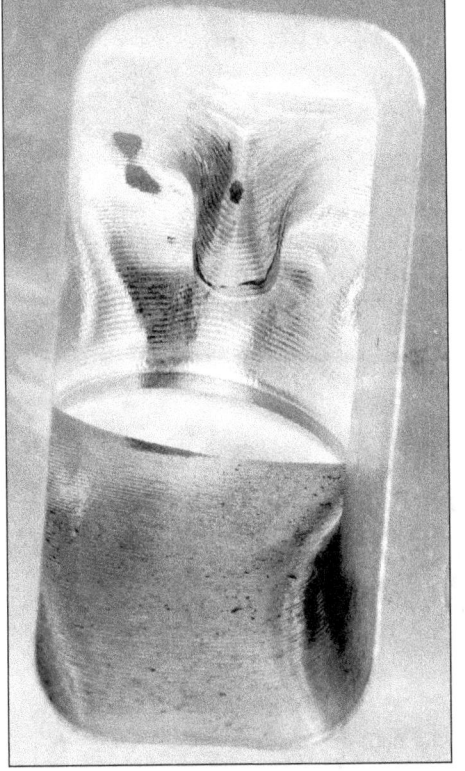
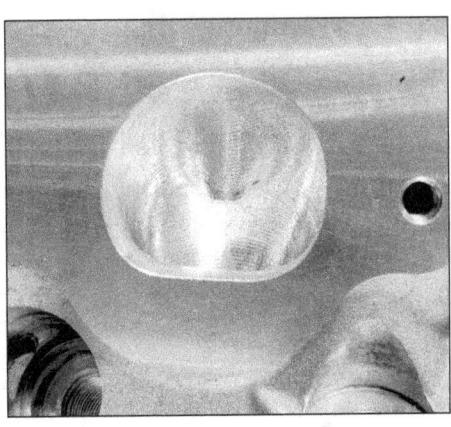
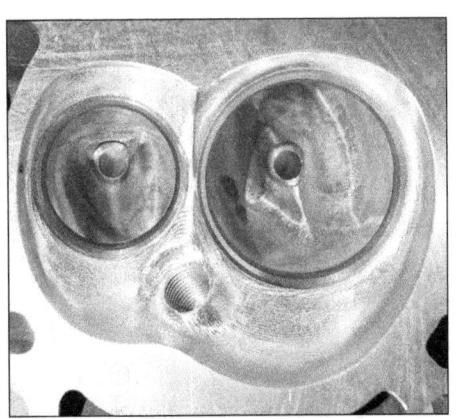

CHAPTER 3

Scoggin-Dickey Parts Center
LS3, CNC

Scoggin-Dickey Parts Center, the largest GM Performance Parts dealer, has a program of its own for LS3 heads that is definitely worth a look. The price is what makes these heads so attractive. Throw in some great flow numbers, and naturally aspirated builds can support plenty of power. As with any LS3/L92 head, a 4-inch-or-larger bore is required (with no other special considerations). For a pair of assembled heads, Scoggin-Dickey offers the CNC LS3s for $750 (that is not a typo). (Photos Courtesy Scoggin-Dickey)

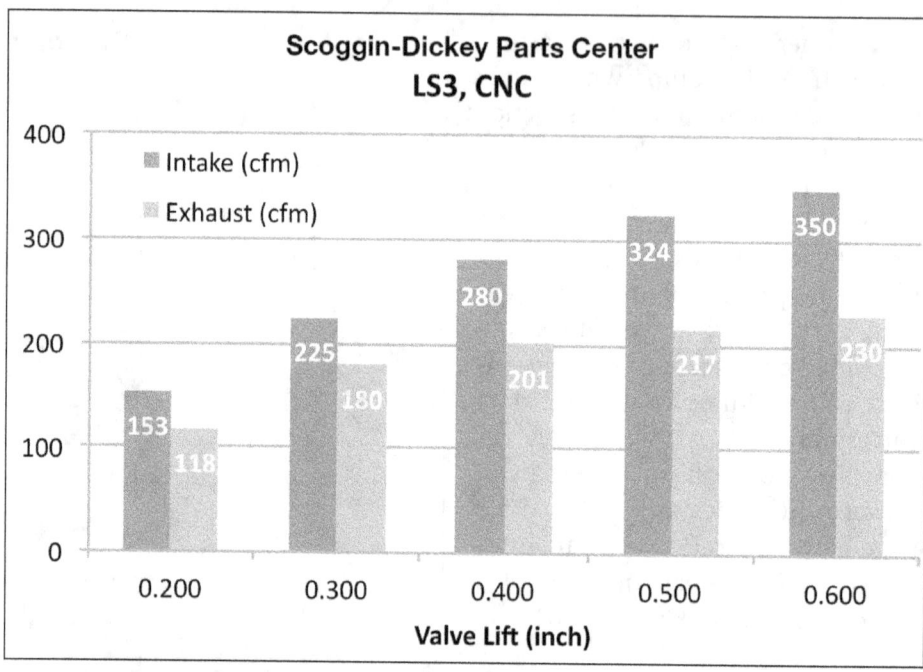

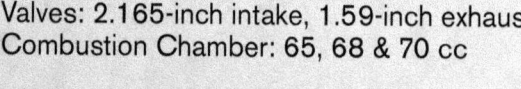

Valves: 2.165-inch intake, 1.59-inch exhaust
Combustion Chamber: 65, 68 & 70 cc

Intake Runner: 279 cc
Intake:

Lift (inch)	.200	.300	.400	.500	.600
Flow (cfm)	153	225	280	324	350

Exhaust Runner: 99 cc
Exhaust:

Lift (inch)	.200	.300	.400	.500	.600
Flow (cfm)	118	180	201	217	230

Recommended Use: 364 to 427 ci, forced induction or naturally aspirated
Additional Features: factory hollow-stem valves, titanium retainers, 7-degree locks, .600-inch lift valvesprings

RECTANGULAR PORT CYLINDER HEADS

Texas Speed/Precision Race Components

Includes:

LS3/L92, CNC

LS3, 250 cc

LS7, CNC

LS7, 285 cc

PRC offers its own aftermarket casting. The company is known for extensive flow and dyno testing of all its heads as well as affordability. PRC is hard to beat in terms of quality and performance per dollar. PRC cylinder heads have several long-standing records in the LS drag race community. (Photos Courtesy Texas Speed)

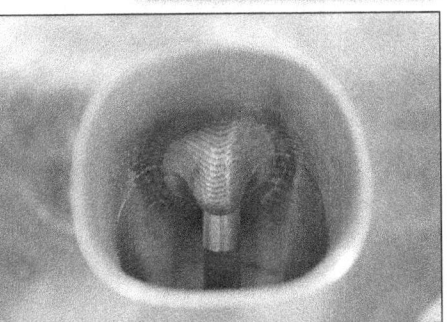

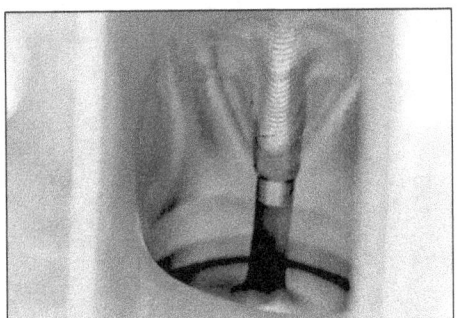

CNC LS3/L92 and 250-cc LS3

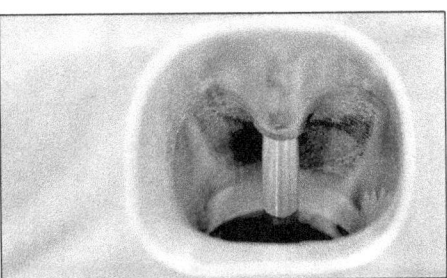

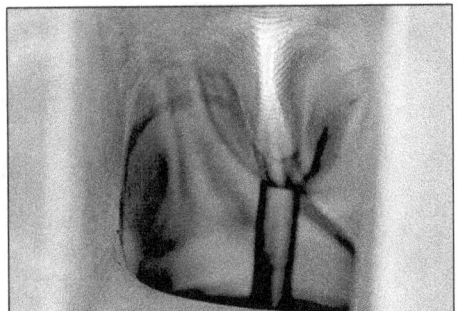

CNC LS7 and 285-cc LS7

HIGH-PERFORMANCE GM LS-SERIES CYLINDER HEAD GUIDE

Texas Speed/Precision Race Components
LS3/L92, CNC

PRC was one of the first to jump on the L92 bandwagon, developing a CNC program to take the GM casting to the next level at a very comfortable price. The flow numbers speak for themselves; however, it is worth noting how extensively these heads have been dyno-tested prior to their release. Many different options are available, from the GM L92 valves to the lighter hollow-stem LS3 valves and aftermarket stainless-steel variations on both. Two different valvespring options allow up to .675-inch-lift cams, and these heads can also be purchased without springs. A 4.00-inch bore is required. Prices start at $900 with a customer-supplied core, or $1,330 (outright).

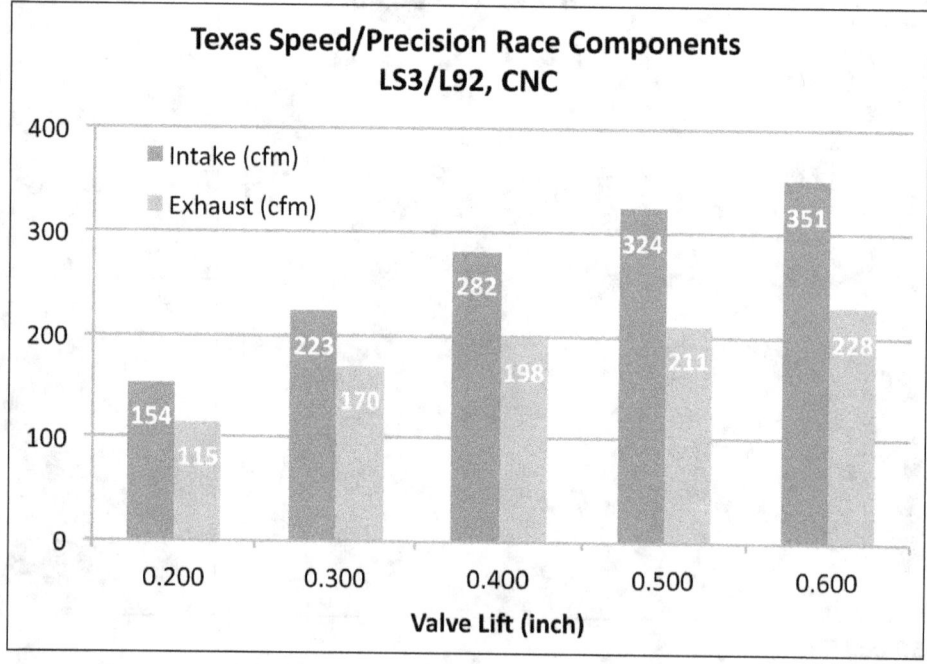

Valves: 2.165-inch intake, 1.59-inch exhaust
Combustion Chamber: 68 cc

Intake Runner: 270 cc
Intake:
Lift (inch)	.200	.300	.400	.500	.600
Flow (cfm)	154	223	282	324	351

Exhaust Runner: 92 cc
Exhaust:
Lift (inch)	.200	.300	.400	.500	.600
Flow (cfm)	115	170	198	211	228

Recommended Use: 364 to 427 ci, forced induction or naturally aspirated
Additional Features: GM valves, stainless steel (122 grams), GM hollow-stem (106 grams) or stainless-steel hollow-stem valves (91 grams) available, PRC .650-inch-lift double or .675-inch EHT valvesprings

RECTANGULAR PORT CYLINDER HEADS

Texas Speed/Precision Race Components
LS3, 250 cc

PRC's own casting of the LS3 head utilizes a 13-degree valve angle and revised runner shape to make a similar flowing intake runner with much less volume (and much more velocity). Meanwhile, the exhaust runner, which is very restrictive on the stock casting, is uncorked considerably. This head was designed with stock cubic-inch builds in mind; however, their flow capabilities also make them a good match for strokers. The rolled valve angle allows greater piston-to-valve clearance (.040 inch) for higher compression and larger camshafts. Available valvesprings handle either .675- or .700-inch lift, where this head peaks in flow (361 cfm). A 4.00-inch-or-larger bore is required. Retail price is $2,200 fully assembled.

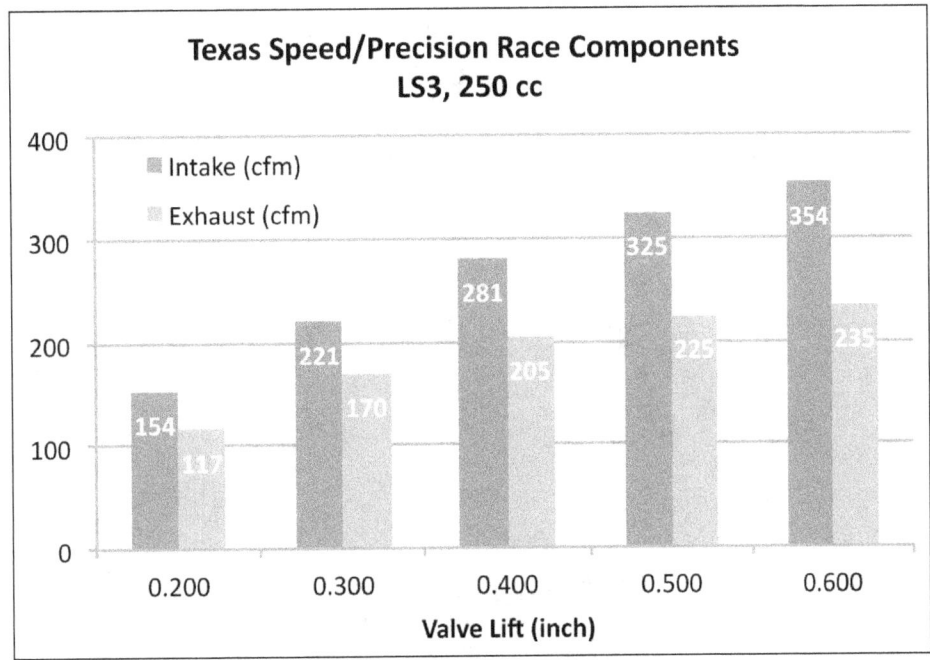

Valves: 2.165-inch intake, 1.59-inch exhaust
Combustion Chamber: 60 to 68 cc

Intake Runner: 250 cc
Intake:
   Lift (inch)   .200   .300   .400   .500   .600
   Flow (cfm) 154   221   281   325   354

Exhaust Runner: 90 cc
Exhaust:
   Lift (inch)   .200   .300   .400   .500   .600
   Flow (cfm) 117   170   205   225   235

Recommended Use: 364 to 427 ci, forced induction or naturally aspirated
Additional Features: Manley stainless-steel valves, PRC .675-inch EHT or .700-inch dual valvesprings

Texas Speed/Precision Race Components
LS7, CNC

PRC improves upon the factory CNC porting by up to 40 cfm, allowing the intake to reach 393 cfm at .700-inch lift while still keeping the intake runner at a fairly conservative 270 cc (perfect for street cars). The high-flowing exhaust runner also makes this head a good choice for boost or nitrous, especially if you check the box for six head bolts (and PRC's own casting), which is a cheap upgrade. Choose from three different valve options, starting with the basic stainless-steel to hollow-stem and titanium (like stock). Several different valvesprings are available as well, for up to .700-inch-lift cams. An LS7-size bore or larger is required. The stock castings cost $2,000 (with no valvesprings) and the 6-bolt version adds only $400.

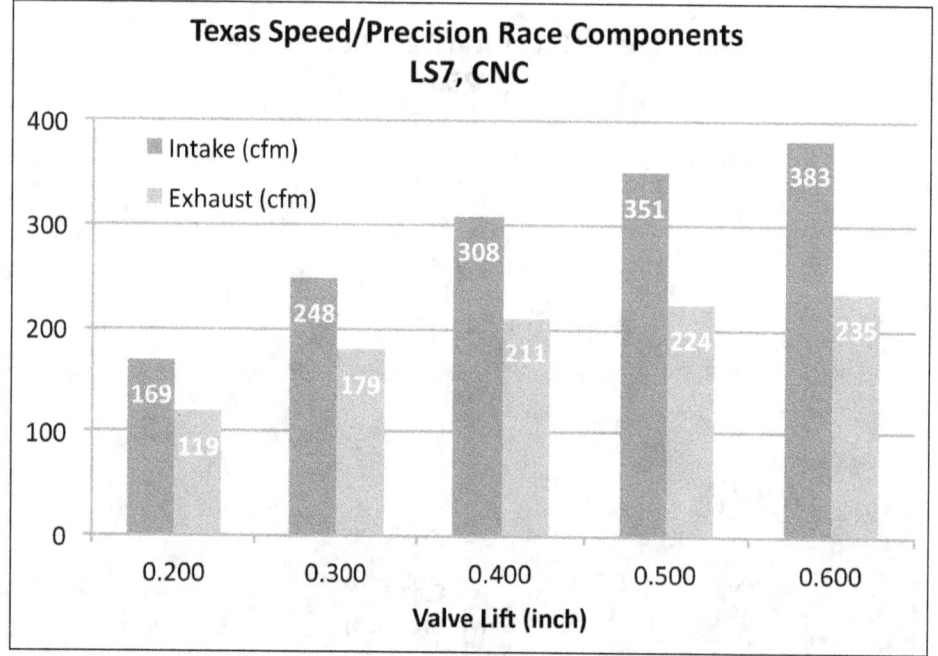

Valves: 2.20-inch intake, 1.61-inch exhaust
Combustion Chamber: 70 cc

Intake Runner: 270 cc
Intake:

Lift (inch)	.200	.300	.400	.500	.600
Flow (cfm)	169	248	308	351	383

Exhaust Runner: 87 cc
Exhaust:

Lift (inch)	.200	.300	.400	.500	.600
Flow (cfm)	119	179	211	224	235

Recommended Use: 388 to 440 ci, forced induction or naturally aspirated
Additional Features: stainless-steel, hollow-stem, or titanium valves available, PRC .650-inch-lift double, .675-inch EHT, or .700-inch dual valvesprings, 6-bolt aftermarket casting available

Texas Speed/Precision Race Components
LS7, 285 cc

PRC's highest-flowing head provides enough airflow for very extreme applications, hitting a magic 407 cfm at .700-inch lift. The aftermarket castings afford several advantages, such as the extra material to make a 285-cc intake runner, a thicker deck surface, and 6-bolt provisions for aftermarket blocks. The massive 2.250-inch intake valves are available in standard stainless steel; however, the sheer weight limits cams to just .616-inch lift. With this type of flow, a higher-lift cam and the lighter hollow-stem or titanium valves are recommended. A 4.125-inch-or-larger bore is required. The 285-cc LS7s start at a reasonable $2,400.

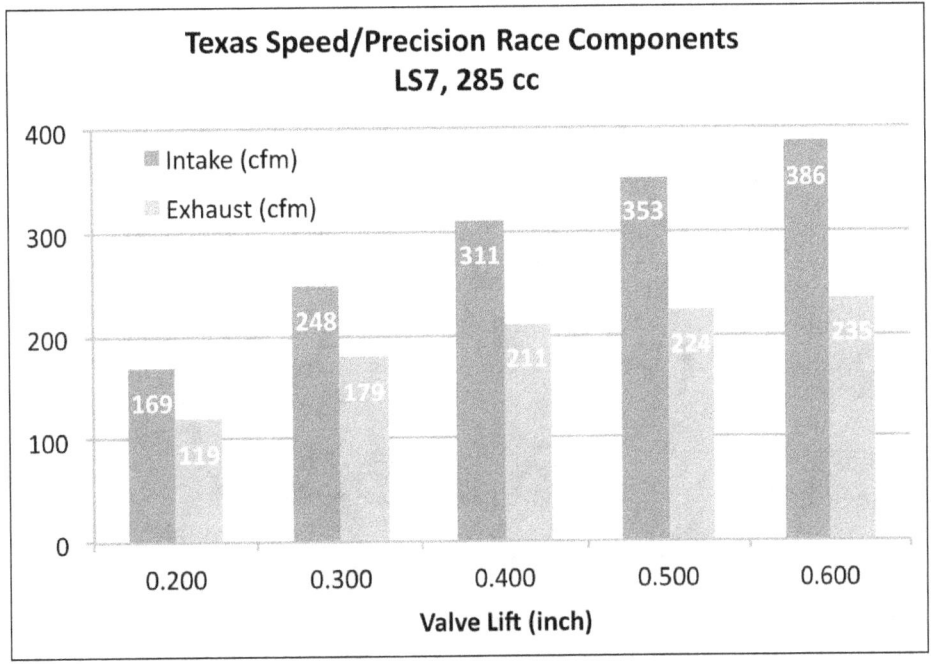

Valves: 2.250-inch intake, 1.61-inch exhaust
Combustion Chamber: 70 cc

Intake Runner: 285 cc
Intake:
Lift (inch)	.200	.300	.400	.500	.600
Flow (cfm)	169	248	311	353	386

Exhaust Runner: 87 cc
Exhaust:
Lift (inch)	.200	.300	.400	.500	.600
Flow (cfm)	119	179	211	224	235

Recommended Use: 427 to 502 ci, forced induction or naturally aspirated
Additional Features: stainless-steel, hollow-stem, or titanium valves available, PRC .650-inch-lift double, .675-inch EHT, or .700-inch valvesprings available

CHAPTER 3

VMAX Motorsports
LS3, CNC

VMAX has made its name porting top-end components such as throttle bodies, intake manifolds, and cylinder heads for the LS market. So it should come as no surprise that the company put together an impressive CNC program for the L92/LS3 head. Using either stock or REV valves, VMAX has a very cost-effective package with a good combination of flow and velocity. Each head is ported with a 5-axis CNC machine and then flow tested, resurfaced, and assembled in-house with the customer's choice of components. The heads can be flat-milled to .040 (maximum) inch, or angle-milled to the high 50s or low 60s. A 4-inch bore is required, with no other special requirements. These heads go for $1,950, plus an additional $240 charge for angle milling.

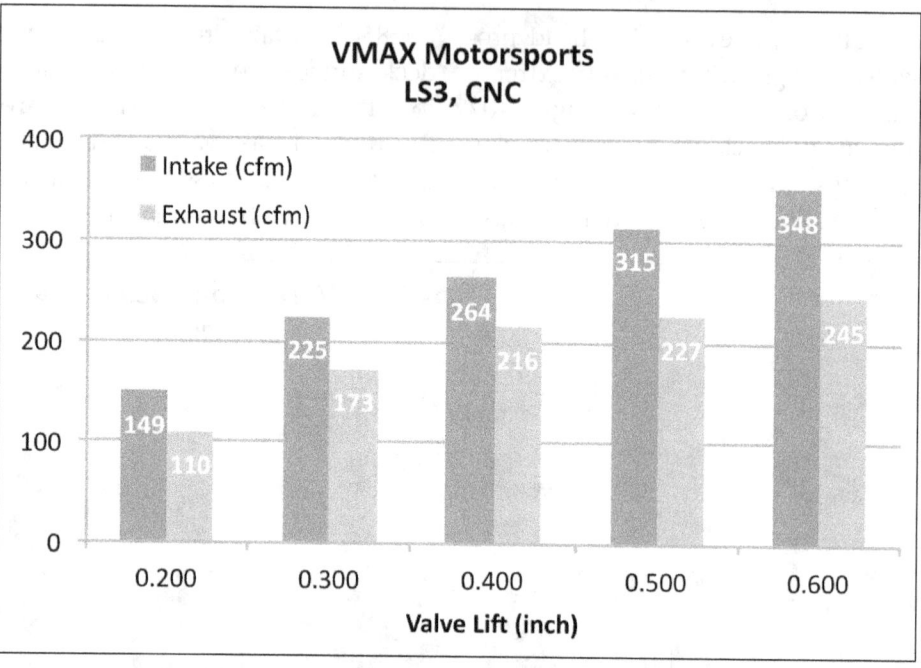

Valves: 2.160-inch intake, 1.60-inch exhaust
Combustion Chamber: 67 cc

Intake Runner: 279 cc
Intake:
Lift (inch)	.200	.300	.400	.500	.600
Flow (cfm)	149	225	264	315	348

Exhaust Runner: 95 cc
Exhaust:
Lift (inch)	.200	.300	.400	.500	.600
Flow (cfm)	110	173	216	227	245

Recommended Use: 408 to 427 ci, forced induction or naturally aspirated
Additional Features: Comp Cams 918 or Patriot dual valvesprings available, stock GM or titanium retainers, stock GM or REV valves

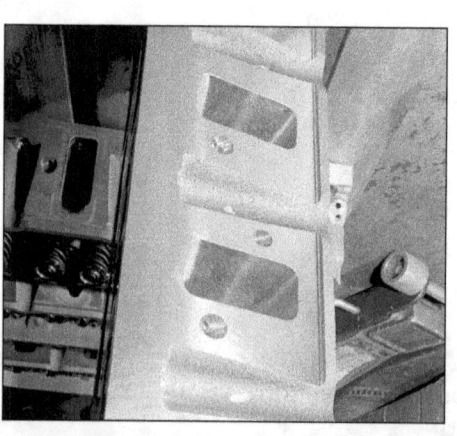

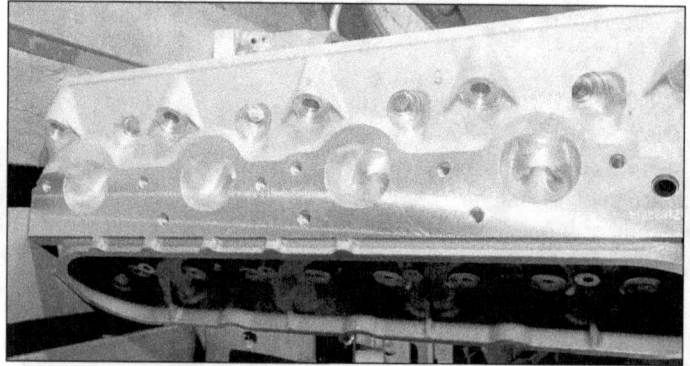

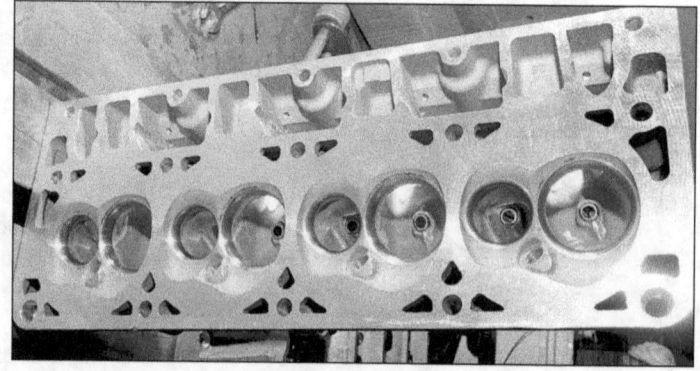

Wegner Motorsports LS3/L92, CNC

NASCAR fans may be familiar with Wegner, but for the uninitiated this Wisconsin-based builder started in the 1970s in a backyard shed building hot rods. As the demand for Wegner engines grew, so did the customer base and facilities to satisfy them. Eventually, the reputation grew, and Wegner engines found their way into every division of NASCAR. Wegner-spec LS engines can be seen in racing classes throughout the country, which led to several products including these CNC-ported heads. With this sort of background, durability is a concern, which is why Wegner ensures that there is plenty of material beneath the spring pockets where ported LS3 heads can break through using heavier valvesprings. The valveguides are honed for proper clearance, and the deck is resurfaced (chamber size varies as needed). Wegner also ports LSA and LS9 heads with very similar flow, which peaks at .700-inch lift with 360.5 cfm. All heads require a 4.00-inch bore or larger. Retail price is $1,650.

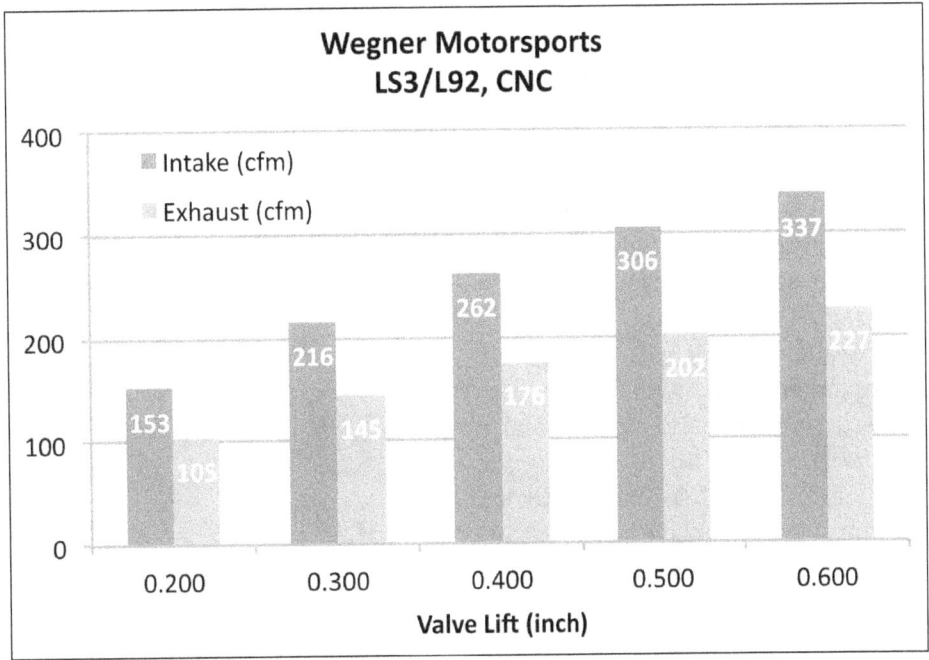

Valves: 2.165-inch intake, 1.59-inch exhaust
Combustion Chamber: 67 cc

Intake Runner: 279 cc
Intake:

Lift (inch)	.200	.300	.400	.500	.600
Flow (cfm)	153	216	262	306	337

Exhaust Runner: 96 cc
Exhaust:

Lift (inch)	.200	.300	.400	.500	.600
Flow (cfm)	105	145	176	202	227

Recommended Use: 364 to 427 ci, forced induction or naturally aspirated
Additional Features: several valvespring and valve options; stainless-steel and Inconel valves recommended for boost

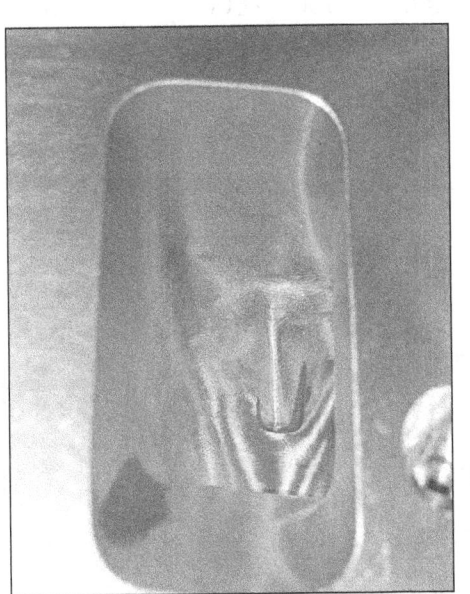

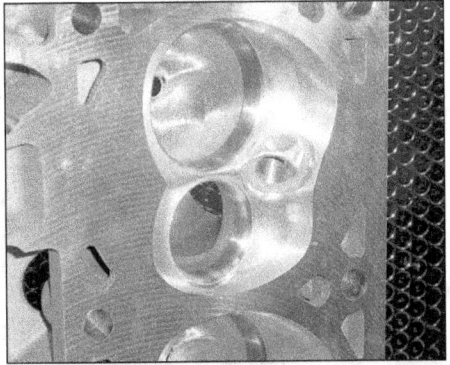

CHAPTER 3

West Coast Cylinder Heads
L92 Stage 2, CNC

WCCH designed this CNC program for the L92 casting for larger-cubic-inch combinations such as 408 and 427 strokers; however, these heads have also proven to be a good source of power on stock-cube, naturally aspirated LS3s. Higher-lift cams can take advantage of up to 363.6 cfm (at .700-inch lift). A Stage 3 is also available, which is designed for even larger-cube engines and uses 2.20-inch intake valves to flow 380.1 cfm at .700-inch lift. Base price for the Stage 2 is $2,045 with Patriot Gold valvesprings. Like any L92/LS3, there is a 4.00-inch bore minimum.

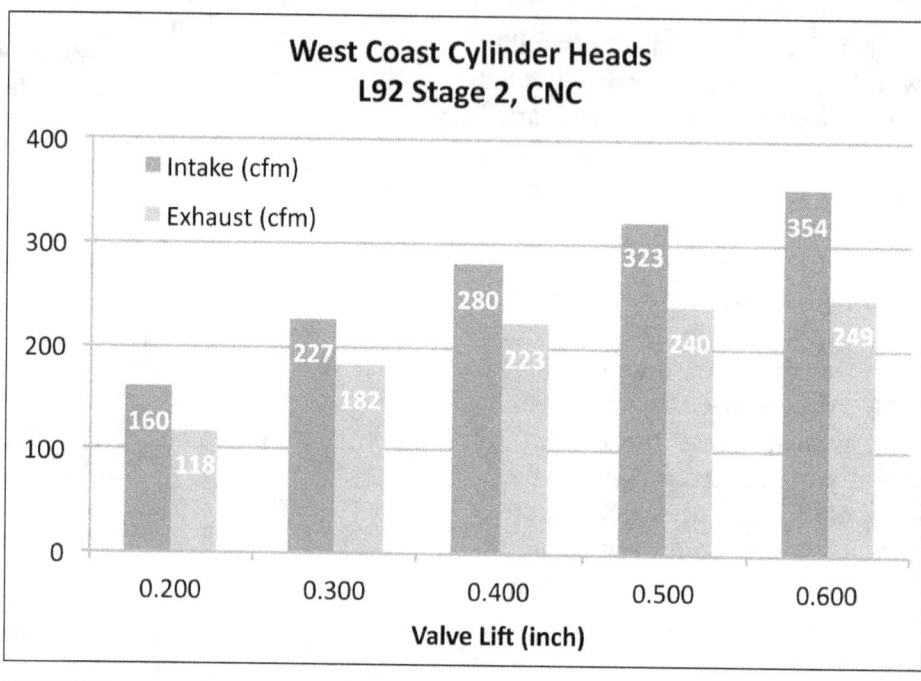

Valves: 2.160-inch intake, 1.60-inch exhaust
Combustion Chamber: 67 cc

Intake Runner: 268 cc
Intake (tested on a 4.155-inch bore):

Lift (inch)	.200	.300	.400	.500	.600
Flow (cfm)	160	227	280	323	354

Exhaust Runner: 99 cc
Exhaust:

Lift (inch)	.200	.300	.400	.500	.600
Flow (cfm)	118	182	223	240	249

Recommended Use: 364 to 427 ci, forced induction or naturally aspirated
Additional Features: Patriot Gold or Extreme valvesprings, REV lightweight stainless valves, titanium retainers, Super 7 locks, Viton seals

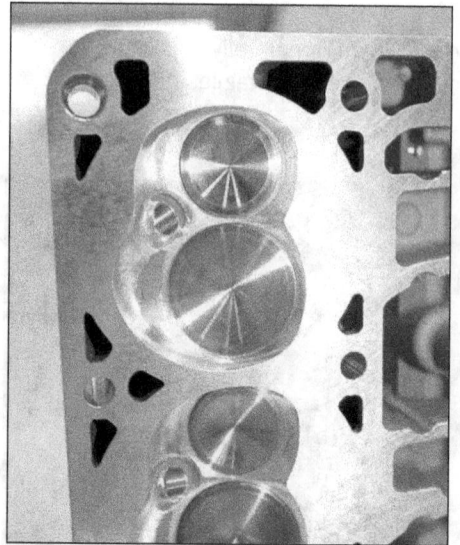

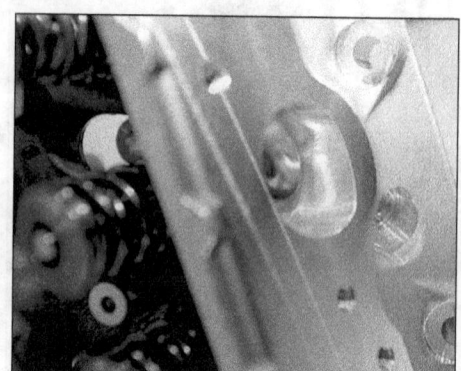

World Products LS7 Warhawk

While also available as-cast (285 cc), which flows 333 cfm, the CNC-ported version delivers the finished product for racers who can utilize the 403 cfm at .800-inch lift. This casting is ideal for high boost or nitrous in particular because of the stronger 355-T6 alloy, raised valve cover rails for aftermarket rocker clearance, and hardened valve seats. These large-runner heads have a 12-degree valve angle, like stock, and are compatible with factory LS7 rocker arms and stands. The heads can accommodate 1.625-inch-diameter springs, and several are available. A 4.125-inch-or-larger bore is required. Base price is $1,130 each, fully assembled, through Summit Racing. (Photos Courtesy World Products)

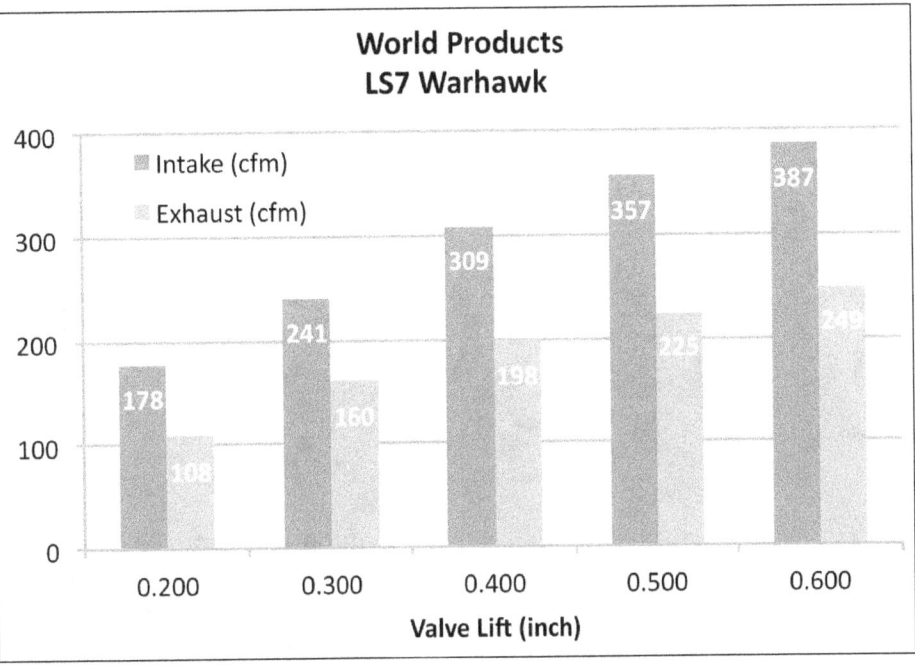

Valves: 2.20-inch intake, 1.60-inch exhaust
Combustion Chamber: 64 or 72 cc

Intake Runner: 296 cc
Intake:

Lift (inch)	.200	.300	.400	.500	.600
Flow (cfm)	178	241	309	357	387

Exhaust Runner: 110 cc
Exhaust:

Lift (inch)	.200	.300	.400	.500	.600
Flow (cfm)	108	160	198	225	249

Recommended Use: 427 to 502 ci, forced induction or naturally aspirated
Additional Features: 12-degree valve angle, Manley stainless-steel 5.500-inch valves, manganese bronze valveguides

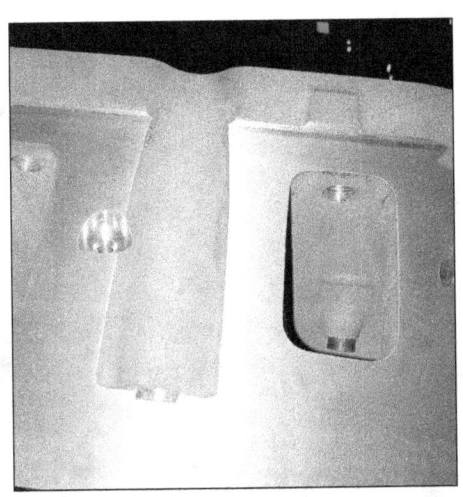

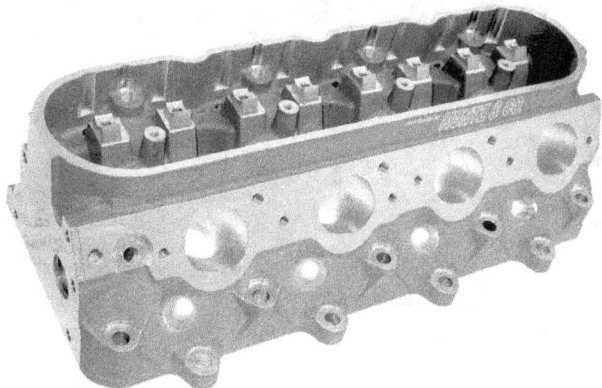

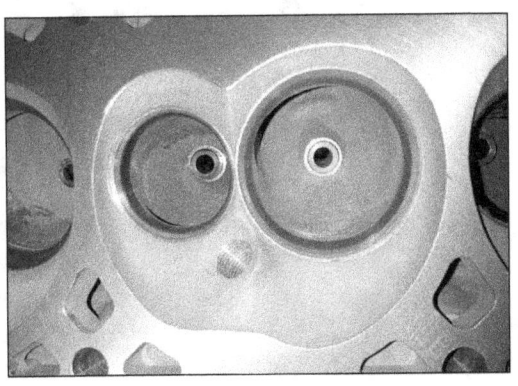

CHAPTER 4

RACE PORT HEADS

This chapter covers any cylinder head that uses an intake or exhaust flange that is not compatible or consistent with OEM patterns. To put it in more simple terms, a typical set of LSX headers and exhaust manifolds do not bolt up and neither do any LSX intake manifolds.

A proprietary intake or exhaust flange, which typically comes with the head, must be used to create a custom intake manifold and headers. Some companies even offer their own cast intake manifold, which limits fabrication to the headers.

Liberating from factory-based designs creates some out-of-the-box thinking with no compromises, and the ultimate performance. The only downside is cost.

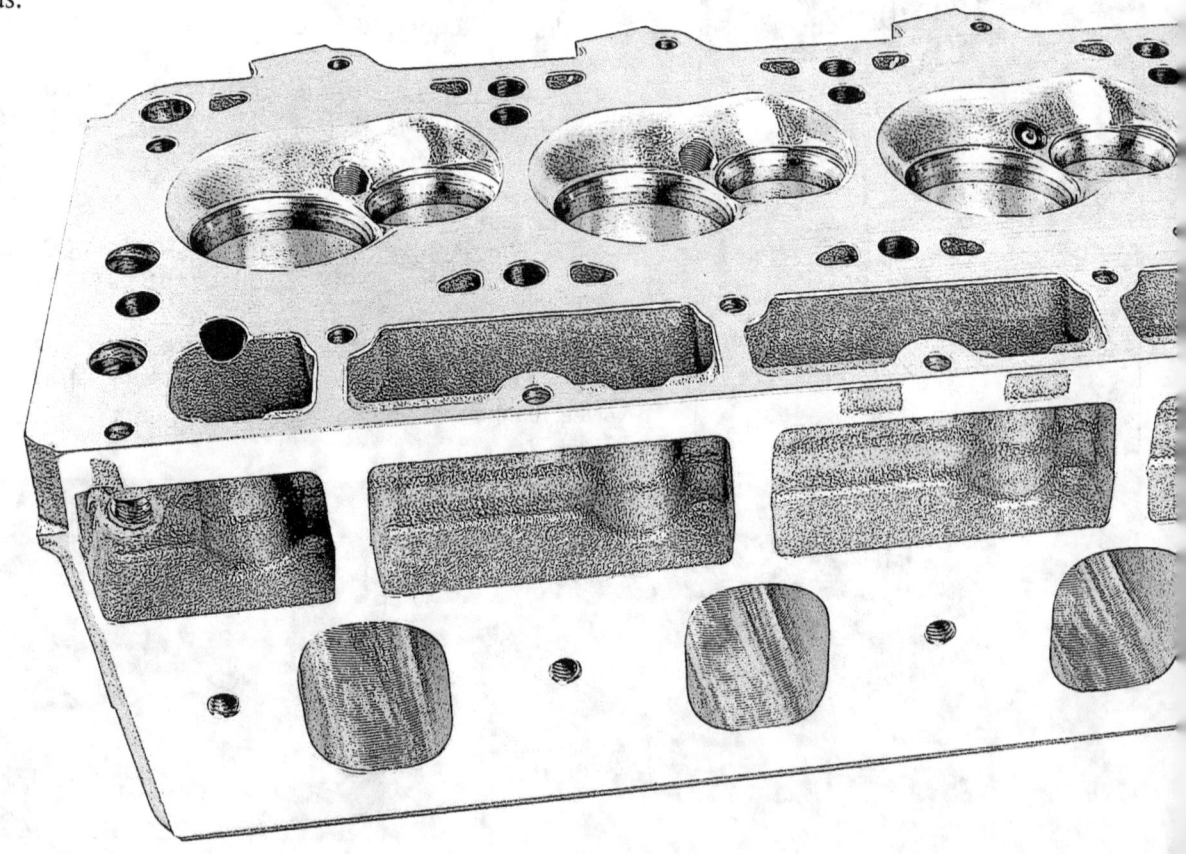

All Pro/West Coast Cylinder Heads
LSW-2

West Coast's program for the All Pro LSW-2 is a game-changer. No longer do you need a canted valve to produce more than 440 cfm. These heads are based on the original LS7 design; however, a proprietary port location (C5R bolt pattern) neccessitates All Pro's cast two-piece intake manifold or a fabricated sheet-metal piece. The exhaust ports are also proprietary and have an 8-bolt flange. Jesel and T&D both make rocker system to accommodate this unique, 12-degree (in-line) head. West Coast has two runner and chamber programs. The larger 330-cc head continues to increase in flow as it hits .900-inch lift with 446.3 cfm. This head is designed specifically for all-out, naturally aspirated builds (hence the small chamber). The 310-cc port leaves more material for greater stability on forced-induction builds while also responding well at high lift, hitting 422.6 cfm at .850-inch lift using a 2.20-inch valve. These heads also have a 65-cc chamber and 116-cc exhaust runner. Both heads have plenty of clearance for 1/2-inch pushrods and utilize the regular LS valve cover pattern. As with all heads in this section, a large (4.125-inch) bore is required. Prices start at $3,290. (Photos Courtesy West Coast Cylinder Heads)

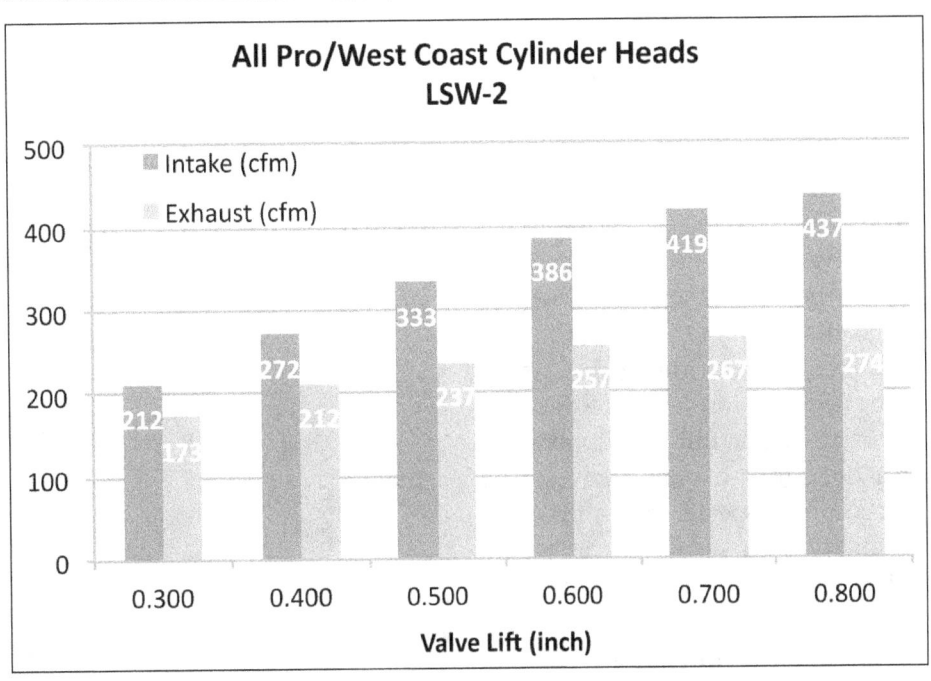

Valves: 2.250-inch intake, 1.60-inch exhaust
Combustion Chamber: 47 cc

Intake Runner: 330 cc
Intake (tested on a 4.155-inch bore):

Lift (inch)	.300	.400	.500	.600	.700	.800
Flow (cfm)	212	272	333	386	419	437

Exhaust Runner: 120 cc
Exhaust:

Lift (inch)	.300	.400	.500	.600	.700	.800
Flow (cfm)	173	212	237	257	267	274

Recommended Use: 427 to 502-plus ci, high RPM naturally aspirated or forced induction
Additional Features: .200-inch raised valve cover rail for rocker clearance

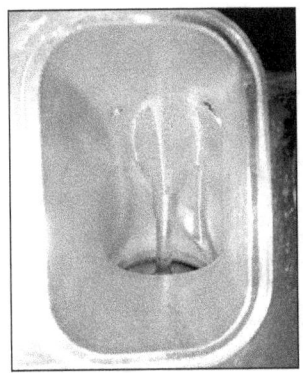

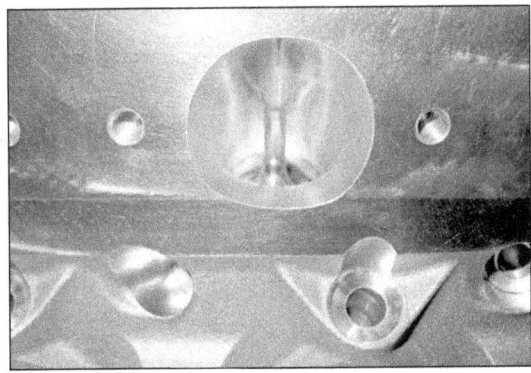

Arias
LS Hemi Chevy

Pro Mods have been running Hemis for decades, so it's no wonder Nick Arias, Jr. developed a casting to adapt this design to an LS engine. These heads were designed for big-power drag racing applications to take advantage of 400-plus cfm. Right out of the box these heads flow 380 (intake) and 268 (exhaust) cfm. The chamber is one of the largest attractions with this head; boost lovers can utilize the large, full-hemisphere. Up to a 1.650-inch-diameter valvespring is accepted. Special pushrods, ARP head studs, investment cast 4340 roller-tip rockers, cast-aluminum valve covers, Cometic head gaskets, oil drain-back line, header flanges (and hardware), and intake/exhaust gaskets are included for $9,975. Hemi pistons, intake manifold, and oil drain bungs are also required. (Photos Courtesy Arias)

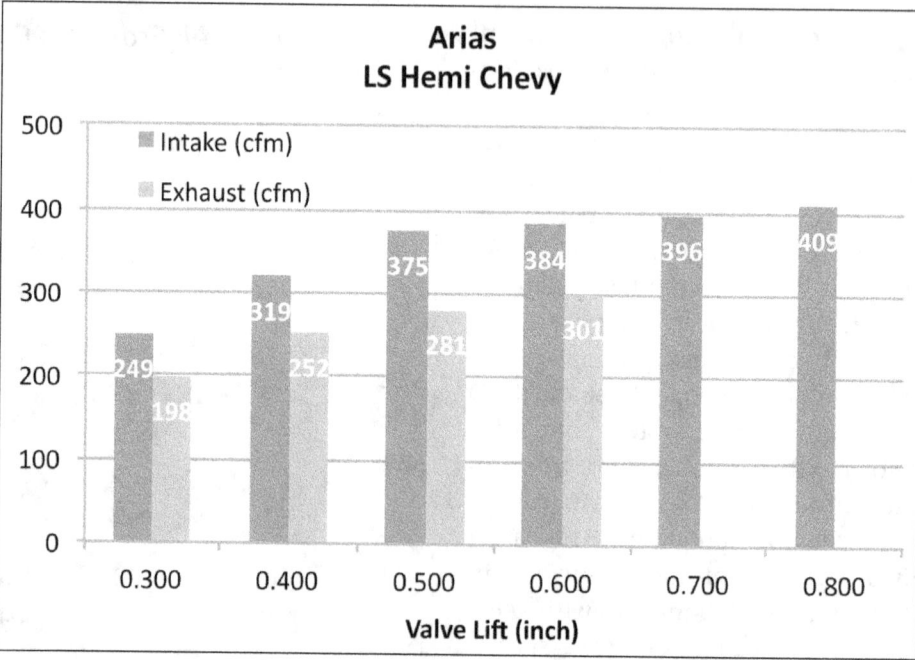

Valves: 2.250-inch intake, 1.600-inch exhaust
Combustion Chamber: 67 & 74 cc

Intake Runner: N/A cc
Intake:
Lift (inch)	.300	.400	.500	.600	.700	.800
Flow (cfm)	249	319	375	384	396	409

Exhaust Runner: N/A cc
Exhaust:
Lift (inch)	.300	.400	.500	.600	.700	.800
Flow (cfm)	198	252	281	301	N/A	N/A

Recommended Use: 427 to 502-plus ci, high-RPM naturally aspirated or forced induction
Additional Features: manganese bronze valveguides, ductile iron valve seats

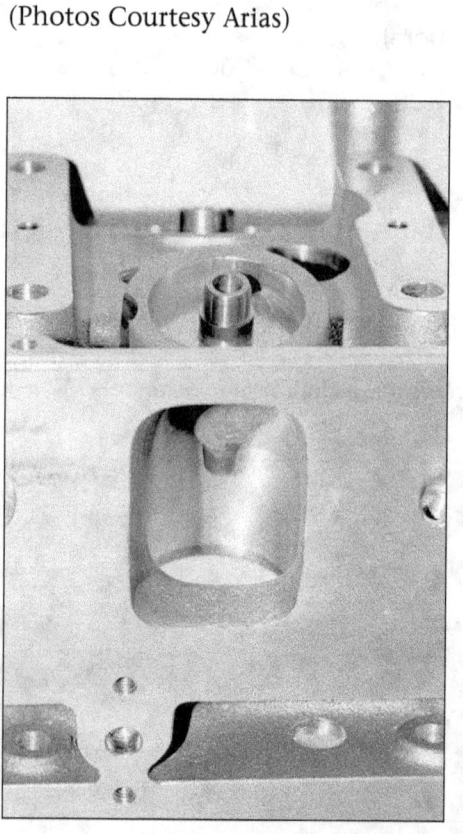
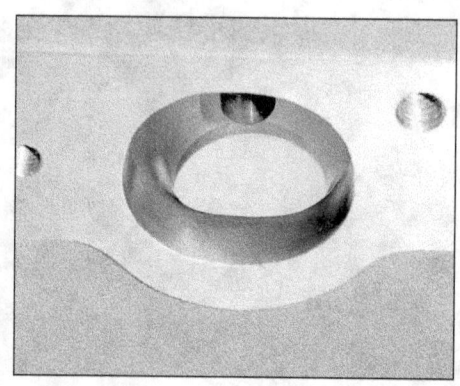
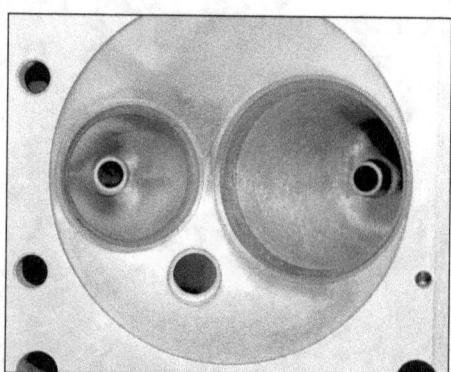

Race Port Heads

Includes:

C5R

LSXDR/Livernois Motorsports

LSXCT/Livernois Motorsports

Chevrolet Performance

Believe it or not, Chevrolet Performance (formerly GM Performance Parts) was a little late to the game in terms of aftermarket product development for the Gen III/IV. But as this market took off, GM was quick to make up ground. Today it boasts an impressive catalogue from budget to high-performance street and full-on (drag and circle track) racing parts. Its resources for testing and development is unparalleled, making it easy to achieve such high-quality parts. Yet the ability to cast its own heads, and in large quantities, allows a low price point. The LSX line was designed with help from not only GM's talented engineering team, but drag racing legends such as Warren Johnson and LS industry insiders.

 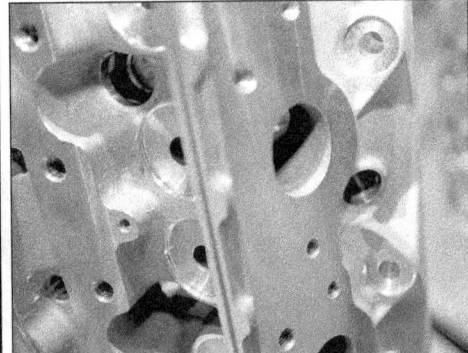 

C5R

  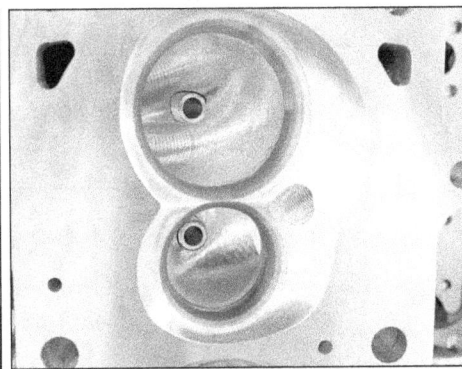

LSXDR

  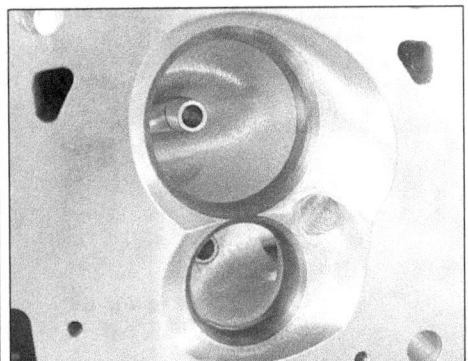

LSXCT

Chevrolet Performance C5R

These are the first race heads ever created for an LS engine, developed for the Corvette C5R Racing program. The raised rectangular port later inspired the LS7; however, no factory intake manifold bolts up to it. Most opt for a custom sheet-metal intake; however, many have modified an SB2 to work. These heads combine high flow with excellent velocity, and when ported properly they can support more than 1,000 hp (and 9,000 rpm) naturally aspirated. The runners and chambers come "as cast" and rough, requiring professional machining; there are no valve seats or guides. The exhaust port is standard LS1, so any regular LS exhaust flange bolts right up. The 11-degree valve angle, however, requires aftermarket rocker arms. Retail price is around $1,978 from Chevrolet Performance dealers such as Scoggin-Dickey.

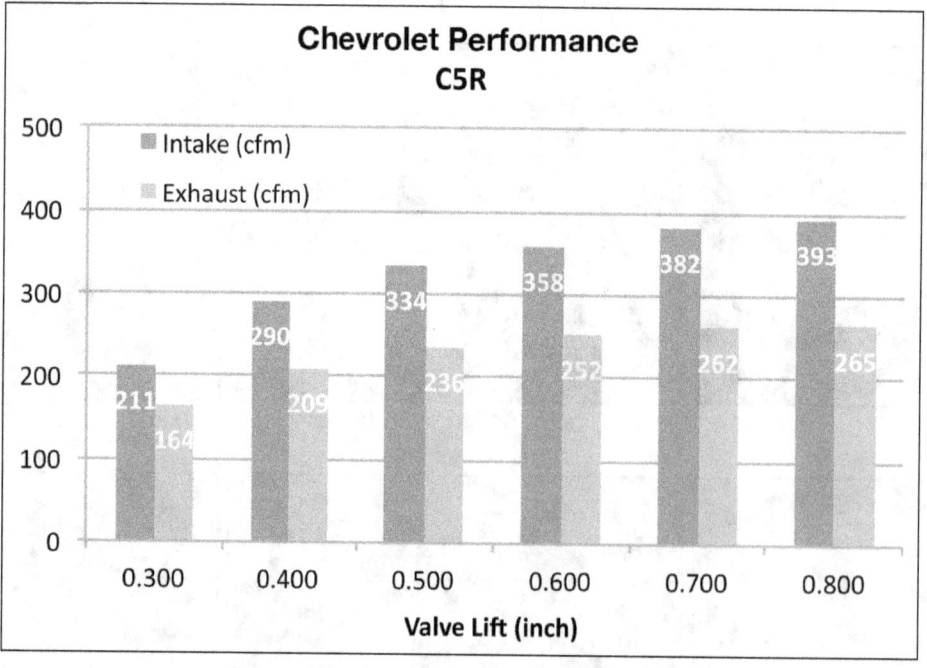

Valves: 2.18-inch intake, 1.625-inch exhaust
Combustion Chamber: 30 cc

Intake Runner: 210 cc
Intake (tested on a 4.155-inch bore with a typical 255-cc CNC porting):

Lift (inch)	.300	.400	.500	.600	.700	.800
Flow (cfm)	211	290	334	358	382	393

Exhaust Runner: 70 cc
Exhaust (tested with typical CNC program):

Lift (inch)	.300	.400	.500	.600	.700	.800
Flow (cfm)	164	209	236	252	262	265

Recommended Use: 427 to 502-plus ci, forced induction or naturally aspirated
Additional Features: 11-degree valve angle

Chevrolet Performance LSXDR/Livernois Motorsports

The LSXDR heads were the perfect follow-up to releasing the short- and tall-deck LSX block by Chevrolet Performance. Developed specifically for drag racers pushing the limits, the DR head has proven to be a good match for high boost and nitrous while still utilizing inline 11-degree valves like its C5R predecessor. The small chambers make these heads particularly valuable on a nitrous car, which is probably why they have high 6-second and low 7-second passes to their credit. Just like the C5R, a 4.125-inch bore is required. The intake runners are raised and the exhaust ports are spread, so the head requires proprietary intake manifolds and flanges as well as rocker arms. The CNC program, done by Livernois, is said to be capable of 900 hp on the engine alone (thanks to its incredible 424.5 cfm at .900-inch lift). Retail price is around $1,600 each (bare).

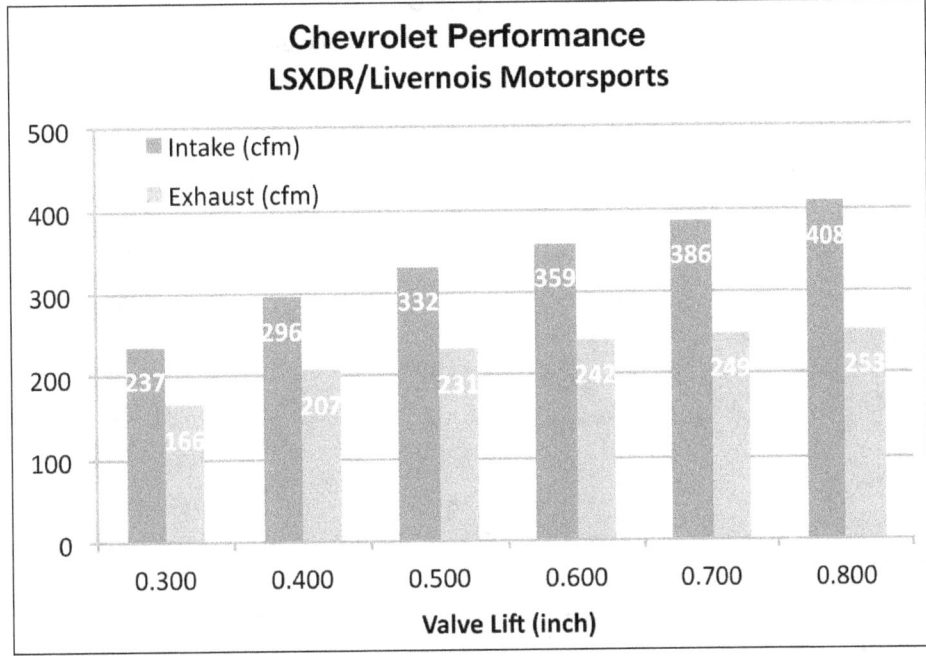

Valves: 2.250-inch intake, 1.650-inch exhaust
Combustion Chamber: 50 cc

Intake Runner: 313 cc
Intake:

Lift (inch)	.300	.400	.500	.600	.700	.800
Flow (cfm)	237	296	332	359	386	408

Exhaust Runner: 116 cc
Exhaust:

Lift (inch)	.300	.400	.500	.600	.700	.800
Flow (cfm)	166	207	231	242	249	253

Recommended Use: 427 to 502-plus ci, high RPM, naturally aspirated or forced induction
Additional Features: 11-degree valve angle, 5/8-inch-thick deck, machined for 1.660-inch valvesprings

CHAPTER 4

Chevrolet Performance LSXCT/Livernois Motorsports

The "CT" stands for Circle Track, and these heads bear plenty of resemblance to their DR cousin. Derived from the C5R, the CT head also uses the same 10-mm raised intake runner and spread-port exhaust pattern (proprietary flanges required). The smaller runners enhance velocity and make the heads suitable for circle-track racing. Special 356-T6 alloy ensures longevity, and the combination of a 5/8-inch-thick deck and LSX-style 6-head-bolts-per-cylinder ensures plenty of clamping. These heads (like the DR) are available prior to machining, and a complementing intake manifold and rocker system is available through Chevrolet Performance. Just like the DR heads, these go for around $1,600 each (bare).

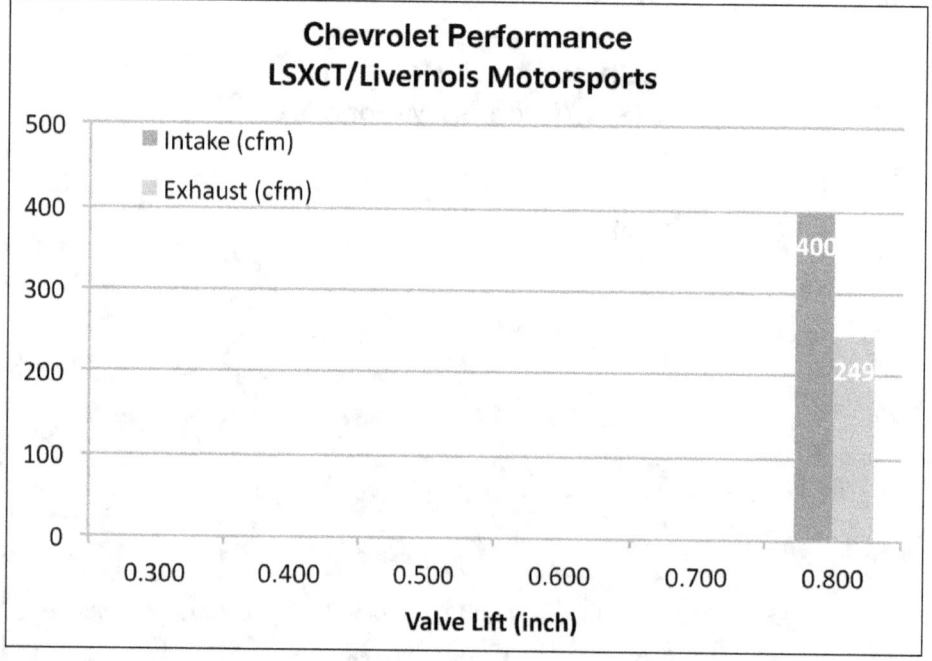

Valves: 2.200-inch intake, 1.610-inch exhaust
Combustion Chamber: 45 cc

Intake Runner: 302 cc
Intake:

Lift (inch)	.300	.400	.500	.600	.700	.800
Flow (cfm)	N/A	N/A	N/A	N/A	N/A	400

Exhaust Runner: 109 cc
Exhaust:

Lift (inch)	.300	.400	.500	.600	.700	.800
Flow (cfm)	N/A	N/A	N/A	N/A	N/A	249

Recommended Use: 427 to 502-plus ci, high RPM, naturally aspirated
Additional Features: 11-degree valve angle

Edelbrock Victor LSR/Race Flow Development

Edelbrock's Victor LSR is one of only two canted-valve heads on the market, and with more testing these could be the heads to beat. Race Flow Development has several different programs with different valves (2.20- to 2.26-inch intake) and runner cross-section to accommodate various combinations. RFD says it has three to five different variations on the LSR's intake runner, but only two on the exhaust runner (usually the smaller is used for naturally aspirated, and the larger for forced induction). There are another two or three different chambers; however, the heads can be milled as needed to achieve the desired compression. A custom intake manifold is required for the proprietary runner shape and location, as with the exhaust and rocker arms. These heads have made more than 1,000 hp naturally aspirated with 2.25- and 1.6-inch valves that help flow 450 and 298 cfm, though they are capable of more than 465 cfm. Prices vary from $4,800 bare to $7,200 assembled. (Photos Courtesy Race Flow Development)

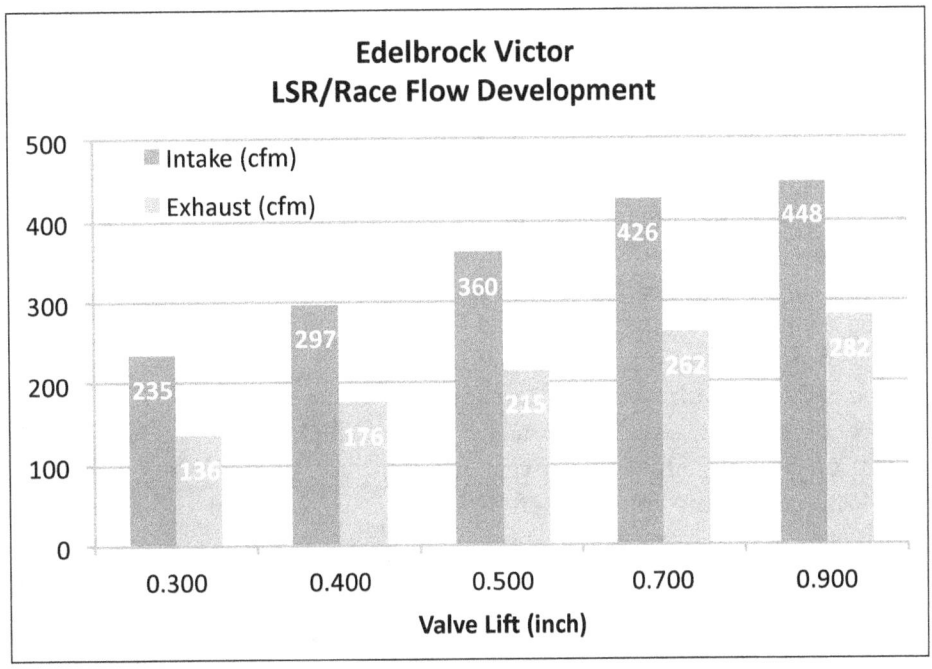

Valves: 2.20- to 2.26-inch intake, 1.58 to 1.625-inch exhaust
Combustion Chamber: 52 cc

Intake Runner: 300+ cc
Intake:

Lift (inch)	.300	.400	.500	.600	.700	.800	.900
Flow (cfm)	235	297	360	393	426	437	448

Exhaust Runner: 95+ cc
Exhaust:

Lift (inch)	.300	.400	.500	.600	.700	.800	.900
Flow (cfm)	136	176	215	238	262	272	282

Recommended Use: 427 to 502-plus ci, high RPM naturally aspirated or forced induction
Additional Features: 9x3-degree canted intake valve, 6x2-degree canted exhaust valve, uses SB2 valve cover, bronze alloy valve seats, titanium valves, various springs available, HIP-process casting

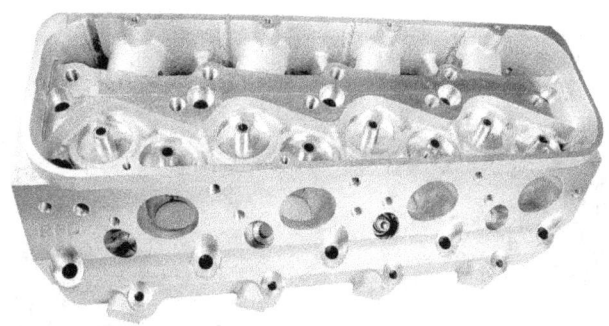
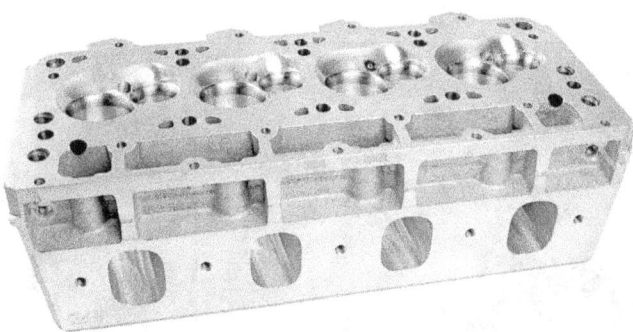

Mast Motorsports
Mozez Canted Valve

Easily one of the highest-flowing heads out there, Mast's canted-valve head is used by the fastest nitrous LSX cars and even a few turbo cars. A 10-degree valve angle with a 4-degree cant on the intake and a 7-degree angle on the exhaust with a 2.5-degree cant make the runners a straight path in and out. The raised intake runners have a perfectly oval shape, which requires either Mast's 2-piece intake or a custom sheet-metal piece. Only SB2 valve covers, or Mast's cast racing covers are compatible. A 4.125-inch-or-larger bore is required. Retail price is $2,500 each (bare).

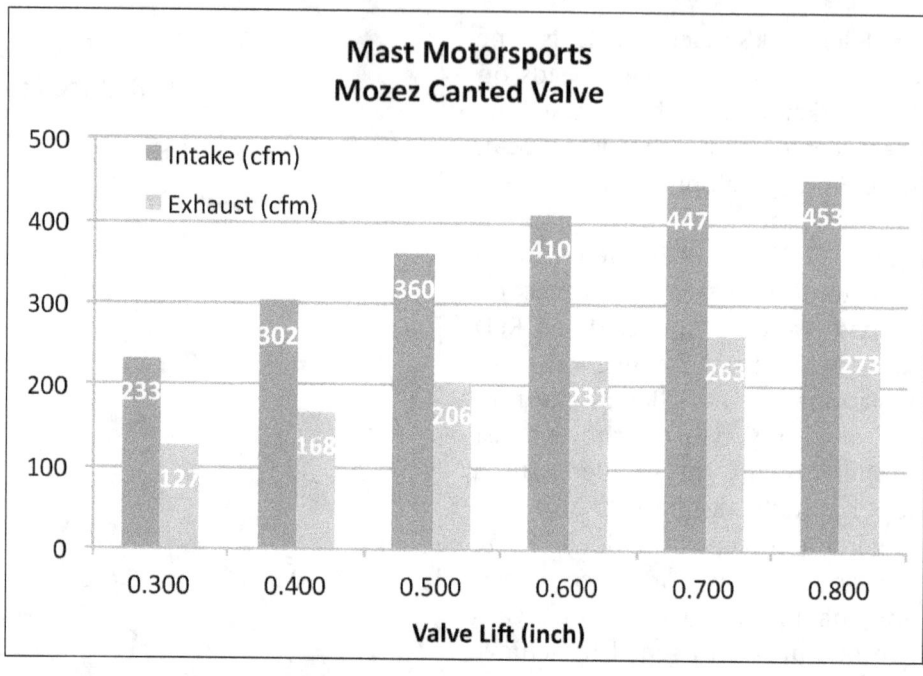

Valves: 2.250-inch intake, 1.600-inch exhaust
Combustion Chamber: N/A cc

Intake Runner: 352 cc
Intake:

Lift (inch)	.300	.400	.500	.600	.700	.800
Flow (cfm)	233	302	360	410	447	453

Exhaust Runner: N/A cc
Exhaust:

Lift (inch)	.300	.400	.500	.600	.700	.800
Flow (cfm)	127	168	206	231	263	273

Recommended Use: 427 to 502-plus ci, high RPM, naturally aspirated or forced induction
Additional Features: copper valve seats (50-degree intake, 55-degree exhaust), .750-inch-thick deck, 6-bolt provisions for aftermarket blocks, milled rocker mounts (TRD, Jesel, or Mast rockers)

CHAPTER 5

SUPPORTING COMPONENTS

Of course no book on cylinder heads would be complete without discussion of its supporting components.

Available intake manifolds and rocker arms should also be considered when choosing cylinder heads. It may add to the cost or help save money; it may add to the performance or take away from the performance of the heads.

Unlike with other engines, aftermarket does not necessarily mean better. The OEM designs are durable, light, and well made. However, the more modified the engine—meaning higher RPM and higher-lift cam—the more likely OEM parts hinder the performance.

Intake Manifolds

There are now a wide range of intake manifolds available for LS-series engines of all power levels. Both front-fed and top-fed (carb-style) intakes are offered. The factory intakes and several aftermarket offerings are made of composite, which is lightweight and sheds heat. Traditional aluminum castings also exist, as do high-end custom sheet-metal units. No matter what your needs, there is certainly an intake available to suit it.

Factory Intakes

For most street cars, it is hard to go wrong with an OEM GM intake manifold. All are made of a very durable composite material (glass-fiber-reinforced nylon) that disperses heat much better than aluminum, which helps keep heat soak and resulting detonation to a minimum. The original LS1 intake manifold used in the 1997–2000 Corvette and 1998–2000 F-Body is one of the least desirable for cathedral ports; however, it is still quite capable. It features long, 262-mm runners with a decreasing cross-section to increase velocity as the air moves into the cylinder head; this design is considered to be of little sacrifice to high-RPM power with a gain in low-RPM torque.

Like the LS1, the LS6 intake manifold, originally designed to complement the LS6 head for the 2001 Corvette Z06 and completely replace the LS1 intake on all models, was also designed for low hood clearance. In addition to the lack of EGR provisions and steam-tube clearance, the LS6 intake differs from the LS1 in its plenum volume, runner shape, and volume. Jumping from .536 to .541 liters proved much more suitable for higher-revving applications such as the new LS6, and with the revised camshaft and cylinder head specs on the later LS1s. The increased plenum volume (5.19 liters in the LS6) made it the largest among cathedral intakes.

Though not the most aesthetically pleasing, many of the truck intake manifolds have some of the most desirable runner lengths for producing torque. Unfortunately, the longer runner lengths most often mean decreased plenum volume. On the LQ4, LR4, LM7, and LQ9 (4.8, 5.3, 6.0, and 6.0 liters), the plenum volume is only 4.0 liters, though the runners are 263 mm and only .513 liters. Although great for throttle response and velocity, this design strains the engine to pull air through the entire intake system instead of having it readily available (in the plenum).

However, all of this may spell the perfect complement to a centrifugal supercharged application. The rectangular-port L92 truck intake follows this exact same formula, and as

HIGH-PERFORMANCE GM LS-SERIES CYLINDER HEAD GUIDE 117

a result gives up as much as 43 cfm at high lift when bolted to a set of ported heads.

If higher RPM power is your goal, the L76 and LS3 intake manifolds clearly have the advantage. Designed for a 7,200-rpm redline, the LS7 intake also excels at high RPM. However, both the LS7 and LS3 leave room for improvement in even street-based combos.

Among the factory intake manifolds, it is important to note three very important differences. All Gen IV engines (LS2, LS3, L76, L92, etc.) utilize electronic, or "drive-by-wire," throttle bodies. All of these intakes also utilize larger 90-mm throttle bodies, up from the Gen III's 75 mm. Last, but not least, Gen IV intakes are constructed utilizing a traditional plastic-injected molding process with three separate pieces, instead of the single piece, that are vibration (or sonic) welded. Time and again, the LS2 and LS6 intake manifolds have been dyno'd back to back, and the LS6 always comes out on top despite the LS2's substantially larger throttle body, slightly larger plenum, and revised runners.

Pete Incaudo at VMAX Motorsports has conducted several tests comparing the LS2 and LS6 intake manifolds, from which he concluded that a miniscule amount of air leaks past those welds internally and this effect is amplified with increased head flow and higher RPM. His solution was to simply port the intake to allow it to flow more air since repairing (by sealing it) was deemed too difficult, and adhesives would have too high a rate of failure.

Aftermarket Intakes

There are plenty of alternatives to running an OEM intake

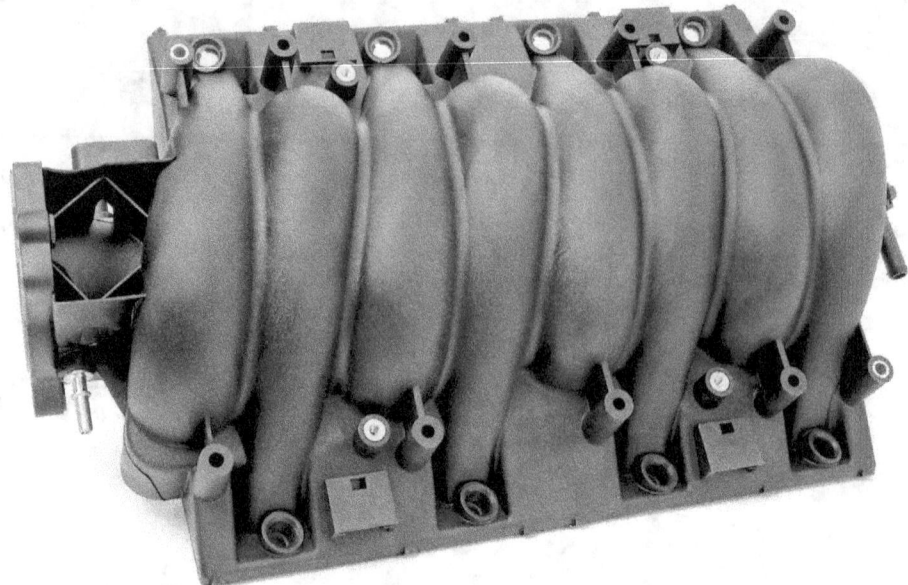

The LS6 intake manifold has stood the test of time as one of the best intake manifolds GM has made to date, and even compared to aftermarket offerings it is hard to beat (especially when price is a factor). In addition, porting can yield an additional 20 hp. Whether you have a mostly stock LS1, ported heads and aftermarket cam, boost or nitrous, the LS6 intake is worth significant power over the original LS1 intake, which is why GM started using it on all Corvettes and F-Bodies starting in 2001.

Despite its larger plenum, throttle body, and revised runners, the LS2 intake manifold is no match for the LS6. GM's new molding process, and use of nylon 6 instead of nylon 66, came with some inherent issues that make the LS2 intake particularly problematic with modified engines.

SUPPORTING COMPONENTS

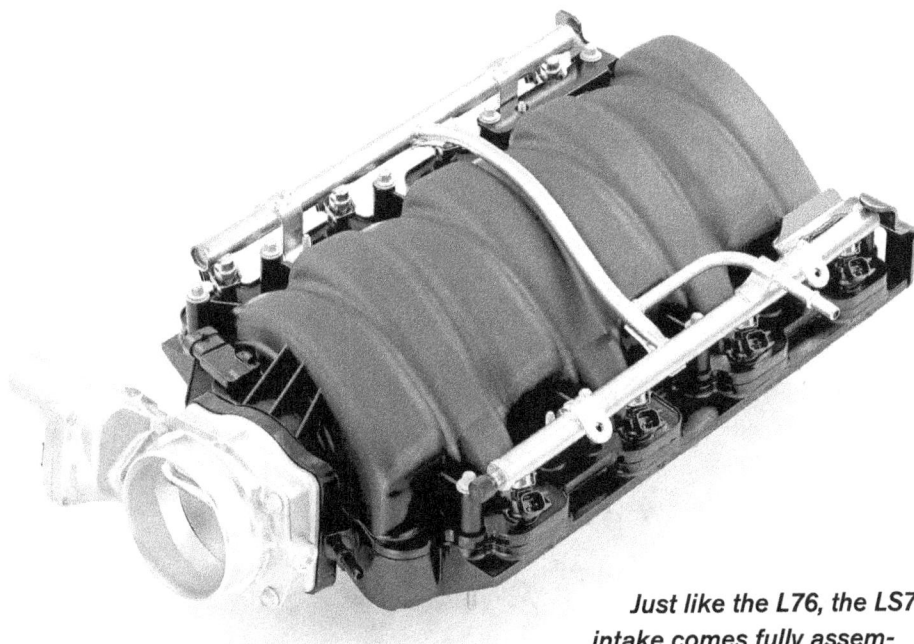

Just like the L76, the LS7 intake comes fully assembled with throttle body, fuel rails, and injectors. It is a well-designed piece that keeps up with aftermarket cams, ported stock heads, and big cubic inches. However, if you are looking to spin 7,500 rpm or more, use a tall-deck block for 480-plus-ci, or simply add boost, you should consider other alternatives.

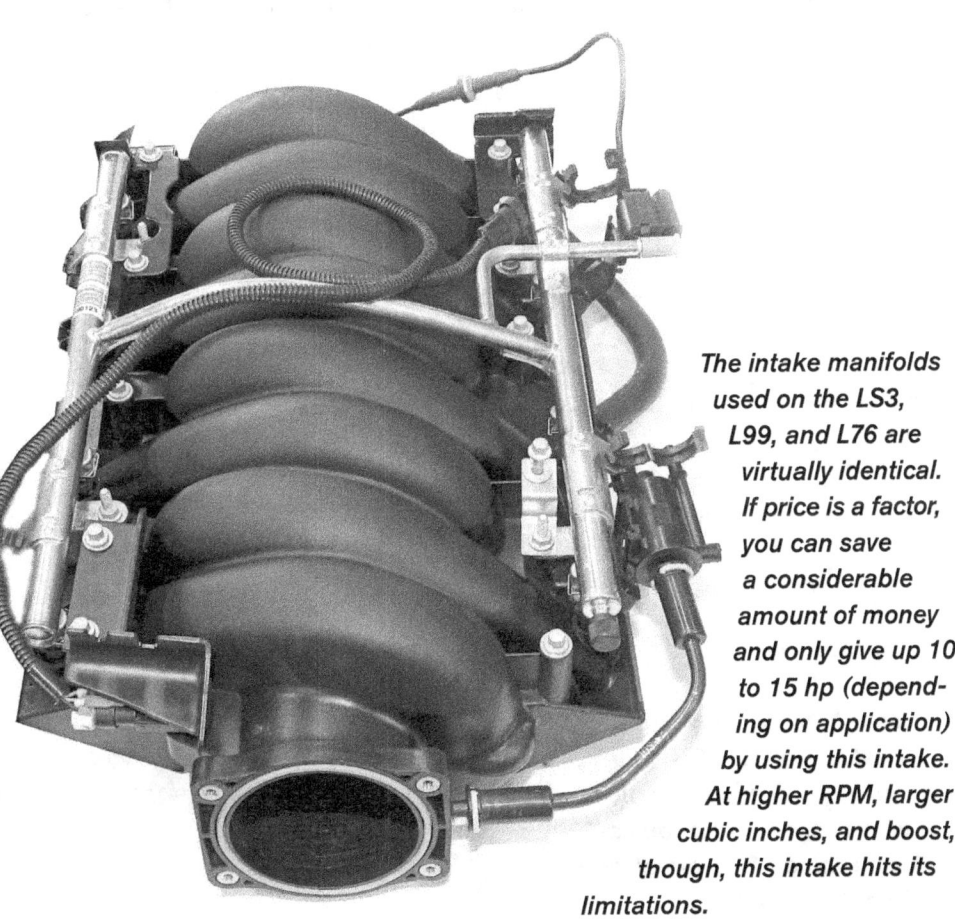

The intake manifolds used on the LS3, L99, and L76 are virtually identical. If price is a factor, you can save a considerable amount of money and only give up 10 to 15 hp (depending on application) by using this intake. At higher RPM, larger cubic inches, and boost, though, this intake hits its limitations.

manifold that are still suitable for a street car, and that can even keep a similar look and fitment. The perfect example, and quintessential upgrade for most people, is the FAST LSX series of intakes. Originally, Wilson Manifolds had developed a 78- and 90-mm LSX intake, which became the gold standard for street cars and even worked well for many race cars. FAST improved upon the design years later, adding the 92-mm Big Mouth throttle body. However, a complete revamp stepped up the game considerably. The 102-mm LSXR intake for the LS7 and LS3 was the first to market, followed by the LSXRT cathedral truck manifold and LSXR cathedral.

Unparalleled plenum volume and removable and tuneable individual runners separate the LSXR from every other intake on the market. Stock cubic-inch combos typically see gains of 8 to 15 hp, and boosted or large-cube strokers can see as much as 50 hp with no loss in low-RPM power. If you simply don't like plastic, BBK Performance and Weiand each make a great upgrade to the factory LS1 that is made from aluminum but with the factory profile. They are both available in several finishes, offer a 10- to 15-hp improvement out of the box (over an LS1 intake), and are also able to be ported for further gains.

As good as the stock-style intakes are, they have several inherent flaws. The front entry is known to cause airflow distribution issues that can pose a serious problem on high-boost or nitrous combinations. Those constructed of plastic are also known to come apart at high boost and during a nitrous backfire. Even the 102-mm FAST LSXR fails to keep up at 7,800-plus-rpm. To solve all of these issues, and even allow the use of a carburetor, several companies are producing some great cast-aluminum alternatives.

Chevrolet Performance makes several 4-barrel intake manifolds for the LS2 (cathedral), LS3/L92, and LS7 that come with (un-tapped) injector bosses cast in, and a whole new line-up of LSX manifolds that are thicker to allow more material for porting. Chevrolet Performance has race-only intake manifolds to accompany the unique port design of the LSX-CT and LSX-DR heads, which have an extra set of injector/nitrous bosses and a 1-inch raised mounting pad.

All Pro and Mast Motorsports each make two-piece cast intake manifolds to accompany each of their own unique port designs, and Mast also has intakes for standard-port designs (LS1, LS3, and LS7). Both are designed for purpose-built race engines and ease of porting.

Edelbrock's line of manifolds is a little more flexible in use. The Performer RPM is designed for 1,500 to 6,500 rpm (as is the RPM Air-Gap Dual-Quad), and the Victor Jr. (3,500 to 7,500 rpm) and Super Victor (3,500 to 8,000 rpm) hit a higher range and are more competition-only.

Holley also has a few manifolds in this ilk, such as the 2X4 Dual Plane Mid-Rise for mid-range and top-end power (up to 7,000 rpm).

All of these intakes (All Pro, Mast, Edelbrock, and Holley) are available for EFI or carbs.

Extreme Intakes

Let your head start to spin when you realize that we haven't even hit the tip of the iceberg yet when it comes to manifolds. The latest generation of intakes combines race car and OEM technology to help build

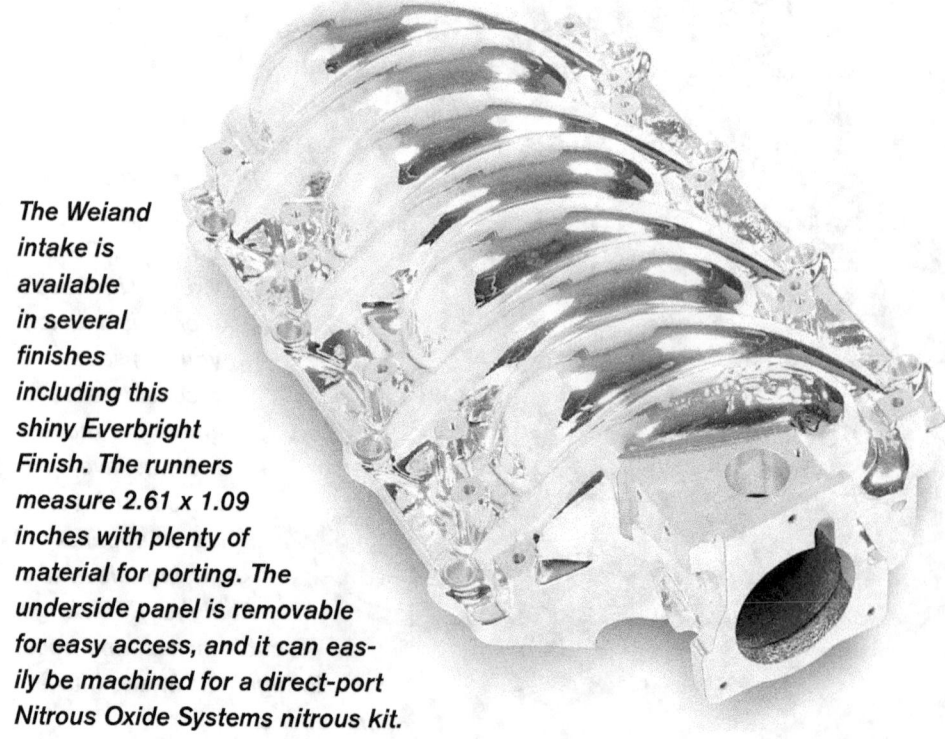

The FAST LSXR is the baddest street intake manifold on the market (for EFI). Its 102-mm throttle body and enormous plenum make for a very efficient design. The runners are removable and therefore able to be ported and tuned per application. Adapters are available to run a smaller throttle body if necessary, as are high-flow fuel rails. The LSXR is available in cathedral, LS3, and LS7 ports. LSXRT is a truck version of this intake that is not concerned with Corvette or F-Body hood clearance, and it allows for much straighter runners and even more power.

The Weiand intake is available in several finishes including this shiny Everbright Finish. The runners measure 2.61 x 1.09 inches with plenty of material for porting. The underside panel is removable for easy access, and it can easily be machined for a direct-port Nitrous Oxide Systems nitrous kit.

SUPPORTING COMPONENTS

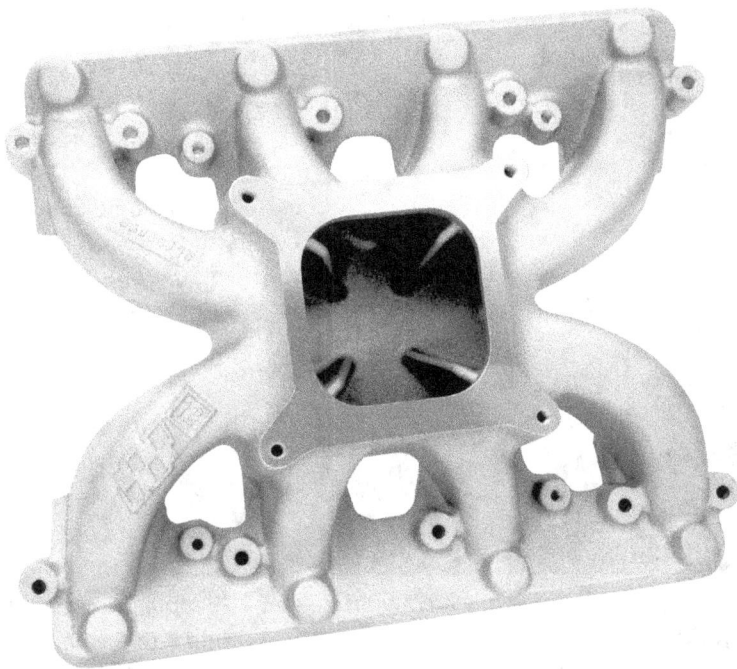

The Chevrolet Performance LS2 4-barrel intake manifold was designed to allow a 4150 carb to bolt up to any cathedral port LS engine, while also providing injector bosses in case the EFI crowd found use for it. To run a carb, though, a front-mount distributor conversion or an ignition controller is needed to fire the individual coils. Versions are available for the LS7 and LS3/L92.

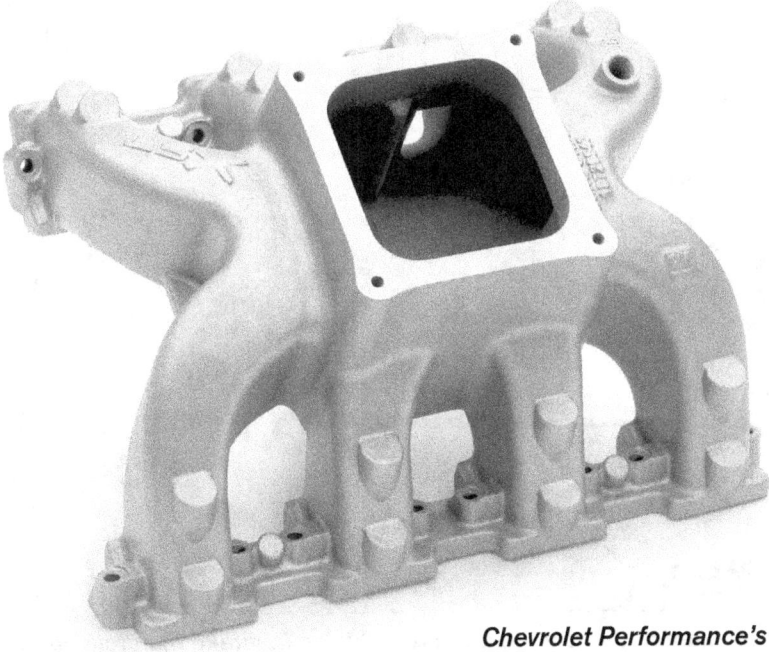

Chevrolet Performance's LSX-DR manifold is for high-RPM, large-displacement race applications only. It matches the unique intake port design and provides plenty of material for porting. Two sets of injector or nitrous bosses are cast in, making its intentions obvious. A version is available for the standard and tall-deck LSX block.

the most extreme street cars, and some just beyond the mark. Harrop and Kinsler both make individual throttle body (ITB) setups that look amazing and perform equally well. You can't beat an ITB intake for throttle response and "wow" factor. Kinsler makes a cross-ram and vertical style, depending on hood clearance, for all standard ports and even the C5R. The Harrop Hurricane intake is only available for cathedral port (currently), but is compatible with factory drive-by-wire electronics or mechanical throttle cables. The ITB intakes are very tunable, complicated, and therefore expensive. However, the latest trend seeks to reduce cost.

Wilson Manifolds and Holley have been producing more cost-effective alternatives to custom manifolds. The Wilson Billet Bank intake is essentially a CNC-made sheet-metal intake that utilizes F1-style trumpets, and is ideal for forced induction.

The Holley Modular Hi-Ram intake is a cast version of what is typical of custom sheet-metal intakes. The Hi-Ram is revolutionary in its flexibility of use. The base, flange with runners, is available with or without injector bosses and can be used with a variety of tops. Whether you plan on running dual 4150 or dual 4500 Dominator carbs, dual 4150 or 4500 throttle bodies, a single 92- or 102-mm throttle body, or want a blank top to do whatever you want, Holley has you covered. Depending on the configuration, the Hi-Ram can handle high RPM, high boost, or whatever you want it to.

Last but not least the custom sheet-metal option. For extreme racing (or oddball) combinations, it is hard to compare to a custom manifold. And if you have certain cylinder heads, such as the Chevrolet Performance C5R or Edelbrock LSR, you have little choice. Artists, such as Tom Nelson (Nelson Racing Engines), John Beck (Beck Mechanical), and John Marcella (Marcella Manifolds), have been crafting some of the most beautiful pieces of aluminum to ever sit atop an engine for decades. Things like runner length and taper, plenum volume, carb or throttle body location, and injector location can all be customized to suit your application. Their years of experience can help determine which best suits your engine size, RPM range, use, and choice of induction. To field a competitive heads-up drag racing effort, their services are highly recommended when class legal.

Rocker Arms

The LS-series engines, unlike so many engines before them, can actually boast of a really good factory rocker arm setup. The stock units are commonly retained on most street-based performance engines and are good for hundreds of thousands of miles. But, once you begin making serious power or spinning to high RPM levels (6,500 plus) for extended periods, it's time to upgrade.

Factory Arms

Traditionally the LS crowd has made very good use of factory rocker arms. However, despite being very light and strong, factory rocker arms suffer two fatal flaws. The first and most alarming problem with factory rockers is that they contain needle bearings in the trunnion that tend to fail with increased RPM, spring pressure, and lift. When these needle bearings fail, the result can be catastrophic as they escape into the oil

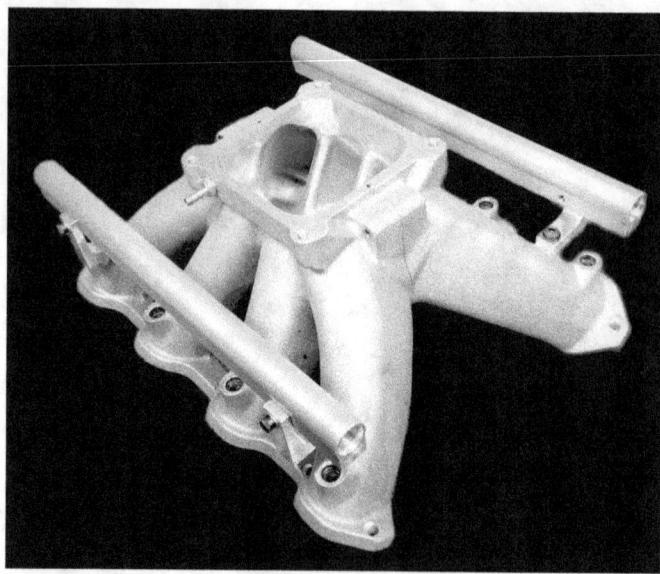

There has yet to be a better cast manifold than Mast's CNC two-piece intake. It's CAD-designed, CNC-machined, hand-finished, and hand-flowed before it leaves the factory. You can practically see your reflection inside the manifold, which is why this intake was later put on Late Model Racecraft's twin-turbo Outlaw Drag Radial Firehawk, which went 7.24 at 209 mph. Though it works on this 2,000-hp turbo application that spins more than 8,000 rpm, the Mast intake has also worked well for naturally aspirated combinations by making surprisingly great torque and power under the curve due to its long runners. On another Late Model engine, this intake made 720 hp at 6,800 rpm on a big-cube, naturally aspirated motor, which was some 47 hp over the stock LS7.

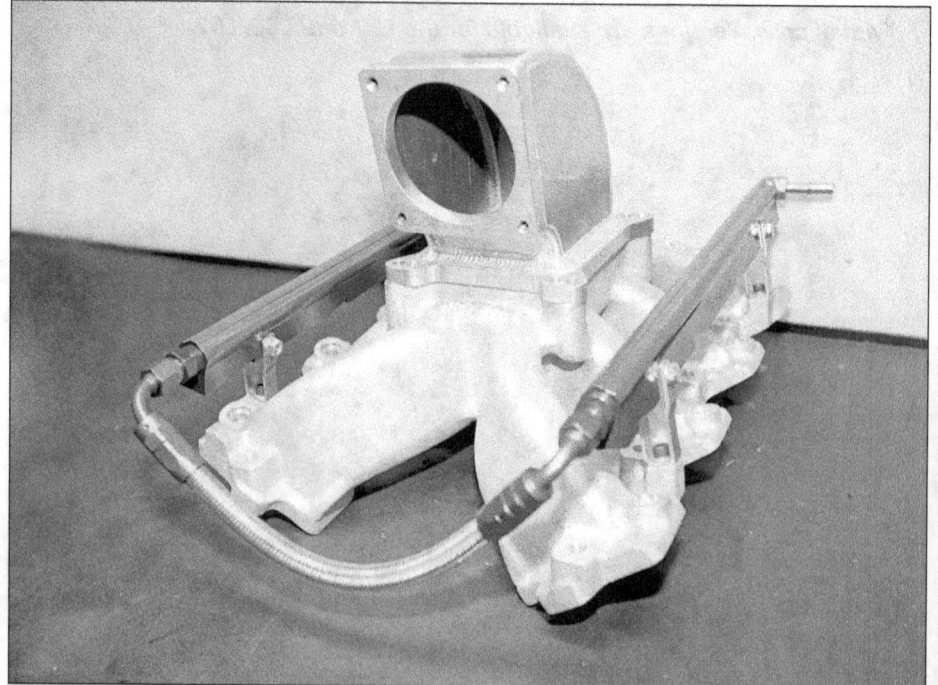

Here is an example of how the Edelbrock Victor Jr. intake manifold can be used in an EFI application: a 2000 Camaro SS with Strictly Performance–ported LS1 heads and a large camshaft. The sheet-metal elbows are from IntakeElbows.com, but Edelbrock has since come out with its own regular and low-profile elbows (which are cast aluminum). Though it does give up some torque down low, this setup improved over an LS6 by almost 40 hp at peak.

galley. Both Comp Cams and Harland Sharpe have captured roller trunnions to upgrade factory rockers, which solves this problem. More than 1,500 hp has been made using this setup.

The second problem is that with high-lift camshafts, the factory rocker arms are known to cause excessive wear on the valveguides, even more so with certain aftermarket castings.

Aftermarket Arms

Aftermarket rocker arms with a roller tip not only have less friction, but they also push more evenly on the valve tip. Economical steel-body, stud-mount rockers are available from Comp Cams; however, a stud-mount aluminum rocker may be worth a little bit of extra dough to reduce valvetrain weight. The technology has come a long way, so no longer are aluminum rocker arms a liability when it comes to durability or stiffness. Comp Cams, Crane Cams, Scorpion, Yella Terra, Harland Sharpe, and Summit Racing all make quality pedestal or stud-mount aluminum roller rockers.

The next step up from a pedestal-mount rocker arm is a shaft-mount version, which is required for all high-RPM builds. With shaft-mount rockers, a shaft connects the rocker arm bodies, which acts as the fulcrum, increasing mounting stiffness and creating a more stable valvetrain. There is also quite a bit of adjustability, which can help optimize geometry.

Whereas every other Edelbrock intake has a very small plenum, the Pro-Flo XT was created for a more broad torque band up to its 7,000-rpm limit. This intake appeals to the street car crowd, though its height makes some applications difficult. With some cutting of the cowl and hood it actually fits in a Gen IV F-Body (reference dimensions available online). Edelbrock says in its testing that it exceeded the LS6 intake by 30 hp at 6,500 rpm. Versions are available for cathedral and LS3 port.

Individual throttle body (ITB) intakes have been around for decades, but are seldom used on later-model engines for some reason (perhaps price). However, the likes of Kinsler and Harrop have changed all that when it comes to the LS1. The Harrop Hurricane (seen here) uses 55-mm inlets for each runner to draw in air. These inlets are tuneable, produce amazing throttle response, and are a great combination of mid-range and top-end power since the runners are obviously as straight as can be. This C5 Corvette has run low 9s naturally aspirated and made more than 600 rwhp with a solid-roller camshaft and Trick Flow heads, but should have an 8-second pass with its new bottom-end combination.

CHAPTER 5

The folks at Wilson Manifolds know a thing or two about intake manifolds, and clearly the Billet Bank intake was made with plenty of experience behind it. While gorgeous to look at with its CNC-machined billet aluminum, F1-style trumpets on the ends of the runners, and engraved top, it is also a great performing piece for a highly boosted street car. Wilson says it was designed for larger displacements and higher RPM than your typical street intakes, and they are more than happy to outfit it with a Nitrous Pro-Flow direct-port kit or high-flow fuel rails.

Holley's brand-new Modular Hi-Ram looks like a cast version of the high-end sheet-metal intakes we've been seeing on race cars for years. The big difference, though, is the price and flexibility of usage. Its various tops allow so many options for induction, making it a builder's dream. So far, this intake is available for LS3/L92 ports only, with or without machined injector bosses, but I am told other versions will be available.

HIGH-PERFORMANCE GM LS-SERIES CYLINDER HEAD GUIDE

SUPPORTING COMPONENTS

Some aftermarket castings, especially in the race port section, require shaft-mount rockers and have plenty of clearance built in. Factory castings usually require milling off the pedestals and sometimes clearancing along the valve cover rail. Taller valve covers or spacers are usually required as well. With the machining, aftermarket valve covers, and the actual cost of shaft-mount systems, they are usually reserved for high-end builds. T&D, Lunati, Mast Motorsports, Comp Cams, and Jesel are some of the most popular and well-made examples.

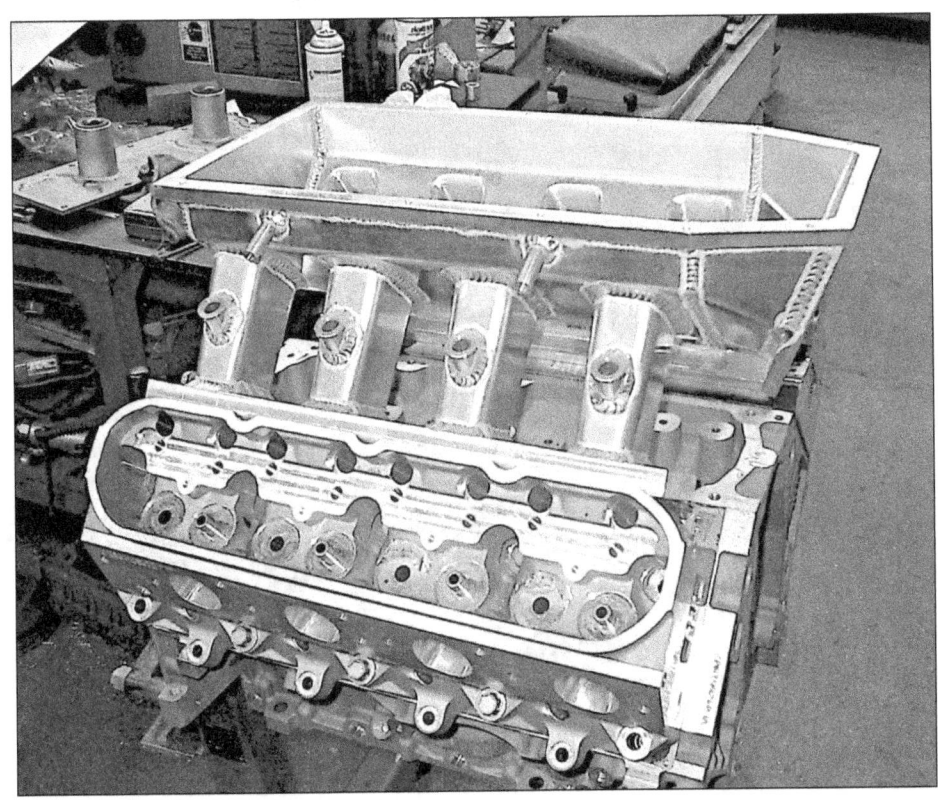

RaceKrafters built this custom intake manifold from aluminum sheet metal for a 440-ci naturally aspirated LSX (drag race only). This particular engine has All Pro LSW-2 heads and an operating range of 5,500 to 8,500 rpm. It is capped off with a lid and custom-CNC'd 125-mm throttle body. The unique port configuration, high-RPM range, and hood clearance limitations necessitated the custom manifold. Bob Wise of RaceKrafters says experience is crucial for knowing what runner shapes work, and the cross-section area and runner taper are critical for a well-designed manifold. He also added that port velocity in the head can be heavily influenced by runner shape and length, so much so that the manifold design is sometimes used to compensate for weak cylinders. (Photo Courtesy RaceKrafters)

John Beck designed this manifold for the School of Automotive Machinists and its record-setting All Motor Camaro SS. This 433-ci LSX uses a 16:1 compression ratio and heavily worked C5R heads to make more than 1,000 hp at more than 9,000 rpm and run as fast as 8.2 in the quarter. A few different configurations of the intake have been used with either two 4-barrel throttle bodies or a single Braswell 7825. The latest version is composite on the upper half, where it meets the throttle body, and could help the Camaro become the first door-slammer to run 7s. (Photo Courtesy T.J. Atkins)

HIGH-PERFORMANCE GM LS-SERIES CYLINDER HEAD GUIDE

CHAPTER 5

Upgrading the trunnions on a set of factory rocker arms with Comp Cams' upgrade is great insurance on your engine build. Comp uses a caged or captured bearing set, which does not fall victim to failure like the OEM rockers with increased spring pressure and RPM. While not recommended, 7-second time slips have been achieved using this upgrade on forced-induction builds.

SLP Performance Parts makes these OEM-style steel rockers as a means of increasing the ratio from 1.7 to 1.85:1 on cathedral-style heads. They are economical, lightweight, and strong—and a great option if you're looking to get more lift out of your current cam (whether stock or aftermarket).

Comp Cams' Ultra Gold rockers are like jewelry for your engine. It's a shame you have to cover them up with valve covers. They are the perfect example of a pedestal-mount aluminum rocker. The roller tip alone can add 5 to 15 hp due to decreased friction, and prevent excessive valveguide wear with higher-lift cams.

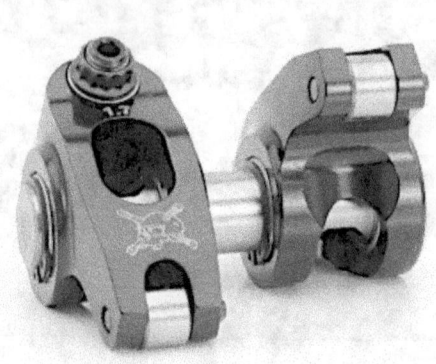

Lunati Voodoo shaft-mount roller rockers are the next step up, providing increased rigidity, but at one-third the price of typical shaft-mount setups.

SUPPORTING COMPONENTS

T&D Machine specializes in shaft-mount systems, whether for high-horse LS7s (shown) or for the small-block Chevy, circle track, or turbo Buick crowds. These rockers have plenty of adjustability built in to optimize geometry and set valve lash in a solid-roller application.

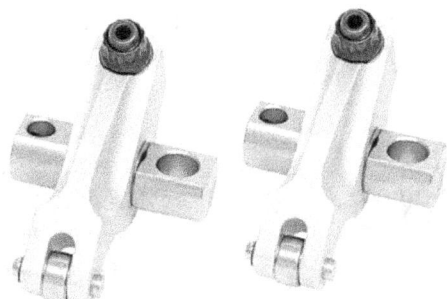

Some of the highest horsepower and most expensive LS builds (from actual C5R race engines to 2,000-horse turbocharged LSXs) have sported Jesel shaft-mount rockers such as these Pro J2Ks. The MoHawk design significantly decreases mass on the valve tip, which allows increased RPM without increasing spring pressure. The design is carefully calculated by balancing strength and weight, and they are custom built based on spring pressure. They can even be machined for valvespring oiling. Jesel also makes more economical Sportsman and Pro series lines.

CHAPTER 6

LS CYLINDER BLOCKS

The cylinder block is the foundation the rest of the engine is built upon. If incredibly high horsepower, torque, and RPM are the goal, the needs may surpass the capabilities of even the best factory offerings.

This chapter briefly reviews factory and aftermarket offerings, providing the basic engineering and capabilities. While all LS blocks are impressive when compared to vintage designs, the important thing to today's LS enthusiasts is what their block is capable of, or what block they need to reliably handle their target power level. That information is here, so you know what you have or what you need.

Factory

By now you know that it all began with the LS1, a block that was cast of 319-T5 aluminum with centrifugally cast iron cylinder liners. Although by today's standards an aluminum block is common, in 1996 few production vehicles had them, let alone one as mass-produced as the LS1 (in both the Corvette and then the Camaro and Firebird a year later). The added cost and questionable durability of cylinder coatings such as Nikasil, needed for proper ring seal and resistance to wear and distortion, made aluminum blocks undesirable for OEMs. However, by casting the iron liners in place with the block, GM was able to create a reliable method with little weight penalty. As a result, the LS1 block weighs a svelte 107 pounds; its iron-block cousins weigh an additional 88 pounds.

The LS1 block design has many features that help make it superior to its predecessors and capable of handling plenty of power. The overall design is robust; it's a deep-skirted block with (iron) six-bolt mains and extra ribbing in critical areas (designed with finite element analysis, or FEA, modeling). These features

All LS1 and LS6 blocks have the same basic construction, cast from 319-T5 aluminum with centrifugally spun iron cylinder liners in place. They have a 3.898-inch bore with knock sensor provisions located in the lifter valley. Powdered metal (steel) main caps are used in each of these deceptively strong blocks, though only the LS6 block has bulkhead windows that enhance bay-to-bay breathing in the crankcase. These blocks only tolerate a light hone to the cylinders and have short cylinders that don't respond well to stroker cranks because of their undersquare nature and the dreaded "piston rock."

LS CYLINDER BLOCKS

The 6.0 iron truck block has a long history of use in racing, due to its extremely heavy-duty construction; however, its price and 4.00-inch bore make it a great candidate for budget strokers like this one. With machining, a 4.060-inch (maximum) bore can be achieved. When GM transposed the original LS1 design, the block was never reengineered to remove material, which may be excessive in a stock application (but was previously necessary with the softer aluminum). This makes these iron blocks sturdy and reliable.

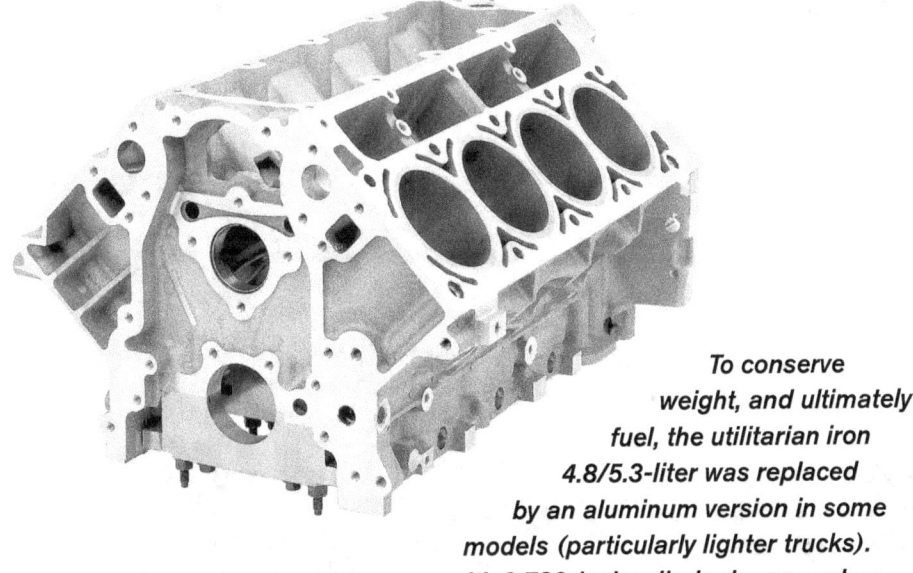

To conserve weight, and ultimately fuel, the utilitarian iron 4.8/5.3-liter was replaced by an aluminum version in some models (particularly lighter trucks). Like all small-bore blocks, these came with 3.780-inch cylinder bores and a maximum of 3.910 inches with machining. The Gen IV version also has provisions for displacement on demand, and some even use variable valve timing.

are found throughout all LS blocks, as well as the standard small-block Chevy 4.400-inch bore spacing and a 9.240-inch deck height. But all blocks were not created equal; bore diameter, cylinder length, head bolts, and oiling are just a few of the variations.

The original aluminum LS1 block used in 1997–1998 Corvettes and the 1998 Camaro and Firebird (casting # 102550592) is thought to be the least desirable of all variations. The cylinder liners are particularly thin, and can only tolerate a light hone (.005 inch) during a rebuild (the later blocks allow .010 inch). The early blocks also have a disadvantage in the oiling department, which makes them easy to spot if bare and on a shop floor. Two small holes make up the rear oil passage above the cam instead of the later blocks' open passage.

The early blocks and the 1998–2000 version (casting # 12559846, 12559090) utilize what is characterized as "medium-length" head bolts, in contrast to the 2000–2002 LS1 (casting # 12559378, 12560626) and 2001–2004 LS6 (casting # 12564243), which have longer head bolts. Neither is said to be an advantage or disadvantage.

The LS6 block boasts the best bay-to-bay crankcase breathing of the bunch. Rather than small machined holes, bulkhead windows were cast in place to more effectively relieve crankcase pressure, which escalates at higher RPM. As a result, most racers and hot rodders installing big cams prefer this among all the 3.89-inch-bore aluminum blocks. All of the above are fairly plentiful used, though new LS6 blocks are still available for $990. Gen III truck blocks share many of the nuances of their cousins with two critical differences: All but one is made of iron and they have different bore sizes. The 1998–2004 (casting # 12551358) and 2002–2004 (casting # 12567392, 12567393) block used in the 4.8- and 5.3-liter LR4, LM7, and L59 utilize a 3.779-inch-bore iron-block. The 5.3 LM4 (casting # 12566910), as well as its current Gen IV counterparts, the LS4 (casting # 12569004) and LH6/LC9/L33 (casting # 12572733), were the few to be made of aluminum because of cost and NVH (noise vibration harshness) issues. These blocks were given the updated LS6 design.

The 4.8/5.3 blocks have become a hot rodder's dream, as they are plentiful in many boneyards and quite cheap. The aluminum versions are more rare, and therefore costly. They can be bored out to the standard 3.89-inch bore for a 327- or 346-ci monster.

It should be noted that the LS4 was designed for a front-wheel-drive application, is the most rare, and is not desirable because of the casting differences, which only make it useful for a front-wheel-drive or rear-engine trans-axle setup.

Historically, the 6.0 iron block has been a formidable basis for serious horsepower as well as budget strokers. Mike Moran's tube-chassis Camaro became the first LS1 to run 6s in the quarter-mile prior to the availability of aftermarket blocks, thanks to its 6.0 truck-block-based, twin-turbo combination built by Wheel 2 Wheel Powertrain.

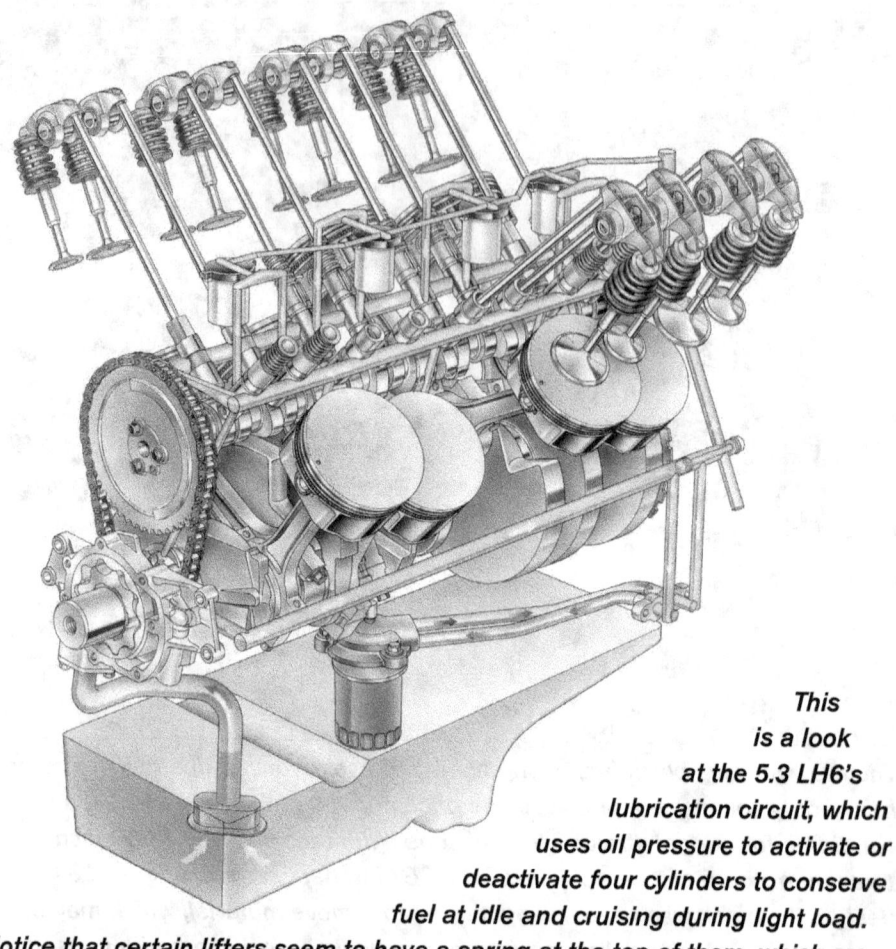

This is a look at the 5.3 LH6's lubrication circuit, which uses oil pressure to activate or deactivate four cylinders to conserve fuel at idle and cruising during light load. Notice that certain lifters seem to have a spring at the top of them, which are the cylinders that can be deactivated for active fuel management. This technology debuted years ago in a Cadillac, but has since been perfected for use in cars and trucks with automatic transmissions. Take that, CAFE.

This is the mighty LS7, the first factory aluminum 427 block since the ZL1. Unlike its big-block cousin, the small-block's 4.400-inch bore spacing makes the cylinders particularly thin. A massive, by today's standards, 4.125-inch Siamese bore is an OEM version of the C5R. Provisions for dry-sump lubrication and improved casting and machining methods make this block a formidable competitor, though not ideal for forced induction.

LS CYLINDER BLOCKS

Of course, when viewing from the front, the year is cast into the block. This is one is from 1998, and is thought to have been cast in Canada (as opposed to Mexico) because the appearance of the aluminum is noticeably different than that on typical LS1 blocks.

The valley is a dead giveaway for the early-style LS1 blocks, which makes the later-LS6-style valley cover incompatible.

The L92 and LS3 block was the next evolution in Gen IV block design, bridging the gap in bore size between the previous 4.00-inch LS2 and the 4.065-inch LS7. The larger bore gave even more clearance for the massive valves in the L92/LS3 heads. GM later decided that the L92 heads would in fact work quite well on the 6.0 block, as they did for the L76 and truck engines. Thick cylinders allow up to a 4.085-inch bore.

The LS9 is a sturdier version of the L92/LS3, adding piston oil squirters and forged-steel main caps. The internal structure (the webbing) was also beefed up considerably in critical areas, which allowed the supercharged LS9 to endure some grueling endurance tests. For better clamping with boost, larger head bolts are used.

CHAPTER 6

These bulkhead windows were improved for the LS9 to increase bay-to-bay breathing.

When the 1998–2004 LQ4 block (casting # 12551364) was first designed it was done the most economic way possible, by transposing the LS1 design to a 4.00-inch bore, iron-block version. As a result, these blocks are perhaps overly reinforced (and heavy), which makes them great for forced-induction builds. The cylinders abide by a traditional .030-inch bore and hone, and with machining can accept aftermarket 1/2-inch head studs for better clamping. Best of all, the cylinder length and large bore make it extremely rewarding to use a longer stroke crank (such as a 4.00-inch for a square motor). These engines and blocks are also fairly common in junkyards and cheap (though not quite as cheap as a 4.8/5.3), though they are also still in production in the L96 (Silverado/Sierra HD) and cost $773.

The Gen IV block production kicked off with the LS2 (2005–2009), which utilized the same bore and stroke as the 6.0 truck engine except it had an aluminum block with iron cylinder liners like the LS6 and similar internal structure. A few notable differences between the LS2 (casting # 12568950) and the LS6 include provisions for active fuel management, or displacement on demand, and a set of lifter towers located in the valley, which necessitated moving the knock sensor to the (left) outside of the block. The relocation of the knock sensors as well as the cam sensor (to the front timing cover), must be accounted for with the wiring harness. The plastic lifter trays on the LS2 are also unique to Gen IV blocks, but are also reverse-compatible with Gen III blocks (Gen III lifter trays do not work in Gen IV blocks).

Like the truck block, the LS2 responds really well to 4.00-inch-stroke cranks, allowing 402 ci or more at a price that won't break the bank. No more than a .020-inch hone is recommended. New blocks cost around $1,100 and are still in production thanks to various other engines such as the L76 and LZ1 hybrid. A healthy

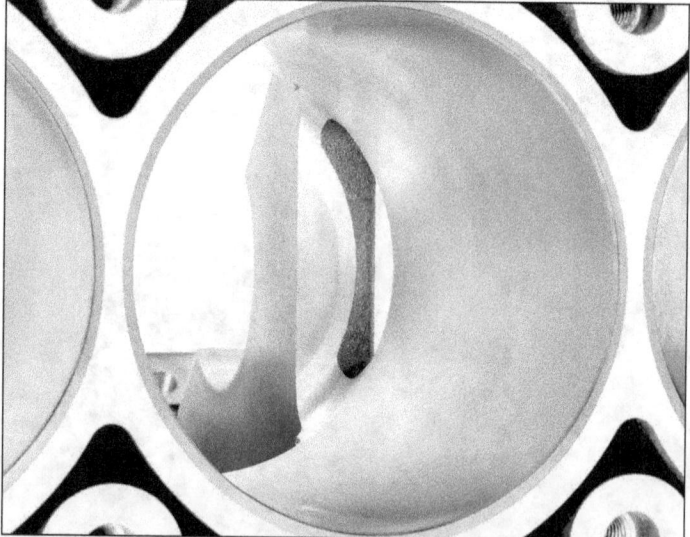

Like all LS blocks, the LS9 has deep-skirted six-bolt mains. However, unlike other factory aluminum LS blocks, the LS9 has forged-steel main caps. And though the iron cylinder liners are spun cast like all factory aluminum blocks, they are housed in a stronger casting of 319-T7 alloy.

LS CYLINDER BLOCKS

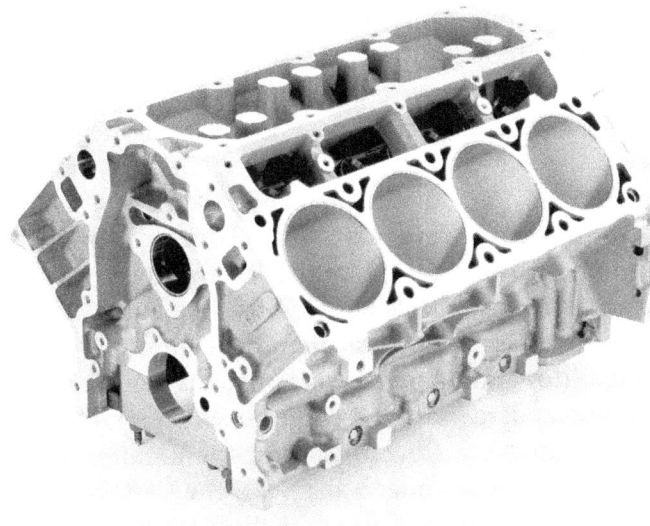

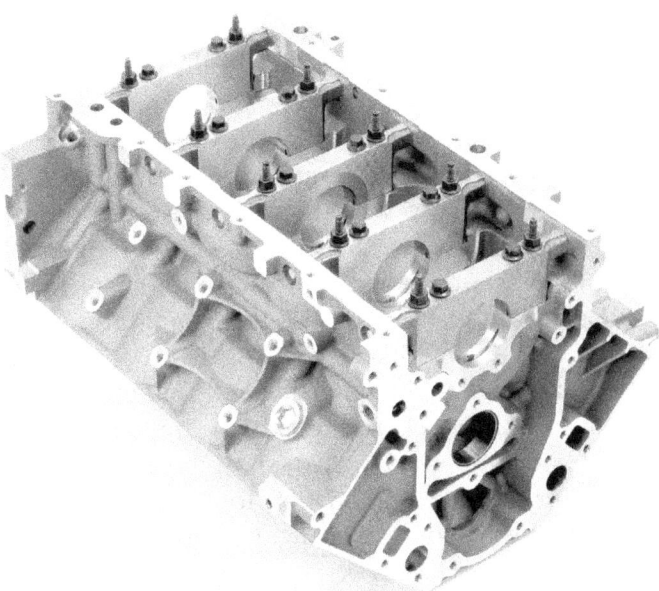

The LSA block (used in the supercharged Cadillac CTS-V and Camaro ZL1 models) is an excellent stop-gap between the LS9 and the L92/LS3. It boasts piston oil squirters and other improvements without the more costly measures.

The LSA block is nearly identical to the LS3 and L92 casting, and has the same basic features of all-aluminum LS blocks spun cast-iron cylinder liners and deep-skirted six-bolt powdered metal main caps.

HIGH-PERFORMANCE GM LS-SERIES CYLINDER HEAD GUIDE 133

CHAPTER 6

production run also means they are fairly abundant used.

A year after the LS2 debuted in the sixth-generation Corvette, the 7.0 LS7 upstaged it in the Corvette's Z06 model. In many ways the LS7 was a stop-gap between the LS2 and the C5R block developed for the GM Racing program. The LS7 has Siamesed cylinders (like the C5R) with pressed-in 4.125-inch-diameter iron liners. The large bore and extra-long cylinders were designed specifically for a 427-ci combination to withstand the heat of road racing. An improved water jacket for better thermal balance and an oiling system that better feeds the bearings and lifters, plus chilled bulkheads, help give the engine longevity.

This block is capable of up to a 4.125-inch stroke, though only a light hone (.005 inch) is possible with the necessarily thin liners. The only knock on this block is that its liners are not durable enough for substantial boost and can easily crack with detonation.

The LS7 brought about many improvements to the machining, casting, and production methods used by GM. The next evolution in the Gen IV design, which benefitted from this substantially, was the 6.2 L92 and LS3 block (casting # 12584727). By increasing the bore size to 4.065 inches, GM was able to provide less shrouding for the massive valves in its revolutionary new heads. The thick cylinder liners allow for a .020-inch bore increase, and these blocks have proven to be very durable.

The LSA block used in the supercharged 6.2 Cadillac CTS-V (2009+) and Camaro ZL1 (2012+) take the LS3 design a bit further by adding piston oil squirters, which help cool the pistons for better durability and to reduce detonation. The LS9 (casting # 12621983) also uses this technology, necessary for factory durability standards in a 638-hp supercharged engine. The LS9, developed for the 2009 Corvette ZR1 supercar, is by far the strongest OEM block and a great candidate for a high-horse boosted application. Like its heads, strength was a concern, so the bulkhead windows were redesigned (to also improve breathing) and the standard powdered metal main caps, used in all LS blocks, were substituted for forged steel. Last but not least, the head bolt provisions went from 11 mm to 12 mm for better clamping. The improvements, though, come at a premium—a $3,800 price tag. The LS3/L92 is only $1,435 and the LSA is priced between them at $2,538.

Modified Factory

It should come as no surprise that since day one, the aftermarket has been looking for ways to build a larger-cubic-inch LS1. At its initial release, there was little choice but to develop a method for resleeving the factory cylinders. Many attempts were made with varying degrees of success. However, Darton was one of the first to develop some reliable methods, which have since been perfected by the likes of shops such as Race Engine Development (RED).

The premise is simple: The cylinders are bored (as you would a normal engine), which removes the iron liners and the aluminum cylinder wall. Next, the Darton ductile iron liners, which are much stronger than the factory centrifugal cast iron units, are installed. With Gen III blocks, where there is a coolant passage between the cylinders this process gets a bit tricky. The Darton Modular Integrated Deck (MID) liner system solves past issues with resleeving by integrating each sleeve yet still encircling the liners with coolant (known as a wet sleeve). Bore sizes are available for 4.125 to 4.160 inches and 4.170 to 4.200 inches.

The cheapest and easiest method of increasing the bore size on an LS block is called "dry sleeving." Because there are no water passages between the cylinders, only Gen IV blocks can utilize this technique. Darton's ductile iron sleeves are also three times as strong as the factory iron liners, which are known to come apart on LS7 and C5R blocks with boost and detonation. (Photo Courtesy Race Engine Development)

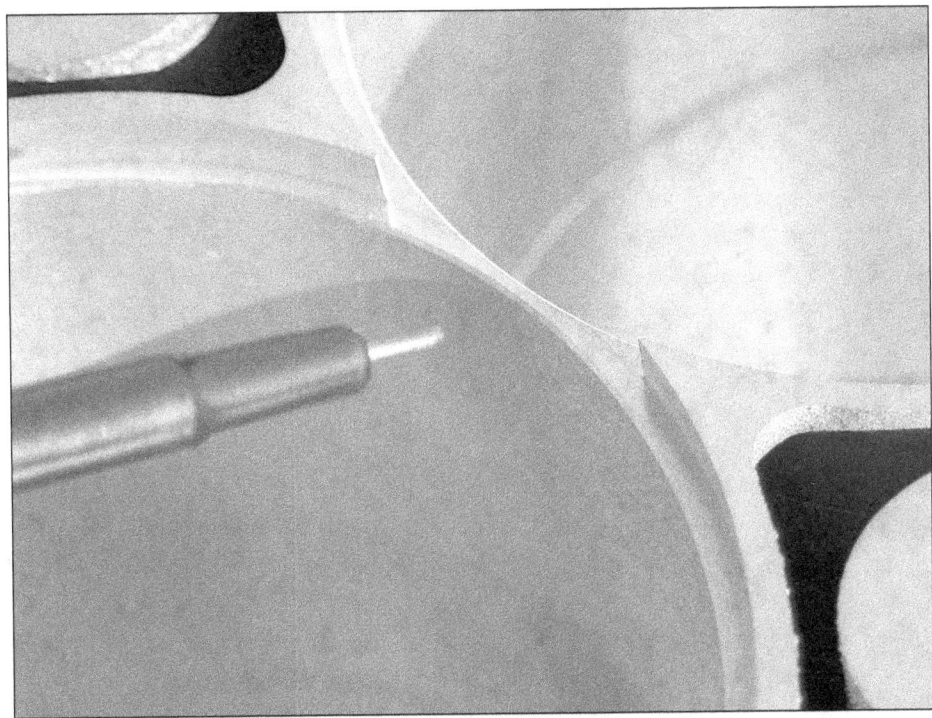

Race Engine Development is one of the best in the business at installing sleeves in LS blocks. Shown here is a Gen IV block prior to sleeve installation and after machining out the factory liners and enlarging the flange.

Here you can see the Darton dry sleeves after installation and decking, which ensures a flat surface.

The Gen IV blocks, by comparison, may utilize either the wet MID sleeves or the more economical dry sleeves to obtain larger bore sizes. With the dry sleeves, the process of removing the old cylinder liners is not much different. However, the machine work and labor involved in installing the new sleeves is much less extensive (read expensive). The LS7 in particular is a great candidate for dry sleeves such as Darton's Seal Tight, which has a phosphate coating, cooling fins, and boasts triple the strength of the factory liners.

There are a surprisingly large number of LS7 blocks left for dead with cracked liners and even cylinder walls as the result of detonation, and could easily be brought back to life and made stronger than ever with Darton sleeves. All Darton LS sleeves boast 5.800 inches of length, too, making them more suitable for stroker cranks. RED charges $2,650 for MID installation (ready for finish hone), and $1,845 for dry-sleeve installations.

Since the development of aftermarket blocks, particularly those that are more cost effective than the C5R and/or made of aluminum, resleeving Gen III and IV blocks has become less common. However, there are still plenty making as much as 2,000 hp with factory-based blocks thanks to ERL Performance and its Superdeck I. ERL takes Darton's and RED's efforts a step further by welding in aluminum trusses (with coolant holes) that connect each pair of head bolts to spread the clamping load across the deck surface to prevent distortion.

After ERL is finished with its internal strengthening, it uses similar ductile iron sleeves to increase strength and wall thickness. ERL also has the ability to machine for

CHAPTER 6

Installing the Darton Modular Integrated Deck (MID) sleeves takes quite a bit more machining, but it is the only way to go on a Gen III block and is even stronger than the dry sleeve technique. It allows for the largest bore possible without sacrificing strength, thanks to the interlocking design. The extensive and precise machining required makes this method particularly difficult to install. Note that the bulkhead windowing on LS6 blocks makes these less desirable from a strength standpoint, though no issues are present with the LS2 or LS7 blocks. (Photos Courtesy Race Engine Development)

It is evident why these are called wet sleeves. The cooling holes at the top effectively remove heat from the cylinders (notice there are more holes on the exhaust side), making it a full Siamese bore. RED recommends using Evans Waterless Coolant to prevent corrosion with these liners, and enhance the reworked coolant system. (Photo Courtesy Race Engine Development)

1/2-inch head studs and add two more head bolts per cylinder (like an aftermarket block). In this variation, billet steel main caps are also used, which make the engine capable of 1,500 hp (for $3,500 not including core). ERL also makes a main girdle for an additional $500. The basic Superdeck I starts at $2,900. Dry-sleeved blocks are also available ($2,250), as are Superdeck II shortblocks, which integrate a deck plate extension into the sleeves to allow a 4.500-inch-stroke crank (and up to 500ci).

ERL has emerged as another major player in the resleeving market, using its own proprietary ductile iron. The company offers dry sleeves, and is the only one with a method to improve strength in the factory blocks with the Superdeck I and II series (a "semi-wet" design).

This cutaway demonstrates some of the improvements that are made with trusses to connect and reinforce the head bolt area, which help spread the clamping load over a larger area. ERL says this allows better clamping with the factory block and its thinner deck than an aftermarket block. The red and blue are ERL's improvements.

CHAPTER 6

With the Superdeck II, ERL has also created the first tall-deck "stock" block. Integrated sleeves and a deck plate spacer allow up to 500 ci of displacement. This block has continued to live in the School of Automotive Machinists' True Street Camaro, which must complete a 30-mile cruise before making its three 9-second passes.

Aftermarket

The capability for larger displacement and withstanding higher cylinder pressure makes aftermarket blocks particularly appealing.

Chevrolet Performance

The Chevrolet Performance LSX block is easily the most recognizable and affordable aftermarket block. However, it certainly is not the first. It all began with the C5R, which is still in production and available today. This heavy-duty aluminum race block was designed for dry sump oiling systems, large cubic inches, and plenty of abuse. It was the first LS engine to have a large bore (4.125 inches), which can even be increased by .035 inch for rebuilds. It was also the first block to have Siamesed cylinders, and GM even outfitted it with billet steel main caps. These blocks still command a $6,980 price, which created a large demand for the more affordable, ironclad LSX block ($2,665). The use of iron not only keeps the cost down, but it boasts excellent rigidity and withstands extremely high cylinder pressure. Increased clamping force is also achieved due to the six head bolts per cylinder.

Legendary NHRA racer Warren Johnson helped develop the LSX

The Superdeck I and II have also been tested in some 30-psi boost applications such as Mark Koehler's 2,000-hp drag radial Firebird. Mark and Mike Brown (aka the Ohio Boys) race in the National Muscle Car Association's LSX Challenge Series, making mid-7-second passes with their ERL combinations.

block, perhaps that's where its priority main oiling came from. The maximum bore is a whopping 4.250 inches, though most stay safely around 4.185 inches, and longer cylinders allow for up to a 4.200-inch stroke. GM's encore to the standard, 9.26-inch-deck LSX block was a tall-deck (9.70-inch) version to allow a 4.350-inch-stroke crank (or more).

Some of the fastest LS-powered cars in the world use LSX blocks as their foundation.

World Products

The World Products Warhawk debuted around the same time as the LSX block, except it is modeled more off the C5R and cast from 357-T6 aluminum (the strongest alloy available). The sleeves are .100-inch thick and backed by more than .300 inch of aluminum (compared to the C5R's .070-inch-thick sleeve and .170-inch support). The Warhawk's main caps are made from billet 1045 alloy steel, and it also has priority main oiling. Six bolts per cylinder (and a .600-inch-thick deck) clamp the cylinder head better than the C5R and OEM blocks, though it is worth noting the pattern is slightly different than the LSX and RHS blocks.

The extra-long sleeves accommodate up to a 4.250-inch-stroke crank,

The C5R was the first aftermarket block, which was developed for the Corvette Racing program. It boasted an unheard of 4.125-inch bore and sleeves long enough to handle a 4-inch stroke with no sacrifice of durability. Drag racers willing to shell out big bucks have been using this tried-and-true piece of aluminum for decades. A Siamese bore, billet main caps, and dry sump oiling provisions are just a few of its features.

The LSX block, from Chevrolet Performance, was developed in conjunction with legendary NHRA racer Warren Johnson to meet and exceed 2,500 hp. Some of the fastest and most powerful LS engines of all time have used this block. Its cost-effective iron uses six head bolts per cylinder, and it's hard to beat. The slightly increased deck height (9.260 inches), longer cylinders, and cylinder design allow for large cubic inches.

for up to 454 ci. Maximum bore size is 4.155 inches. The standard deck (9.24 inches) retails at $4,700, and the tall-deck (9.800 inches) commands $5,690. The ability to add a 4.500-inch-stroke crank makes near 500 ci a reality.

Dart Machinery

Dart Machinery was next to introduce its billet aluminum block. This block has the most potential. Because it is a billet block, pretty much anything can be changed (deck height, cam height, bore spacing, cam journal, etc.). It offers the light weight of aluminum, but with uncompromising strength. Dart chose forged 6061 aerospace alloy with a proprietary heat treatment as the basis for creating a maximum-effort bullet that is seven times stronger than its cast counterpart, and then added billet steel main caps.

Virtually every potential issue can be solved with Dart's billet block, from core shift to cam interference and bore or stroke limitations. Racers enjoy the custom-spec head-bolt pattern and sizing, full or uncut water jacket, ability to do a 60-mm cam tunnel, custom lifter diameters, and ability to raise the cam journal in taller deck configurations. Expect to pay a minimum of $8,000.

The tall-deck LSX block was the follow up, or encore, performance. With 9.70 inches of deck height, a 4.350-inch-stroke (or larger) crank can be used to achieve near 500 cubes.

Jim Filipowski is one of several drivers with a very fast car running the LSX block in drag race competition. Jim's 1993 Camaro (aka White Lightning) has run as fast 7.65 at 199 mph with a 101-mm turbo. For class reasons, Filipowski uses a 3.90-inch stroke to stay just under 400 ci with a carburetor and All Pro heads to top it off.

LS CYLINDER BLOCKS

Racing Head Service

Some will certainly argue that the best was saved for last. Racing Head Service's LS Race Block is somewhat of a deceptive name since it is easily as at home on the street as it is on the track. Cast from A357-T6 aluminum, it uses press-in spun cast-iron cylinder liners and has a .500-inch-thick deck. The water jacket also bears resemblance to the LS7, with Siamesed bores; however its extra-long sleeves and six-head-bolt provisions help give it a significant edge. The cam tunnel can house a standard or 60-mm roller bearing camshaft, and there is extra material in the lifter bore and around the head bolts for larger-than-standard sizes. The lifter area has also been opened up to permit removal of the lifters without removing the heads. Provision for dry sump lubrication is also one of many great features (too many to list).

The RHS block is available in standard-deck (9.240 and 9.250 inches) and tall-deck (9.750 and 9.760 inches). Tall-deck versions have a raised camshaft tunnel (.388 inch), which increases rod clearance with the longer crankshaft stroke. These blocks are available unfinished or bored and ready to hone for $4,977. Those completely machined are ready to put together for $5,082.

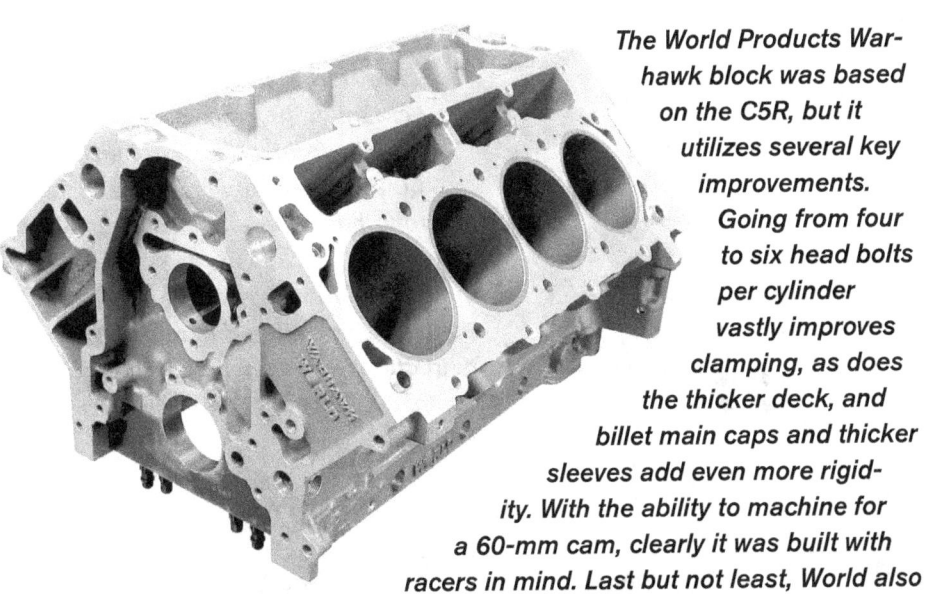

The World Products Warhawk block was based on the C5R, but it utilizes several key improvements. Going from four to six head bolts per cylinder vastly improves clamping, as does the thicker deck, and billet main caps and thicker sleeves add even more rigidity. With the ability to machine for a 60-mm cam, clearly it was built with racers in mind. Last but not least, World also added a tall-deck version to allow for obscene cubic inches.

Paul Major used a tall-deck Warhawk block to go 7.11 at 204 mph in his 2001 Corvette Z06, one of the fastest times ever recorded by an LS engine. Paul's setup included the 454-cube (tall-deck) Warhawk short-block with C5R heads and twin 91-mm turbos.

CHAPTER 6

The Dart Billet LS Block is the cream of the crop. Because it is CNC'd from a chunk of forged 6061 aluminum, and not cast, its strength is unparalleled by any other aluminum block, as is its potential for power and modification. Nearly every aspect can be altered per customer instruction from deck height to bore spacing, cam location, and lifter bore size.

Block	Bore (inches)	Material	Cylinder Length (inches)
LR4/LM7	3.780	Iron	5.485
L33	3.780	Aluminum	5.455
LS1	3.898	Aluminum	5.455
LS6	3.898	Aluminum	5.475
LQ9/LQ4	4.000	Iron	5.420
LS2	4.000	Aluminum	5.475
LS7	4.125	Aluminum	5.900
LS3/L92	4.065	Aluminum	5.460
RED/Darton	3.90 to 4.200	Aluminum	5.800
ERL SD I	3.90 to 4.200	Aluminum	5.800
ERL SD II	3.90 to 4.200	Aluminum	6.525
LSX	3.99 to 4.250	Iron	5.575
C5R	4.11 to 4.160	Aluminum	6.000
RHS (std)	4.10 to 4.165	Aluminum	5.900
RHS (tall)	4.10 to 4.165	Aluminum	6.378
Warhawk (std)	4.00 to 4.125	Aluminum	5.365
Warhawk (tall)	4.00 to 4.125	Aluminum	5.925
Dart Billet*	Any	Aluminum	5.425

*With 9.240-inch deck height

Chart Courtesy of School of Automotive Machinists

LS CYLINDER BLOCKS

Ductile iron sleeves are pressed into the block in-house after heat treating and can accommodate a 4.185-inch bore. Nikasil coating is also an option, which allows just over a 4.20-inch bore, but it is costly to apply and machine afterward (diamond stones are needed for honing). While not prudent in an OEM application, Nikasil has been used with success in many racing applications.

Billet steel main caps are used to secure the crankshaft in place.

The RHS LS Race Block was the last to be developed, so it should come as no surprise that it boasts the most features of any of the cast variants. It has increased access to lifters (yes, you can actually remove them with the heads on), .500-inch-thick deck, longer sleeves, six head bolts, provisions for dry sump lubrication, cam tunnel that supports a 60-mm roller bearing, and several different machining and finishing options. Perhaps best of all, though, is the raised cam tunnel on the tall-deck block. Many other large camshafts have clearance issues with longer-stroke crankshafts, so this makes big cubic inches possible in a race application.

Source Guide

Advanced Induction
6841 Belt Road
Concord, NC 28027
704/918-5526
www.advancedinduction.com

Air Flow Research
28611 W. Industry Drive
Valencia, CA 91355
877/892-8844
www.airflowresearch.com

Arao Engineering Inc.
818/709-4781
www.araoengineering.com

Chevrolet Performance
www.chevroletperformance.com

Edelbrock, LLC
2700 California Street
Torrance, CA 90503
310/781-2222
www.edelbrock.com

Lingenfelter Performance
   Engineering
1557 Winchester Road
Decatur, IN 46733
260/724-2552
www.lingenfelter.com

Livernois Motorsports
2500 South Gulley Road
Dearborn Heights, MI 48125
313/561-5500
www.livernoismotorsports.com

Mast Motorsports
330 NW Stallings Drive
Nacogdoches, TX 75964
866/551-4916
www.mastmotorsports.com

Nick Arias Jr. Racing Components
310/323-Race
www.nickariasjr.com

Patriot Performance
103 Rainbow Industrial Boulevard
Rainbow City, AL 35906
888/462-8276
www.patriot-performance.com

Procomp Electronics
1101 W. Rialto Avenue
Rialto, CA 92376
909/605-1123
www.procompelectronics.com

Race Flow Development
545 South Birdneck Road, Suite 109
Virginia Beach, VA 23451
757/222-9717
www.raceflowdevelopment.com

Scoggin-Dickey Parts Center
5901 Spur 327
Lubbock, TX 79424
800/456-0211
www.sdparts.com

Texas Speed & Performance
5619 FM 1585
Lubbock, TX 79424
806/698-0365
www.texas-speed.com

Total Engine Airflow
285 West Avenue
Tallmadge, OH 44278
330/634-2155
www.totalengineairflow.com

Trick Flow Specialties
285 West Avenue
Tallmadge, OH 44278
330/630-1555
www.trickflow.com

Vmax Motorsports
813/469-4665
www.vmaxmotorsports.com

Wegner Motorsports, Inc.
N2258 Hilltop Road
Markesan, WI 53946
920/394-3557
www.wegnerautomotive2.com

West Coast Racing Cylinder Heads
18405 Hart Street
Reseda, CA. 91335
818/705-5454
www.proheads.com

World Products
51 Trade Zone Court
Ronkonkoma, NY 11779
631/981-1918
www.worldcastings.com

www.ingramcontent.com/pod-product-compliance
Lightning Source LLC
Chambersburg PA
CBHW081451070526
44586CB00019B/2302